AF600363

THE CATHOLIC UNIVERSITY OF AMERICA
CANON LAW STUDIES
Number 83

A COMPARATIVE STUDY OF THE COUNCILS OF BALTIMORE AND THE CODE OF CANON LAW

A DISSERTATION

Submitted to the Faculty of Canon Law of the Catholic University of America in Partial Fulfillment of the Requirements for the Degree of

DOCTORATE OF CANON LAW

BY

JOHN DANIEL MARY BARRETT, A.M., J.C.L.
Priest of the Society of Saint Sulpice

THE CATHOLIC UNIVERSITY OF AMERICA
WASHINGTON, D. C.
1932

Nihil Obstat:

VALENTINUS T. SCHAAF, O. F. M., J. C. D.,
Censor Deputatus.

Washingtonii, D. C., die XXIV Augusti, 1932.

Imprimatur:

MICHAEL J. CURLEY, D. D.,
Archiepiscopus Baltimorensis.

Baltimorae, die XXIV Augusti, 1932.

PRINTED BY
J. H. FURST COMPANY
BALTIMORE, MD.

TO

MY MOTHER AND FATHER

TABLE OF CONTENTS

FOREWORD

Until the Feast of Pentecost of 1917 the American clergy had looked unquestioningly to the Councils of Baltimore for their Particular Canon Law. What effect the Code, which was promulgated on that date and which was to go into force on the same Feast the following year, would have upon our local legislation became a matter of varied conjecture. Some felt that the new common law should become our only source of ecclesiastical procedure and that the laws of Baltimore should all pass automatically into desuetude. Others judged the Councils quite adequate to local conditions and believed that the Code should not be considered as applying to the United States. Still others were of the opinion that we should be governed by both the Code and the Councils and in cases of conflict should petition the Holy See to uphold our local statutes. Those more familiar with the new common law arguing particularly from canon 6, § 1 maintained that while the Code in its entirety would apply here, the Councils, too, must continue to be observed except in so far as they are opposed to the Code.

It is known now authoritatively that this last view is correct. However, though some of the points of conflict between the two laws have been considered and settled, they have never been collected in one treatise nor has there been an exhaustive comparison made between the Code and the Councils to ascertain completely the present status of the latter.

For the first annual meeting of the American Hierarchy which was held in 1919 Doctor Creagh prepared and printed a brochure dealing with the Code and the Councils. Herein the Author showed in general the effect of the new common law upon our local legislation and in particular the changes it brought about regarding the most important parts of the *De Personis* of the Third Plenary Council.

This brief study inspired and has been a helpful guide in the preparation of the present volume, the purpose of which is to institute a thorough comparison between the two laws in order to answer not only generically but specifically the question: "How has the Code effected the decrees of the Councils of Baltimore?"

The task, indeed, has not been an easy one owing in the first place to the large number and great variety of subjects to be treated, and secondly to the fact that it has been necessary to study carefully the full text of the Councils in order to determine the matter that should come properly under consideration, that is, to separate what is strictly law from the admixture of Dogmatic, Moral, Ascetic and Pastoral Theology and of directive statutes.

To the study of only these laws properly so called and as contained within the decrees enacted by the Fathers of the Councils this treatise has been limited.

In making the comparison between the Councils and the Code the decrees of the former have been examined in their proper order, but in recording the results the more logical and now more familiar order of the Code has been followed.

The author takes this opportunity of thanking the Faculty of the School of Canon Law of the Catholic University and all others who have in any way assisted him in the preparation of this work.

CHAPTER I

BEGINNING AND GROWTH OF OUR NATIONAL LEGISLATION

In its laws as in all else clemency has ever been the policy of the Church. The Master said, "I will have mercy," [1] "I am come to save," [2] and the Church still does and will forever echo these sentiments. Peter in the Church's first council asks: "Why tempt you God to put a yoke upon the necks of the disciples which neither our fathers nor we have been able to bear?" [3]

So the Church has always been slow to impose her laws upon her weaker children. The Catholic Church in America struggled for years under a great handicap by reason of circumstances. The faithful were few in number, scattered, with very restricted means of ministration and suffering extremely violent opposition and even oppression.[4] The purely essential common laws of the Church were all that the Hierarchy could hope to enforce. The necessary lack of centralization made any kind of local legislation at first out of the question, and even though it might have availed something, there was little facility before the time of Bishop Carroll for the making and enforcing of laws.[5]

With the appointment of the Reverend John Carroll to the simultaneously erected See of Baltimore [6] in 1789 a new era began in

[1] Matt., XIX, 13.

[2] John, XII, 47.

[3] Acts, XV, 10.

[4] Guilday, *Life and Times of John Carroll*, p. 152.

[5] The Church in America was from 1688 presumably, and from 1757 certainly under the jurisdiction of the Vicar Apostolic of the London District. (Cf. Guilday, *Life and Times of John Carroll*, pp. 137, ff.; Shea, *Life and Times of Archbishop Carroll*, p. 50.) The Reverend John Carroll was appointed Prefect Apostolic on June 9, 1784 (Shea, *op. cit.*, p. 223; Guilday, *op. cit.*, p. 202) and Bishop on November 6, 1789. (Shea, *op. cit.*, p. 337; Guilday, *op. cit.*, p. 356.)

[6] *Acta S. Congr. de Prop. Fide*, 1789 (Extract in Shea, *Life and Times of Archbishop Carroll*, pp. 337, ff.; Guilday, *Life and Times of John Carroll*, p. 356.)

American Church History. Almost the first official act of the Bishop was the calling of a synod for November 1791. This was at the suggestion of the Holy Father [7] though Bishop Carroll himself certainly realized the need of it. Letters summoning the priests of his "widely extended diocese" were issued on September 27, 1791. On the seventh of November the formal opening took place and the five sessions comprising the meeting were spread over four days, the last being held on November 10.[8]

The Synod after formal preparation in the first session devoted the next three to legislation on the Sacraments with the exception of Holy Orders. The last session dealt with the regulation of divine offices and the observance of the holydays of obligation, regulations on the life and support of the clergy and on the burial of those persons who had neglected to approach the Sacraments at Easter.[9] Finally, the question of a division of the diocese or of a coadjutor was raised and it was decided to ask the Holy See to make some provision so that the young Church in America might not have to suffer the evil effects of the necessarily long delay if the procedure then followed in the appointment of Bishops were begun only after Bishop Carroll's death.[10] A full account of the proceedings was sent to Rome where they were received with the highest commendation [11] and approved with slight modification on August 13, 1792.[12]

The acts of the Synod which form the first body of laws adopted for the government of the Church in this country have always excited the admiration of those who study them. Bishop Bruté in writing of them some years later said: "We must read over the synod of 1791

[7] Shea, *Life and Times of Archbishop Carroll*, p. 394.

[8] Twenty priests were present on the first day. Two more came later. (*Conc. Prov. Balti. Habita*, pp. 11 and 19.)

[9] *Conc. Prov. Balti. Habita*, pp. 12-24.

[10] Shea, *Life and Times of Archbishop Carroll*, pp. 397 and 398; O'Gorman, *The American Church History*, X, 277 and 278; Guilday, *Life and Times of John Carroll*, p. 441.

[11] Cardinal Antonelli writing to Bishop Carroll on August 16, 1794, says: "They have been read with great pleasure by all for they give most luminous proofs of your piety, prudence and pastoral vigilance, since what you have deemed proper to enact will apparently be most profitable to the people of your diocese."—Shea, *Life and Times of Archbishop Carroll*, p. 403, footnote 2.

[12] Guilday, *Life and Times of John Carroll*, p. 443.

for the form and its authority will be a good standard. In every line you see the Bishop. In all you see how extensively he had studied and the spirit of faith, charity and zeal in that first assembly has served as a happy model for its successors."[13] The Fathers of the First Provincial Council of Baltimore expressed their appreciation by ordering the Acts of the Synod to be printed at the head of those of the Council.[14] The request for a helper and successor to Bishop Carroll was answered by allowing the American clergy to elect a coadjutor for the See of Baltimore and their choice fell ultimately upon the Reverend Leonard Neale who was consecrated December 7, 1800.[15] Perhaps it was from force of circumstances, but Bishop Neale seems to have been a disappointment as Coadjutor. For this reason among others the only practical solution of the existing difficulties seemed to be the division of the diocese and for this Bishop Carroll petitioned Rome. Finally, and only after a second appeal did the Holy See consent and on April 8, 1808, by the Briefs, "*Pontificii Muneris*" and "*Ex Debito Pastoralis Officii*," Pope Pius VII divided the then only existing diocese making Bishop Carroll Metropolitan in the See of Baltimore and erecting the suffragan sees of New York, Philadelphia, Boston and Bardstown.

The first Bishops appointed for the new dioceses were the Right Reverend Richard Luke Concanen, O. P., for New York, the Right Reverend Michael Egan, O. F. M., for Philadelphia, the Right Reverend John Cheverus, for Boston and the Right Reverend Benedict Joseph Flaget, S. S., for Bardstown.[16] Bishop Concanen was consecrated in Rome on April 24, 1808, but died before he could sail for the United States.

Owing to the difficulties of communication at that time between Italy and this country more than two years elapsed before our first Archbishop received his pallium and the documents authorizing him to consecrate the other Bishops.[17] Bishop Egan was consecrated in

[13] Shea, *Life and Times of Archbishop Carroll*, p. 398; Guilday, *Life and Times of John Carroll*, p. 446.

[14] *Conc. Prov. Balti. Habita*, pp. 9 and 10; Shea, *Life and Times of Archbishop Carroll*, p. 398; Guilday, *Life and Times of John Carroll*, p. 446.

[15] Guilday, *op. cit.*, pp. 569, ff.

[16] Guilday, *Life and Times of John Carroll*, p. 583.

[17] Guilday, *op. cit.*, pp. 587 and 588.

St. Peter's, the pro-Cathedral of Baltimore, on October 28, 1810, Bishop Cheverus in the same church on November 1 and Bishop Flaget in St. Patrick's Church, Fells Point, Baltimore, on November 4.

The Suffragans did not depart immediately after their consecration but remained for two weeks[18] in consultation with their venerable Metropolitan and his Coadjutor, Bishop Neale to discuss a number of points of "regulation and discipline" that, as they wrote later, "we may form an uniform practice in the government of our Churches and likewise to take into consideration the present state of the Catholic Church, its visible Head, our Venerable Pontiff, and the consequence of his being withdrawn from his captivity, either by violence, or the ruin of his constitution by interior or exterior sufferings."[19] As a result of their deliberations "several articles of ecclesiastical discipline were adopted." Those of their enactments now published with the decrees of the Provincial Councils deal with *exeats,* the faculties of the clergy regular and secular, the adoption of the Douay Bible as revised by Bishop Challoner two editions of which had already appeared, parochial registers, the Sacraments of Baptism and Matrimony, the Mass stipend, the warning of the faithful against the dangers of theaters, dances and novel reading, and lastly the exclusion of Freemasons from the Sacraments until they had renounced all connection with the association and promised no more to attend the meetings.[20] Over and above these, as we learn from original documents in the Archives of the Baltimore Cathedral (Case 2-J 1) the Fathers further considered the provincial council, diocesan synod, visitation of the diocese, nomination of Bishops, the ministry of strange priests, the use of the vernacular in public service, the taking of vows by others than religious and the Benediction of The Most Blessed Sacrament.[21] The faithful were acquainted with the result of these deliberations through what Shea calls the Pastoral of 1810,[22] but which was rather only copies of this "agreement" sent out to the clergy.[23] These enactments with those of the Synod of 1791 consti-

[18] Griffin, *op. cit.*, p. 44.

[19] Shea, *Life and Times of Archibishop Carroll*, pp. 632 and 633.

[20] *Conc. Prov. Balti. Habita*, pp. 25-28.

[21] Cf. also Griffin, *op. cit.*, pp. 44-48 and Guilday, *Life and Times of John Carroll*, pp. 589, ff.

[22] Shea, *Life and Times of Archbishop Carroll*, p. 633.

[23] Guilday, *Life and Times of John Carroll*, pp. 589 and 593.

tuted the statutes of the Church in the United States for the next twenty years and form the earliest code of Canon Law in the American Church.

This meeting constituted no formal council. There was, indeed, immediate need for one, as the Fathers themselves implicitly admitted; but at the time they were unprepared, as the new Bishops had not yet become conversant with the condition of their respective sees. They gave promise, however, for the future, saying: "The Most Reverend Archbishop and Right Reverend Bishops . . . not being able to extend their enquiries and collect full information concerning many points which require uniform regulation and perhaps amendment they reserve to a future occasion a general review of ecclesiastical discipline now observed throughout the different dioceses and the reducing of it everywhere to as strict conformity with that of the Universal Church as our particular situation, circumstances and the general benefit of the faithful will allow." [24] They even decided upon November of 1812 as a proximate, tentative date for this meeting,[25] but circumstances conspired to delay the fulfillment of this promise nineteen years.

In the year 1829 was held the first of a series of seven councils which were somewhat unique in that the first six, while provincial in form, were national in authority,[26] whereas the seventh was strictly speaking neither provincial nor plenary [27] although it has always been referred to as the Seventh Provincial Council of Baltimore and ultimately received universal application to this country; for the Fathers of the First Plenary Council explicitly state that the decrees of the seven Councils of Baltimore have the force of law for the whole United States and its possessions.[28]

[24] Shea, *Life and Times of Archbishop Carroll*, p. 633.

[25] Guilday, *Life and Times of John Carroll*, p. 591.

[26] The whole territory of the United States formed but one province until July, 1846.—Cf. O'Gorman, *op. cit.*, p. 346.

[27] It was not strictly provincial since more than one province was concerned, nor plenary since Archbishop Eccleston in presiding did not act in the capacity of Apostolic Delegate, nor did the Fathers of this assembly intend that it should be our first National Council as is evident from their Acts and Decrees.

[28] "Quae in septem conciliis Baltimorensibus decreta sunt, ad omnes dioeceses Foederatorum Statuum, et regionum omnium generali gubernatione sub-

This First Provincial Council fulfilled one of Archbishop Carroll's most cherished wishes, one that he had carried unfulfilled to his grave. He had urged it at the Meeting of 1810 and an early date had been set,[29] the new Bishops being given some time in which to become acquainted with conditions in their dioceses. For reasons about which historians are not agreed,[30] the wished-for day came and went without a meeting of the American Hierarchy. On July 22, 1814 Bishop Egan of Philadelphia died and on Sunday, December 3, 1815 Archbishop Carroll passed away.

Archbishop Neale, successor in the See of Baltimore, put on the pallium with hands enfeebled with age and sickness and so it was out of the question to expect him to preside over an assembly before which was to come so much weighty business. Moreover, in view of the disorder that took hold of a number of the Church's principal centers about this time, it would seem that a meeting of the Hierarchy would have done more harm than good.[31]

No sooner, though, had Archbishop Mareschal, the next incumbent, received his metropolitan authority[32] than the long pending council was again urged. In the meantime other sees had been created[33] and all the vacant ones had been filled again.[34] The new Archbishop preferred postponement for reasons about which again authorities differ.[35] Bishop Cheverus did not favor a council and wrote: "I cannot see even now any necessity for holding a council and I cannot help doubting even the expediency of it."[36] Bishop Conwell began

ditarum, extendi statuimus eaque ubique vim obtinere."—*Conc. Plen. Balti. Habit. 1852*, p. 44.

[29] November 12, 1812.

[30] Shea, *Hist. of the Cath. Church in the U. S.*, I, 407, ff; Guilday, *Life and Times of John Carroll*, p. 816 and *Life and Times of John England*, II, 69 and 70.

[31] Guilday, *The Life and Times of John England*, II, 70.

[32] He was consecrated December 4, 1817.

[33] At Richmond and Charleston on July 11, 1820, and at Cincinnati on June 19, 1821.

[34] New York on November 6, 1814 and Philadelphia on August 24, 1820.

[35] Shea, *Hist. of the Cath. Church in the U. S.*, III, 408; Guilday, *Life and Times of John England*, II, 68, ff.

[36] Letter to Archbishop Carroll, January 5, 1813.—Cf. Shea, *Hist. of the Cath. Church in the U. S.*, I, 407.

to advocate it during the Hogan trouble.[37] Bishop England was heartily in favor of it and indeed was the prime mover.[38] He was very anxious to put an immediate stop to foreign interference in the affairs of the Church in this country by establishment of counciliar regulations with regard to the nomination to sees. Archbishop Mareschal himself was aware of the need but was playing for time. Much discussion on the subject passed between him and Bishop England in letter form. The Sacred Congregation of the Propagation in its letter of May 25, 1822 had suggested to Archbishop Mareschal the advisability of holding at once a provincial council for the purpose of regulating the whole problem of ecclesiastical discipline. This suggestion did not meet with the Archbishop's approval and so there was no Council during his episcopate.[39]

Archbishop Mareschal died on January 29, 1828. Two months later Father James Whitfield was appointed his successor. Just what finally induced the new Metropolitan to call the First Provincial Synod is not known, but on December 18, 1828 he issued letters of convocation appointing October 1, 1829 as the opening date for the Council.[40]

Meantime, a body of theologians set to work to prepare the ground. To this group were submitted the suggestions of the Metropolitan and his Suffragans and the documents which came from Rome. Finally, after nearly two decades of effort our First Provincial Council formally opened on October 3, 1829. For two weeks the Fathers prayed and debated and as a result on October 18 were signed the thirty-eight decrees which Pius VIII approved on September 26 of the following year.[41]

The Council legislated first that a priest should accept any mission to which he is assigned and which affords him suitable maintenance; secondly, that he remain in the diocese to which he belongs either by ordination or by adoption; thirdly, Bishops are urged not to accept priests not presenting proper credentials; fourthly, that in the parish

[37] O'Gorman, *op. cit.*, p. 318.

[38] Guilday, *The Life and Times of John England*, II, 77, ff.

[39] Guilday, *The Life and Times of John England*, I, 359.

[40] Shea, *op. cit.*, I, 408, ff; Guilday, *Life and Times of John England*, II, 112, ff.

[41] *Decree of The Sacr. Cong. de Prop. Fide*, October 16, 1830.—*Conc. Prov. Balti. Habita*, p. 92.

where two or more priests are required, one should be designated pastor and the others assistants; fifthly, that in general all new churches be deeded to the Bishop; sixthly, that the *jus patronatus* and the right of substituting and dismissing pastors is denied to the laity and that no collection of money for the Church gives any right of patronage. It was urged in number seven that Bishops revoke the faculties of any priest instigating or encouraging such usurpation; and in number eight that they interdict churches retaining unapproved or suspended priests or refusing to receive duly appointed priests. Number nine dealt with the use of correct editions of the Bible; ten ordered uniform use of the Roman Ritual; eleven treated of the sponsors for Baptism and Confirmation; twelve and thirteen dealt with the baptismal name; fourteen required parish registers; fifteen treated of the blessing of the water and font on Holy Saturday; sixteen directed Baptism in churches where possible; seventeen dealt with the Baptism of children of non-Catholic parents; eighteen treated of the form in adult Baptism and contained a petition for permission to use the same form for adult as for infant Baptism; nineteen concerned the churching of women; twenty ordered Latin used in the administration of the Sacraments; twenty-one permitted the confirming of children under seven in special circumstances; twenty-two ordered that where a number are to be confirmed each have a card bearing his name; twenty-three treated of the celebration of Mass in private homes; twenty-four regulated the decency of the place where Mass is offered; twenty-five ordered public confessionals and forbade the hearing of women's confessions in private houses; twenty-six urged pastors to prepare the faithful for the proper reception of matrimony; twenty-seven treated of clerical dress; twenty-eight warned clerics against improper pastimes; twenty-nine ordered preaching on Sundays and holydays; thirty exhorted Bishops to impress their clergy with the sense of duty, urging a yearly retreat, daily meditation, spiritual conferences and other exercises; thirty-one ordered the preparation of a proper ceremonial in English; thirty-two urged the use of the Roman biretta and a suitable surplice; thirty-three pronounced against the use of unapproved catechisms and prayer books and ordered the preparation of a catechism suited to this country; thirty-four urged the building of Catholic schools; thirty-five dealt with the preparation of fitting school-books; thirty-six urged the establishment of a society for the spread of Catholic literature; thirty-seven stated that these decrees will be submitted to Rome and exhorted the Bishops to hold synods and to see to the observance of the local laws approved by the Holy See; thirty-eight provided for a Second Provincial Council to be held after three years.[42]

Other topics which have not been embodied in the foregoing decrees were discussed by the Fathers. Chief among these were the reading of forbidden books, the establishment of a Catholic press and the erection of a central seminary.[43]

Besides the request contained in the eighteenth decree the Holy See was further petitioned at this time to allow the use of the shorter form for the blessing of baptismal water outside the Saturdays before the Pasch and Pentecost and to fix for this country as the time for the Easter Communion the period from the first Sunday of Lent to Trinity Sunday both inclusively.[44]

On September 26, 1830 the decrees of the Council with some modifications were approved and all the petitions granted; that, however, concerning the form for adult Baptism only for twenty years.[45] The Fathers of the First Plenary Council, through their twenty-third decree petitioned the Holy See for the extension of this faculty and were granted this favor *ad quinquennium* from September 5, 1852.[46]

So complete was the legislation of this First Provincial Council that it gave general satisfaction and succeeding ones had comparatively little to add.

The Second Provincial Council also presided over by Archbishop Whitfield was held in 1833.[47] Its decrees, eleven in all, treat of the following: the petition for the erection of the new see at Vincennes; the suppression of the vacant see of Richmond and the determining of the geographical limits of the American sees; the mode of nominating to vacant bishoprics in the future; the request that certain of the

[42] *Conc. Prov. Balti. Habita,* pp. 72-85.

[43] *Conc. Prov. Balti. Habita,* pp. 42-43.

[44] *Conc. Prov. Balti. Habita,* pp. 46, ff.

[45] *Conc. Prov. Balti. Habita,* pp. 62, ff and pp. 89, ff.

[46] *Conc. Plen. Balti. Habit. 1852,* pp. 49, 57 and 58.

[47] October 20-27;—cf. Guilday, *Life and Times of John England,* II, 243, ff; Shea, *Hist. of the Cath. Church in the U. S.,* I, 432, ff.

Indian missions and the Liberian mission for the negroes be entrusted to the Jesuits; the new Ritual; the foundation of seminaries in each diocese; the censorship of text-books used in Catholic schools and colleges; the revocation of extra-diocesan faculties; and the convocation of the Third Provincial Council.[48] The decrees of the Council were approved May 17, 1834[49] and all the petitions granted. The see of Vincennes was erected with Bishop Bruté as the first incumbent. Richmond was placed under the administration of the Archbishop of Baltimore. The boundaries of the other dioceses were fixed. The Jesuits were put in charge of certain Indian missions and of the Liberian-negro mission and a definite method of choosing candidates for vacant sees was decided upon.[50] This system continued in vogue until altered by the Holy See at the request of the Fathers of the Seventh Provincial Council in 1849.[51]

Just one year after the Council on October 19, 1834 Archbishop Whitfield died. A month previously the Right Reverend Samuel Eccleston had been consecrated Coadjutor-Archbishop of Baltimore and under his direction were held the next three Provincial Councils.

In accordance with the last decree of the Second Provincial Council which provided for the Third to be convened on the third Sunday after Easter of the year 1837 Archbishop Eccleston summoned his Suffragans to Baltimore. The Council opened on the morning of Sunday, April 16, and lasted until the following Sunday. Eleven decrees were enacted during the sessions. They dealt with ordinations *titulo missionis;* the oath to be taken before Holy Orders; the acceptance of a mission; the duty of the faithful to contribute to the support of their pastors; the clerical fund for the support of old and infirm priests; the uniform use of the Ceremonial provided for in the thirty-first decree of the First Provincial Council; the making secure of ecclesiastical property; the uniform use of the Roman Ritual; the prohibition for priests to bring ecclesiastical cases before the civil courts; the soliciting by priests of financial help outside their own parishes; Church music; the petition for the abrogation as

[48] *Conc. Prov. Balti. Habita,* pp. 100-106.

[49] Guilday, *Life and Times of John England,* II, 265.

[50] *Op. cit.,* pp. 107, ff; cf. Guilday, *Life and Times of John England,* II, 263, ff.

[51] *Conc. Prov. Balti. Habita,* pp. 278 and 290, ff.

holydays of obligation of the major ferials after Easter and Pentecost; the dispensation from the fast and Wednesday abstinence in Advent; and finally, the next Provincial Council to be held in 1840 on the fourth Sunday after Easter.[52] The decrees of the Council were approved and confirmed without change on July 9, 1837.[53] As for the petitions which included besides the foregoing, the request for the erection of the sees of Natchez, Dubuque and Nashville,[54] all were granted absolutely except the dispensation from the fast on the Fridays of Advent. This the Holy See was loathe to abolish but empowered the American Hierarchy to do so if after mature consideration they deemed it necessary for the avoidance of sin. Our Bishops decided to retain the fast.[55]

The Fourth Provincial Council was convened by Archbishop Eccleston on May 16 and solemnly opened on Sunday, May 17, 1840.[56] Through the ensuing week the Fathers met and deliberated. Many questions came under discussion but, as usual, not all were embodied in the actual legislation. The eleven decrees of the Council treat of mixed marriages; the limiting to the pastor of the power of the administering of the parish; the regulating of the division of perquisites; the fitting observance of Sundays and holydays; the combating of intemperance; the safeguarding of the faith and the education of children against the dangers of the public school; the prohibition against secret societies; the protecting of Church property; the keeping of registers of ordinations; the titles and pastors of churches; the exhorting of the clergy to lead edifying lives; and finally, the date of the Fifth Provincial Council which was fixed for the fourth Sunday after Easter of the year 1843.[57]

As in the Third Council so in the Fourth the question of making Pittsburgh a see was discussed but no formal petition was made to the Holy See. Likewise, though the expediency of a bishopric at

[52] *Conc. Prov. Balti. Habita*, pp. 141-144.

[53] *Conc. Prov. Balti. Habita*, p. 147.

[54] The Bishops named were the Reverend Thomas Heyden for Natchez; the Reverend Mathias Loras for Dubuque; and the Reverend Richard Miles, O. P. for Nashville. *Conc. Prov. Balti. Habita*, p. 146.

[55] *Conc. Prov. Balti. Habita*, pp. 148, ff.

[56] Guilday, *Life and Times of John England*, II, 502, ff.

[57] *Conc. Prov. Balti. Habita*, pp. 169, ff.

Springfield, Illinois, was talked of, as was the removal of the episcopal residence from Bardstown to Louisville, no action was taken.[58] It was decided, however, to petition the Holy See to dispense from the fast still observed in some dioceses on the vigil of the feast of Sts. Peter and Paul and *in perpetuum* from the Saturday abstinence which had already been done *ad decennium;* and finally, for the uniformity throughout the United States in the recitation of certain offices. Rome's response to these requests was the denial of the first, an extension of the second to twenty years, and the granting of the third.[59]

The enactments proper of the Council received Papal approval practically without change on November 22, 1840, but the eighth of these which dealt with the safeguarding of Church property called forth from the Sacred Congregation of the Propaganda in the following December a special decree. This was later mitigated somewhat by the Holy See through the petition of the Fathers of the Fifth Provincial Council.[60]

On May 14, 1843 the Fifth Provincial Council was convened under Archbishop Eccleston. Like the three preceding it lasted a week ending on Sunday, May 21, and like its predecessor enacted eleven statutes.[61] It decreed adherence to state laws in the holding of Church property; prohibited the use of the church to lay lecturers; pronounced excommunication *ipso facto* against one who would remarry after a merely civil divorce; determined the extent of the *Tametsi* as regarded the diocese of Detroit; ordered the enforcement of the decrees of the Council of Trent concerning the residence of pastors; forbade the rash incurring of debt in church building; ordered bookkeeping for every church; approved the newly prepared Ritual; ordered the observance of the decree of the First Provincial Council which directed the erection in churches of confessionals for the hearing of women's confessions; approved the establishment of Catholic presses in Baltimore and Cincinnati; and urged upon the clergy prompt and constant attendance upon the sick and assiduity in preaching the word of God.[62]

[58] *Conc. Prov. Balti. Habita,* pp. 125, 162 and 164.
[59] *Conc. Prov: Balti. Habita,* pp. 187 and 190, ff.
[60] *Conc. Prov. Balti, Habita,* pp. 172, 198, ff and 216.
[61] *Conc. Prov. Balti. Habita,* p. 208.
[62] *Conc. Prov. Balti. Habita,* pp. 216-220.

The Fathers further made a formal appeal to the Holy See for the erection of a bishopric in Pittsburgh and requested the new sees of Little Rock, Chicago, Hartford and Milwaukee. They asked, too, that the vacant see of Charleston be filled and that coadjutors to the Bishops of New York and Boston be appointed. They petitioned, finally, that the Oregon Territory be made a Vicariate Apostolic.

The decrees of the Council were approved by Pope Gregory XVI on September 24, 1843.[63] A letter from the Congregation of the Propagation of the Faith dated September 30, 1843 assured the Fathers of the Council that their requests had been granted. To the bishoprics the first choice was appointed in every case. The Holy See preferred, however, to make the Reverend Francis Norbert Blanchet, a Canadian priest, Vicar Apostolic of Oregon.[64]

On May 9, 1846 Archbishop Eccleston summoned his Suffragans to convene for the Sixth Provincial Council of Baltimore. This meeting is memorable most of all for its resolution to petition the Holy See to ratify the Fathers' choice of Mary Immaculate as special Patroness of the United States. In this connection, they asked, too, the transfer of the solemnization of the feast to the following Sunday. The Holy See was further petitioned to extend to the whole United States the prohibition such as already existed in the dioceses of Vincennes and St. Louis whereby clerics ordained to Sacred Orders *titulo missionis* were forbidden to enter a religious Order without the written permission of their Ordinary. The other three of the Council's five decrees provided for the publication of the marriage banns; strictly forbade pastors to assist at marriages and to baptize in the cases of those from other dioceses who could easily approach their proper pastors; and finally, appointed the fourth Sunday after Easter of the year 1849 as the opening date of the next Council.[65]

The Holy See was asked, moreover, that if it were seen fit to grant the request embodied in the first decree of the Council, we be allowed henceforth to join the word, Immaculate, to the word, Conception, in the oration and preface of the Mass and the oration of the Office, and to add to the Litany of the Blessed Virgin the invocation, Queen

[63] *Conc. Prov. Balti. Habita*, p. 228.

[64] *Conc. Prov. Balti. Habita*, pp. 226 and 227.

[65] *Conc. Prov. Balti. Habita*, pp. 244 and 245.

conceived without original sin.[66] The petition for the new sees of Albany, Buffalo and Cleveland with recommendations of candidates for each was also sent to Rome at this time.

The entire work of the Council met with unstinted approval from the Holy See. The petition for the patronage of Our Lady Immaculate with the other formal decrees was approved on February 7, 1847.[67] The erection and filling of the new sees was made known in a letter dated July 3, 1847,[68] while as early as September 13, 1846 the Holy Father had sanctioned the incorporation of the word Immaculate into our liturgy.[69] By briefs dated July 24, 1846 [70] and January 30, 1847 [71] a second and third province, those of Oregon City and St. Louis respectively, were created.

So henceforth, all national legislation had to emanate from plenary councils. It was the universal wish of the Catholics of this country that the Hierarchy take advantage of an early opportunity to come together to mark a day of triumph for the young American Church after its years of struggle. To satisfy this general demand Archbishop Eccleston on September 23, 1848 with the authorization of the Holy See issued the usual letters of convocation naming the following May as a suitable time for our First Plenary Council.[72]

The day came and the meeting was held but expectations for a formal National Council were not realized. Because of their remote position the Archbishop of Oregon City and his Suffragan, the Bishop of Walla Walla, were unable to attend the Council and sent word to this effect thus causing the abandonment of the original plan.[73]

The Archbishops and Bishops of the Provinces of Baltimore and St. Louis, however, met in the former city to discuss matters of import to the American Church. Their deliberations continued through the week and resulted mainly in seven formal decrees and a number of petitions to the Holy See. The matter of the decrees

[66] *Conc. Prov. Balti. Habita*, p. 241.
[67] *Conc. Prov. Balti. Habita*, pp. 254, ff.
[68] *Conc. Prov. Balti. Habita*, pp. 250, ff.
[69] *Conc. Prov. Balti. Habita*, pp. 246, ff.
[70] O'Hara, *Pioneer Catholic History of Oregon*, p. 132.
[71] Rothensteiner, *History of the Archdiocese of St. Louis*, II, 2.
[72] *United States Catholic Magazine*, III, n. 10, 543.
[73] Shea, *Hist. of the Cath. Church in the U. S.*, II, 36.

is as follows: the assurance to the Holy See of the great devotion of American Catholics to Mary Immaculate; the expression on the part of the Fathers of the gratitude that will be theirs when the Holy Father sees fit to define the doctrine of the Immaculate Conception; the slight modifications of the existing method of recommending candidates for the Episcopacy; the determining of ownership for certain Church property; the refusing of *exeats* to all not certain of incardination in another diocese; the prohibition for priests to assist at the marriage of those who have gone or intend to go before a non-Catholic minister; and finally, the expression of hope that with the authority of the Holy See a national council be held in 1852.[74] Another enactment which because of its nature was not included in the above official statutes was the unanimous agreement of the Fathers to have taken up in all the churches of the United States on the Sunday within the octave of the feast of Sts. Peter and Paul a collection for the Holy Father as a testimony of filial love and obedience.[75]

The petitions sent to Rome at this time show the rapid growth of Catholicity in our country. It was asked that New York, New Orleans and Cincinnati be made Archiepiscopal sees and that the Metropolitan See of Baltimore be dignified with the Primacy of honor. The new sees of Savannah, Wheeling and St. Paul were requested. Vicars Apostolic were sought for the territory of New Mexico and a designated section of the Rocky Mountain district; and in a final appeal was expressed the need for a coadjutor for Hartford because of the failing health of the Bishop of that see.[76]

The Fathers of the Council received a favorable reply to all their petitions except that asking the prerogative of Primacy for the see of Baltimore.[77] Regarding this the letter of the Propaganda was silent. The request repeated, however, by the Fathers of the First Plenary and the Eighth Provincial Councils of Baltimore was finally granted by a decree of the Sacred Congregation of Propaganda dated August 15, 1858.[78] The statutes of the Council were approved by

[74] *Conc. Prov. Balti. Habita*, pp. 277, ff.

[75] *Conc. Prov. Balti. Habita*, p. 272.

[76] *Conc. Prov. Balti. Habita*, pp. 269, ff.

[77] *Conc. Prov. Balti. Habita*, pp. 287, ff.

[78] *Conc. Plen. Balti. II Acta et Decr.*, p. 343; Shea, *Hist. of the Cath. Church in the U. S.*, II, 379 and 380.

Pope Pius IX on June 16, 1850,[79] and by the second decree of the First Plenary Council were extended to all the dioceses included within the States and Territories of the Union.[80]

Thus the Seventh Council of Baltimore, a little more than Provincial and a little less than Plenary served as a fitting transition to those of a national character.

Archbishop Eccleston who had been the first to send out letters convoking a Plenary Council in the United States, did not live to see the actual fulfillment of his much cherished wish.[81] His successor, the Most Reverend Francis Patrick Kenrick, appointed August 3, 1851 received not quite three weeks later, on August 19, from Pope Pius IX the Brief "*In Apostolicae Sedis*"[82] appointing him Apostolic Delegate with power to preside over a Plenary Council. This Council was convened on May 9, 1852. Its twenty-five decrees include the acknowledgment of the decrees of all the general councils and the extending of the enactments of the first seven Councils of Baltimore to the whole United States; the legislation regarding the Ritual and the Ceremonial; the residence of Bishops in their dioceses; the appointing of Diocesan Consultors, a Chancellor and a Censor Librorum; the condemning of a too ready reception of foreign priests; the defining of limits for missionary districts; marriage and the publication of banns; the teaching of catechism; the establishing of schools; the founding of at least provincial seminaries; the administration of temporalities; the Ritual for Benediction of the Most Blessed Sacrament; the seeking of the right of worship for our Catholic soldiers and sailors; the spreading of the Society of the Propagation of the Faith and the Association of Prayer; the petition for extraordinary faculties regarding Matrimony; the petition for the extension *ad perpetuum* or for another twenty years of the privilege of using the infant form for adult baptism; the case of those who have gone or who intend to go before a non-Catholic minister for the sake of marriage; and the time of promulgation of the foregoing decrees.[83]

[79] *Conc. Prov. Balti. Habita*, p. 290.

[80] *Conc. Plen. Balti. Habit. 1852*, p. 144.

[81] He died April 22, 1851—cf. Shea, *Hist. of the Cath. Church in the U. S.*, II, 40.

[82] Shea, *op. cit.*, p. 366; *Conc. Plen. Balti. Habit. 1852*, p. 3.

[83] *Conc. Plen. Balti. Habit. 1852*, pp. 43, ff.

Of the many other questions that came up for discussion the most important were the feasibility of having our parishes canonically erected; the preparation of catechisms in English and German; the use of the Roman calendar in our provinces; and the establishment of societies for the maintenance of Catholic schools and for the safeguarding of Catholic rights, proposals for which organizations were rejected.

As usual a number of petitions over and above those embodied in the decrees of the Council were sent to Rome by the Fathers. These were for an indult to ordain *titulo missionis;* that the Holy See forbid any secular priest in the United States to enter Religion without the written permission of his Bishop; the enriching by indulgences of the work of the Sodality of Prayer for converts; a further change in the method of erecting and filling sees in this country; and finally, the erection of the new sees of Portland in Maine, Burlington, Brooklyn, Newark, Erie, Covington, Quincy, Santa Fe, Natchitoches and Wilmington; the making of San Francisco and Boston into Metropolitan sees and the creation of Vicariates Apostolic in upper Michigan and in Florida.[84]

The entire work of the Council met with Apostolic approval. The decrees with little or no change were ratified on September 5, 1852.[85] The petitions were for the most part granted. The indult to ordain *titulo missionis* was given *ad quinquennium* from January 1, 1853. The use of the infant form for adult Baptism was approved for another five years with the recommendation that the Bishops strive during that period to bring about the observance of the Roman Ritual in this respect. Apropos of the Ordinary's permission for seculars to enter Religion the Sacred Congregation called the attention of the Fathers to the fact that their wish had already been granted through the Papal approval of the second decree of the Sixth Provincial Council. All the proposed sees were erected and filled with the exception of that of Wilmington. Likewise, it pleased the Holy See to postpone the forming of the Province of Boston and the creation of a Vicariate Apostolic in Florida.[86]

[84] *Conc. Plen. Balti. Habit. 1852*, pp. 24, ff and 53, ff.

[85] *Conc. Plen. Balti. Habit. 1852*, p. 56.

[86] *Conc. Plen. Balti. Habit. 1852*, pp. 57, ff; cf. Shea, *Hist. of the Cath. Church in the U. S.*, II, 369, ff.

It was the years 1866 and 1884 that saw enacted our greatest national legal achievement, the decrees of the Second and Third Plenary Councils. The former of these convened on October 7, 1866 with the Most Reverend Martin J. Spalding, Archbishop of Baltimore, presiding as Apostolic Delegate.[87]

In the surprisingly short time of two weeks (the Council closing on October 21) the Fathers has passed five hundred and thirty-four decrees. There are included under fourteen titles treating of the orthodox faith, the Hierarchy and Church government, ecclesiastical persons, churches and Church property, the Sacraments, divine worship, uniformity of discipline, regulars and nuns, the instruction of youth, the salvation of souls, books and newspapers, secret societies, the erection of new episcopal sees, and finally, the efficacious execution of the Council's decrees. Forwarded to Rome these decrees were approved with only slight revision on October 6, 1867 [88] and continued to be our most important source of law for about the next two decades.

In the wealth of matter that goes to make up the rather sizeable volume published under the title, "*Concilii Plenarii Baltimorensis II Acta Et Decreta,*" the student of Ecclesiastical Law finds comparatively little to engage him. The specialist in Dogmatic or Pastoral Theology, especially the latter, will find herein a much larger field of interest. It is true that discipline has been given a generous share in the decrees but as a rule the Fathers have hesitated to go beyond mere suggestion and exhortation and so one finds a rather small number of strict commands and prohibitions.

Of the Acts and Decrees of The Third and last of our Plenary Councils the same can be said in a general way though here one finds the proportion of positive statutes appreciably greater. This Council opened on November 9, 1884 and lasted almost a month ending on December 7. Owing to the illness of Cardinal McCloskey of New York, Archbishop Gibbons of Baltimore was appointed Apostolic Delegate.[89] The fruit of its five sessions was three hundred and nineteen decrees divided under eleven titles and treating of the Catholic faith,

[87] *Conc. Plen. Balti. II Acta et Decr.*, p. xix, ff.

[88] *Conc. Plen. Balti. II Acta et Decr.*, p. cxxxvi.

[89] *Conc. Plen. Balti. III Acta et Decr.*, p. xix.

ecclesiastical persons, divine worship, the Sacraments, the education of clerics, the instruction of Catholic youth, Christian doctrine, zeal, Church property, trials, and Christian burial. All these decrees were approved with very little modification on September 10, 1885 [90] and constituted our chief source of law until the Code went into effect on May 19, 1918.

The Second Plenary Council of Baltimore having incorporated into its decrees what of previously existing local legislation was considered still useful became the code of our particular ecclesiastical law.[91] The Third Plenary Council declared that all the decrees of its predecessor which it did not change or abrogate continued to bind. It did not, therefore, replace but only supplemented the existing American statutes.[92] The alterations of the Second Council affected by the Third and the changes of the Third Council brought about by subsequent decrees of the Holy See were very few. Before the promulgation of the Code practically all the decrees of these two Plenary Councils were in force. Which of these laws have survived the Code requires a comparative study to ascertain and to this study the succeeding chapters will be devoted.

[90] *Conc. Plen. Balti. III Acta et Decr.*, p. xv.
[91] *Conc. Plen. Balti. II, Acta et Decr.*, p. 270.
[92] *Conc. Plen. Balti. III, Acta et Decr.*, p. 3.

CHAPTER II

GENERAL PRINCIPLES COVERING THE RELATION BETWEEN THE CODE AND PARTICULAR LAW

The decrees of the Councils of Baltimore canonically fall under what is known as particular law. Now, particular law can be made by every residential Bishop for his diocese either in synod or out of it,[1] by the Bishops of a province for that province either in a provincial council or a meeting,[2] and finally by the Archbishops and Bishops of several provinces, convened with the special permission of the Holy Father and presided over by his Delegate, for their several provinces.[3] To this last group belong the laws of the Plenary Councils of Baltimore under consideration. The decrees of the Third Plenary Council and those of the Second not abrogated by the Third were for the most part certainly in force up to the time of the Code's promulgation. The question now is: How did the new common law affect our local statutes? Nowhere in the Code does one find decreed the total abolition of all particular laws. Nor should this be expected since the very purpose of particular law is to enlarge on the scope of the general[4] and it has always been the policy of the Church to respect and safeguard particular law in so far as consistency would allow.[5]

In Canon 6, §1, however, one finds laid down the general principle according to which is to be determined the status of all particular laws in force at the time of the promulgation of the Code. This principle is summed up briefly in the words: "*Leges quaelibet, sive universales sive particulares, praescriptis huius Codicis oppositae, abrogantur, nisi de particularibus legibus aliud expresse caveatur.*"

This clearly implies, as commentators universally admit, that all

[1] Canons 335 and 362.

[2] Canons 283-291 and 1507.

[3] Canons 281 and 291.

[4] Vering, *Theologische Bibliothek, Kirchenrecht*, p. 346.

[5] Neuberger, *op. cit.*, p. 44.

particular laws opposed to the decrees of the Code are abrogated except those that are expressly kept in force by such phrases as "*nisi aliter pro locis particularibus legitime provisum fuerit,*" "*salvis particularibus constitutionibus,*" "*nisi aliter in casibus particularibus fuerit a Sancta Sede provisum,*" and the like.[6]

Such expressions are immediately manifest and leave no doubt as to the present binding force of the law in question. Opposition on the other hand is not always so evidently conspicuous. Its detection requires a process that is not so simple. A comparison must be made between the general and particular laws and a judgment formed as to their relations, that is, as to whether they are opposed to each other or not. But before making this judgment it is necessary to know what the Code means by the word opposed—*oppositae*—as used in the canon quoted above. Neuberger who has made a thorough study of canon 6 defines the word as used by the Code as "the relation of two laws identical in matter and different in form."[7] This difference may be negative or positive. The former called contradiction is "the introduction of an enactment which is the negation of an erstwhile affirmation."[8] The latter called contrariety is "a positive repugnance which exists between two laws."[9] Opposition, then, is a general term including both contradiction and contrariety. It exists wherever there is incompatibility between two laws, that is, where two laws are mutually exclusive and so cannot be in force simultaneously.

With the ground thus cleared one is prepared to make a judgment. The result will be one of three possibilities. Opposition either will be certainly present or certainly absent or there may exist a doubt. If opposition be certainly present, then the particular law is abrogated. If certainly absent, then the particular law will continue in force. If doubt exists and cannot be dispelled, one must resort to the principle laid down in canon 6, §4 which says: "*In dubio num aliquod canonum praescriptum cum veteri jure discrepet, a veteri jure non est recedendum.*" Though the text of the Code and commentators would seem to restrict this principle to doubt existing between the

[6] Canons 120, 162 and 235.

[7] *Op. cit.*, p. 35.

[8] Suarez, *op. cit.*, p. 450, n. 2, cap. XXVII.

[9] *Ibid.*

old and new common law, still in the absence of any other rule, it may be applied analogously to particular law, being as it is after all only an adaptation of the principle: "*Melior est conditio possidentis.*"

According to the terminology of the jurists a particular statute opposed to the general law is a *jus contra legem.* One not opposed may be either *jus secundum legem* or *jus praeter legem.* The former of these two terms is used for those laws practically identical with the common law while the latter includes all laws that without opposition go entirely or partially beyond the common law. An example of a statute entirely *praeter codicem* is that of our Third Plenary Council decreeing *ipso facto* excommunication reserved to the Ordinary for validly married Catholics who attempt marriage after a civil divorce.[10] While an instance of one partially *praeter codicem* is the decree of the same Council requiring the clergy retreat at least every two years instead of at least every three years as ordered by the Code.[11]

It remains now to make a comparison between the Baltimore statutes and the Code to ascertain to which of the foregoing three classes each of our local laws belongs. Those that can be assigned to the first class, that is those opposed, have lost their binding force, while all the others continue of obligation for us.

[10] N. 124.

[11] N. 75; canon 126.

CHAPTER III

PERSONS

The Second Plenary Council of Baltimore treats of Persons in its second and third Titles wherein it deals from number 42 to number 181 with the Roman Pontiff, Archbishops, Bishops, Diocesan Officials, Priests having the care of souls, Provincial Councils, Diocesan Synods, the Duties of Clerics and other kindred subjects. The Third Plenary Council gives its second Title, number 11 to number 99, to the consideration of Persons. Herein one finds the rules governing the appointment of American Bishops, a rather thorough treatment of Diocesan Consultors, Examiners of the Clergy, Irremovable Pastors, the *Concursus* for appointment to parishes, the Diocesan Clergy in general and finally of Regulars especially as regards the exercising of the sacred ministry and consequent relations to the Ordinary.

The Code devotes to this matter one of its five books including canons 87 to 725. Its treatment, which is more complete, detailed and logical, considers the notion of person, clerics in general and in particular and, finally, religious and the laity. Under the title of "Clerics in Particular" it deals with the Roman Pontiff and those who share with him the administration of the Church, with Bishops and diocesan administration, with pastors and assistants and lastly at great length with religious.

Since, as has been said, the more logical and more familiar order of the Code is to be followed, some subjects included under Persons in the Second Council of Baltimore will be treated later in this work.

TITLE I

Stable Affiliation With Diocese

SECOND PLENARY COUNCIL

93. Censuerunt Patres orandam esse S. Sedem ut declarationem edat pro Statibus Americae Septentrionalis Foederatis, qua statuatur clericos in

CODE

CANON 112

Praeter casus de quibus in can. 114, 641, § 2, ut clericus alienae dioecesi valide incardinetur, a suo Ordinario

sacris, ordinatos titulo missionis, et dioecesibus hisce addictos, non posse absque Ordinarii sui licentia in scripto data, religiosum Ordinem ingredi, prout jam Episcopis Vincennensi et Ludovicopolitano S. Congregatio rescripsit.

Third Plenary Council

60. Hoc praetera fine statutum est, ut quicumque ad sacra ministeria in dioecesi obeunda ab Episcopo proprio, vel cum ejus licentia ab alieno, sive ad titulum missionis, sive ad alium titulum ordinantur, eo ipso huic dioecesi adscripti sint. Hinc et Concilium Provinciale Baltimorense I., n. 2, statuit, et Concilium Plenarium Baltimorense II. confirmavit: "quemlibet sacerdotem qui pro quacumque hujus provinciae dioecesi ordinatus fuerit, teneri vi promissionis in ordinatione factae ad permanendum in eadem dioecesi, et ad se subjiciendum praesuli suo, usquedum canonice dimissus fuerit." Hoc decretum, S. Congregatio de Propaganda Fide (Instr. 16 Oct. 1830.) iis consentaneum declaravit, quae Benedictus XIV. eadem de re docuerat.

61. Imo vero, ii omnes, qui titulo missionis inter sacros ministros cooptari cupiunt, juxta repetitas S. Congregationis declarationes, prius juramentum emittere tenentur, quo spondeant, quod in sua dioecesi perpetuo in divinis administrandis laborem suum et operam, sub omnimoda directione et jurisdictione R. P. D. pro tempore Ordinarii, pro salute animarum impensuri sint. (Instr. S. C. de P. F., 17 Apr. 1871, n. 8.) Unde, qui hoc titulo ordinati sunt, quod in nostris regionibus communiter fit, tam arcto vinculo suae dioecesi obligantur, ut ne ab Episcopo quidem absolvi pos-

obtinere debet litteras ab eodem subscriptas excardinationis perpetuae et absolutae; et ab Ordinario alienae dioecesis literas ab eodem subscriptas incardinationis pariter perpetuae et absolutae.

Canon 114

Habetur excardinatio et incardinatio, si ab Ordinario alienae dioecesis clericus beneficium residentiale obtinuerit cum consensu sui Ordinarii in scriptis dato, vel cum licentia ab eodem in scriptis concessa e dioecesi discendendi in perpetuum.

Canon 542

Firmo praescripto can. 539-541, aliisque in propriis cuiusque religionis constitutionibus,

2.° Illicite, sed valide admittuntur:

Clerici in sacris constituti, inconsulto loci Ordinario aut eodem contradicente ex eo quod eorum discessus in grave animarum detrimentum cedat, quod aliter vitari minime possit;

Aere alieno gravati qui solvendo pares non sint;

Reddendae rationi obnoxii aut aliis saecularibus negotiis implicati, ex quibus lites et molestias religio timere possit;

Filii qui parentibus, idest patri vel matri, avo vel aviae, in gravi necessitate constitutis, opitulari debent, et parentes quorum opera sit ad liberos alendos vel educandos necessaria;

Ad sacerdotium in religione destinati, a quo tamen removeantur irregularitate aliove canonico impedimento;

Orientales in latinis religionibus sine venia scripto data Sacrae Congregationis pro Ecclesia Orientali.

Canon 981

§ 1. Si ne unus quidem ex titulis de quibus in can. 979, § 1, praesto sit,

sint, sed Sanctae Sedis dispensatione opus sit, non illi tantum, qui ad aliam dioecesim cui incorporetur transire velit, sed etiam cui sacram religionem ingredi desiderium sit. (Ibid. n. 10.)

suppleri potest titulo servitii dioecesis, et, in locis Sacrae Congregationi de Prop. Fide subiectis, titulo missionis, ita tamen ut ordinandus, iureiurando interposito, se devoveat perpetuo dioecesis aut missionis servitio, sub Ordinarii loci pro tempore auctoritate.

As a missionary country under the Sacred Congregation of Propaganda we had neither parishes nor benefices and our priests were ordained *titulo missionis.* Accordingly, they were to serve in a diocese or a vicariate-apostolic and be supported by the offerings of the faithful. In some parts of the country living conditions were especially hard and contributions consequently few in number and small in amount. Many of the clergy received scarcely enough for their daily maintenance, and provision for the future was entirely out of the question. As a result, fearing lest old age or infirmity should find them without means of support, a good number of priests became panic-stricken and sought refuge in religious orders where they could be sure of a decent living under any circumstances. The Fathers of the First Provincial Council viewed this situation with concern. Accordingly in their second decree,[1] while insisting on the obligation of priests to remain in their dioceses, they declared themselves nevertheless in no wise wishing to interfere with the liberty of entering Religion granted to the secular clergy by Pope Benedict XIV.[2]

The Fathers of the Sixth Provincial Council saw in this liberty a real menace to the stability of our diocesan clergy in general as it had already proved to be for those of St. Louis and Vincennes in particular. Through the medium, therefore, of their second decree[3] they petitioned the Holy See to extend to the whole United States the rescript already granted to the two above mentioned dioceses; which rescript forbade any cleric in Sacred Orders who had been ordained *titulo missionis* and had become affiliated with any of our dioceses to join a religious order without the written permission of his Ordinary.

[1] *Conc. Prov. Balti. Habita,* p. 73.
[2] *Const. "Ex quo,"* July 11, 1742—*Fontes,* 329.
[3] *Conc. Prov. Balti. Habita,* p. 244.

The Holy See approved the decrees of the Council [4] but made no specific mention of the foregoing request, though of others made similarly at this time and previously the Sacred Congregation was wont to take special cognizance. The matter, therefore, was left at least in doubt and the secular clergy apparently took the benefit of it and continued freely to enter Religion.

In number 93 of the Second Plenary Council the Fathers, employing the identical words of the Sixth Provincial, renewed the petition. The reply of the Congregation was to the effect that the decree of the Sixth Provincial Council which contained this petition had been approved with the others and was to be diligently observed.[5]

On April 27, 1871 the Sacred Congregation of the Propagation of the Faith issued an Instruction requiring of each candidate before ordination *titulo missionis* the taking of an oath of perpetual service to his diocese; release from which oath, whether to enter Religion or to change dioceses, could be granted only by the Holy See.[6] This legislation was incorporated into numbers 60 and 61 of the Third Plenary Council. The Fathers at the same time, however, petitioned Rome to permit the changing from one diocese to another within the same province simply by mutual consent of the Ordinaries concerned without having recourse to the Holy See. This request was granted by a decree dated November 30, 1885.[7]

Regarding change of diocese on the part of diocesan clergy the Code makes no distinction between changes within the same province and those involving two different provinces, but gives two methods of effecting the transfer. The first of these requires the signed excardination and incardination of the Ordinaries concerned.[8] The second provides a kind of substitute for the first and recognizes on the part of the incardinating Ordinary the granting of a benefice and on the part of the excardinating Ordinary his signed consent to this or at least his written permission for the cleric in question to leave the diocese forever.[9] As for entrance into Religion the Code contains

[4] *Conc. Prov. Balti. Habita*, p. 254.

[5] *Conc. Plen. Balti. II Acta Et Decreta*, p. 67, footnote 2.

[6] *Coll. de Prop. Fide*, 1369.

[7] *Conc. Plen. Balti. III Acta Et Decreta*, p. civ.

[8] Can. 112.

[9] Can. 114.

no invalidating clause for diocesan clergy in good standing. But in canon 542, § 2, it declares illicit such entrance as is unknown to one's Ordinary or is opposed by him on the grounds of grave detriment to souls which cannot otherwise be averted.

Since the two laws alike leave to the discretion of the local Ordinaries concerned any changes of diocese within the same province there is no difficulty. But the question arises as to whether our clergy to change from one diocese to another not in the same province or to enter a religious Order still need the permission of the Holy See.

The practice here since the publication of the Code and seemingly before has been to follow the common law in this matter; and this practice now appears definitely justified. Our passing in 1908 [10] from the control of the Sacred Congregation of Propaganda to that of the Consistory and the subsequent change by this latter Congregation of our title of ordination from *missionis* to *servitii ecclesiae* [11] gave rise to some doubts. Among the questions asked of the Congregation of the Consistory was whether or not our *ordinandi* were henceforth to take the oath of service to their church or diocese. The answer of the Congregation was negative, with allowance for any common law prescription to the contrary.[12] This led some to conclude that those ordained under the title of service were obliged to no oath at all,[13] but the Code in canon 981, § 1, states clearly that they are. It must be concluded then, as stated above, that since the common law has supplanted the Council on this point, our secular clerics in changing dioceses or entering Religion must follow the prescription of the Code.[14]

It, of course, goes without saying that here as in other things recourse to the Holy See against the refusal of the Ordinary is always open to the cleric.[15]

A question not touched by the Council or Code, but one none the less interesting and often asked in connection with the entrance of a

[10] *Constitutio "Sapienti Consilio,"* June 29, 1908—*A. S. S.*, XLI (1908), 431.

[11] Jan. 2, 1909—*A. A. S.*, I (1909), 685.

[12] *A. A. S.*, I (1909), 686, ad XIV.

[13] Ayrinhac, *Legislation on the Sacraments*, p. 356.

[14] Vermeersch, *op. cit.*, II, 143; Ayrinhac, *Legislation on the Sacraments*, pp. 352, ff.

[15] Vermeersch, *op. cit.*, I, 355.

secular cleric into Religion, concerns the expenses incurred by the diocese for his education. This topic, a very practical one, has been discussed at length by canonists. Their conclusion, based on the general policy of the Church to extend as much as possible the liberty of seculars to enter Religion and on some of her positive decrees is that such indebtedness is no obstacle to a religious vocation. Since neither the aspirant nor his chosen community is obliged to pay this debt, it remains a liability of the diocese.[16]

TITLE II

Method of Changing Diocese After Ordination

Second Plenary Council

109. Statuimus et declaramus quemlibet sacerdotem qui pro quacumque hujus provinciae dioecesi ordinatus fuerit, teneri vi promissionis in ordinatione factae ad permanendum in eadem dioecesi, et ad se subjiciendum praesuli suo, usquedum canonice dimissus fuerit. Statuimus quoque eadem obligatione pariter adstringi omnem sacerdotem rite co-optatum in aliquam dioecesim: co-optari autem declaramus quemlibet ex aliena dioecesi advenientem, statim ac testimoniales et dimissoriales litterae, praesulis cui proxime subditus erat munitae auctoritate, ab ipso sacerdote, Ordinario cui se subjicere velit exhibeantur, et ab eodem in perpetuum acceptantur. His porro statutis obstare nolumus quin ea servari debeant, quae Benedictus XIV., (Constitutione 25, Tom. 2. Bullarii sui: *Ex quo dilectus.*) luculenter docet circa sacerdotes qui ad religiosum aliquem Ordinem transire volunt.

Third Plenary Council

62. Cum varias ob causas quandoque fieri soleat, ut sacerdos uni dioecesi vi ordinationis adscriptus ad aliam transire cupiat, vel sacerdos regularis ab ordinis sui vinculo solutus, clero saeculari adscribi petat, visum est Nobis certum modum definire, quo in hisce nostris provinciis sacerdos alienus clero dioecesano incorporari debeat. Duplicem itaque statuimus incorporationem, vel ut appellari solet, incardinationem, formalem scilicet et praesumptam.

63. Formalem declaramus eam esse, quae per actum Episcopi documento signatum efficitur, qui sacerdotem alienae dioecesis, dummodo utique literas commendatitias et excardinationis a suo Episcopo afferat atque exhibeat, in clerum suum adscribit. Haec tamen adscriptio non statim facienda est, cum quis admitti in aliquam dioecesim postulat, quocumque titulo ordinatus fuerit, sed Episcopus eum inter trienii spatium in ministeriis sacris exercendo ad

---

[16] Vermeersch, *op. cit.*, I, 354, and *De Religiosis*, II, Nos. 21 and 22; Augustine, *A Commentary on Canon Law*, III, 212; Benedict XIV, *Const.* "*Ex quo*"—*Bullarium*, II, 78.

tempus probabit, exquirendo interim peculiares informationes ab Ordinario, a quo fuerat dimissus. Exigere tamen poterit experimentum ultra triennium, sed non ultra quinquennium, quo in casu Episcopus hoc suum propositum ulterioris probationis sacerdoti in scriptis significare debet, antequam triennium expiret. Priusquam vero triennale vel quinquennale experimentum absolvatur, si illum idoneum reperiat, expresso decreto dioecesi adscribat; idque Episcopo, cui ille proxime subditus fuit, significet. Ex communi vero consilio et concensu utriusque Episcopi atque ipsius sacerdotis, poterit is ex propria dioecesi excorporari et in alteram incorporari absolute et immediate, praetermisso probationis tempore.

64. Si de sacerdote agatur, qui ordinatus est titulo missionis, Episcopus sex mensibus antequam illum absolute dioecesi adscribat, supplices ejus preces S. Congregationi de Propaganda Fide commendet, ut haec a juramento quo adhuc obstrictus est, illum dispenset. Qua dispensatione obtenta, Episcopus novum ab eo juramentum in favorem suae dioecesis recipiat (Conc. Prov. Balt. VIII., decr. III.), illiusque formulam a sacerdote subscriptam in tabulario episcopalis curiae servandam mandet. Episcopum vero, a quo sacerdos discessit, de receptione a se facta moneat.

65. Quod vero pertinet ad sacerdotes religiosos, qui vota solemnia nuncuparunt, atque ex Apostolica indulgentia in saeculo vivere permittuntur; vel qui ediderunt vota simplicia et a suis Congregationibus seu institutis egressi sunt (nisi qui a votis rite soluti jam in presbyterorum saecularium conditione versantur), si ad Episcopum accedant petantque in ejus dioecesim adscribi, primo quidem tantum ad missae celebrationem, dummodo literas saecularizationis ac commendatitias Ordinarii loci a quo dicesserunt exhibeant, admitti possunt, nondum vero ad triennale experimentum in ministerio pastorali. Volumus enim, ut ad hanc probationem in ministeriis hujusmodi subeundam non admittantur, antequam Episcopus, exquisitis ab Ordinis vel Instituti superioribus et Episcopo commendante secretis informationibus, iisque ad S. Congregationem remissis, hujus veniam sciscitatus sit; qua obtenta, peractoque experimento, ii qui non ad tempus, sed in perpetuum S. Congregationis Episcoporum et Regularium rescripto saecularizati sunt, clero dioecesano incardinari possunt, dummodo prius de titulo canonico sibi providerint. Quod si assumunt titulum missionis, simul juramentum dioecesi perpetuo inserviendi praestare tenentur. (Instr. S. C. cit., n. 12.)

66. Praesumptam incardinationem haberi declaramus, si Episcopus elapso triennio vel respectivo quinquennio probationis, actum adscriptionis formalem omiserit. Qui enim eo elapso tempore, clericum qui dioecesi adscribi petierat, nec formaliter admittit nec admittere plane diserteque recusat, jure praesumitur adscripsisse. Quod quidem valet etiam pro ordinatis titulo missionis, quo in casu juramentum praestitum in aliena dioecesi, censetur pro nova esse servandum. Idem valet de regularibus modo quo dictum est saecularizatis, qui consentiente S. Congregatione ad experimentum admissi sunt. Isti enim in hoc casu dioecesi titulo missionis (nisi de alio titulo canonico sibi providerint) adscripti esse praesumuntur, iisdemque tenentur obligationibus ac si juramentum praescriptum revera emisissent.

67. Declaramus porro sacerdotum, sive ad nostras provincias pertineat, sive ex Europa aliundeve advenerit, etsi a proprio suo Episcopo literas excorporationis (*Exeat*) jamjam obtinuerit, a vinculo communionis et subjectionis erga ipsum solutum haberi non posse, donec alteri dioecesi vel formaliter vel praesumptive adscriptus sit; simulque, si de formali adscriptione agatur, Episcopus proprius de ea peracta authenticum monitum acceperit. Ejus enim jurisdictio in sacerdotem tantum cessat post hanc monitionem. Itaque declaramus literas dimissoriales quantumvis dimissionem seu excardinationem plenam et absolutam enuntiare videantur, sensu exposito intelligendas esse, "ne ovis quasi perdita et errans inveniatur." (C. 1, dist. 72.) Simul decernimus quod, sicut nullus sacerdos exterus in dioecesim adscribendus est, priusquam literas dimissoriales proprii Episcopi rite confectas Ordinario loci exhibuerit, ita neque has literas ulli sacerdoti a suo Episcopo dandas esse, nisi certo constet, eum ab alio Episcopo in dioecesim fore admittendum. (Instr. S. C. de P. F., 31 Jan. 1866. Conc. Plen. Balt. II. No. 122.)

69. Quae de sacerdotum excorporatione, et in aliam dioecesim adscriptione sive formali sive praesumpta definivimus, nullatenus obstant consuetudini, juxta quam Episcopi sacerdotes, si qui in sua dioecesi satis abundent, egentioribus dioecesibus ad auxilium in cura animarum ferendum pro longiori etiam tempore concedunt. Quem morem, uti zeli Apostolici indicium, S. Sedes commendavit. (Instr. S. C. C. ad Conv. Epp. Prov. Mediol. 1849.)

Code

Canon 112

Praeter casus de quibus in can. 114, 641, § 2, ut clericus alienae dioecesi valide incardinetur, a suo Ordinario obtinere debet litteras ab eodem subscriptas excardinationis perpetuae et absolutae; et ab Ordinario alienae dioecesis litteras ab eodem subscriptas incardinationis pariter perpetuae et absolutae.

Canon 114

Habetur excardinatio et incardinatio, si ab Ordinario alienae dioecesis clericus beneficium residentiale obtinuerit cum consensu sui Ordinarii in scriptis dato, vel cum licentia ab eodem in scriptis concessa e dioecesi discedendi in perpetuum.

Canon 585

Professus a votis perpetuis sive sollemnibus sive simplicibus amittit ipso iure propriam quam in saeculo habebat dioecesim.

Canon 641

§ 1. Si religiosus in sacris constitutus propriam dioecesim ad normam can. 585 non amiserit, debet, non renovatis votis, vel obtento saecularizationis indulto, ad propriam redire dioecesim et a proprio Ordinario recipi; si amiserit, nequit extra religionem sacros ordines exercere, donec Episcopum benevolum receptorem invenerit, aut Sedes Apostolica aliter providerit.

§ 2. Episcopus religiosum recipere potest sive pure et simpliciter, sive pro experimento ad triennium: in priore casu religiosus eo ipso est dioecesi incardinatus; in altero, Episcopus potest probationis tempus prorogare, non ultra tamen aliud triennium; quo etiam transacto, religiosus, nisi antea dimissus fuerit, ipso facto dioecesi incardinatus manet.

Canon 964

Quod attinet ad ordinationem religiosorum:

1.° Abbas regularis de regimine, etsi sine territorio *nullius*, potest conferre primam tonsuram et ordines minores, dummodo promovendus sit ipsi subditus vi professionis saltem simplicis, ipse vero sit presbyter et benedictionem abbatialem legitime acceperit. Extra hos fines, ordinatio, ab eodem collata, revocato quolibet contrario privilegio, est irrita, nisi ordinans charactere episcopali polleat;

2.° Religiosi exempti a nullo Episcopo ordinari licite possunt sine litteris dimissoriis proprii Superioris maioris;

3.° Superiores professis votorum simplicium, de quibus in can. 574, litteras dimissorias concedere possunt dumtaxat ad primam tonsuram et ordines minores;

4.° Ordinatio ceterorum omnium alumnorum cuiusvis religionis regitur iure saecularium, revocato quolibet indulto Superioribus concesso dandi professis a votis temporariis litteras dimissorias ad ordines maiores.

The Second Plenary Council in number 109 recognizes only one method of changing dioceses. It decrees that a priest coming from one diocese becomes incardinated in another only after he has presented authenticated testimonial and dismissorial letters to the Ordinary of his choice and is accepted by him in perpetuity.

The Third Council has a full treatment of the subject under the title, *De Sacerdotum Incardinatione,* which includes numbers 62 to 69. It gives two methods of effecting a change of diocese, the formal and the presumed or informal.

The incardination in a new diocese is formal when a priest with proper testimonials and *exeat* from his former Bishop has his name formally inscribed on the list of clergy of that diocese; which inscription may be made immediately or after a trial of from three to five years. If, as has just been seen above, this change involved two provinces, the permission of the Holy See would be required.

For the formal incardination of a religious priest who has been secularized or has left his community at the expiration of his temporary vows, the Council prescribes the following: Such a priest presenting himself for admission to a diocese, if he is without letters of secularization and the recommendation of the Ordinary of the place from which he has come, is at first to be permitted only to say Mass. Should he have documents, he may be allowed to exercise the pastoral ministry, but only on trial for three or five years. It is even strongly urged that before this acceptance on probation the incardinating Bishop make secret inquiries about the priest from his former religious Superior and Ordinary and forward this information to the Holy See, whose permission for incardination must be asked. The period of probation completed and the consent of the Sacred Congregation obtained the priest, if permanently secularized, may be formally inscribed among the diocesan clergy and so become formally incardinated.

Incardination is presumed alike for seculars and ex-religious when after the above-mentioned trial period, which is optional for the former and obligatory for the latter, no formal action is taken by either of the parties concerned. The failure of the Bishop to dismiss or of the priest to leave is considered to imply mutual satisfaction and so effects incardination.

The Code deals with incardination and excardination in canons 112, 114, 585 and 641. The first two of these refer to the secular clergy and the last two to religious and ex-religious. According to canon 112 a change of diocese is validly effected for a secular cleric when he has obtained letters of absolute and perpetual excardination and incardination signed by the respective Ordinaries. Canon 114 provides another method for the secular clergy by recognizing a valid change of diocese when a cleric has obtained from the incardinating Ordinary a residential benefice and from the excardinating Ordinary in writing either the permission to accept the benefice or his perpetual release from his diocese.

As for religious, canon 585 provides that only by perpetual vows is one excardinated from his diocese. In further confirmation of this, canon 641, § 1, provides that a religious in Sacred Orders who in accordance with canon 585 has not lost his diocese by perpetual profession, must, if he does not renew his vows or is secularized, return to his Ordinary and be accepted by him. Since according to canon 964, § 4, a religious cannot receive Sacred Orders until after he has made his final vows, this case will arise only with those entering the novitiate after having received at least Subdiaconate and hence will be comparatively rare.

For the incardination of a religious secularized after having taken his final vows, canon 641, § 2, provides the following: The benevolent Bishop may receive the religious unconditionally, in which case he is *ipso facto* incardinated. The Bishop, on the other hand, may accept the religious conditionally on trial for three years, which period of probation may be extended another three years at most. At the end of the six-year period the religious becomes *ipso facto* incardinated in the diocese unless he has been dismissed before the time of trial has elapsed.

We now follow the Code in this matter, since our local discipline is incompatible with the common law and must yield.

A summary of the changes to our former discipline of excardination and incardination wrought by the Code will be interesting. In the first place the Code does not require the permission of the Holy See in any case, whereas the Council did, except for change of dioceses within the same province. Secondly, the Code is silent about a period of probation for the secular clergy, while the Council admitted, though it did not require, one. Thirdly, the Code allows, but does not require, for secularized religious a trial period which is to have a maximum limit of six years, while the Council required such a trial with a limit of five years. Fourthly, according to the Code, presumed incardination takes place in the case of seculars without any prescribed period of probation and only when one has received a benefice; whereas the Council recognized no such presumption without the three or five year trial and accepted any kind of ministry, even a chaplaincy, as sufficient grounds. Lastly, according to the Code presumed incardination for religious takes place only at the completion of the second three-year period of probation, while according to the Council it went into effect at the end of five years at most and even at the end of three years if during that time the Bishop did not signify in writing his intention of requiring two more years.

TITLE III

Privilegium Fori

THIRD PLENARY COUNCIL

84. Omnino vetamus, ne contra laicum de pecunia pro sedium locatione vel alia de causa ecclesiae debita

CODE

CANON 120

§ 1. Clerici in omnibus causis sive contentiosis sive criminalibus apud

coram tribunali civili agant, nisi accepta prius in scriptis Episcopi licentia. Ad tuendam porro immunitatem ecclesiasticam, quatenus inter nos fieri potest, districte iisdem prohibemus, ne contra sacerdotem vel clericum de rebus etiam temporalibus coram judice civili litem intentent sine permissione scripto expressa ipsius Episcopi, cujus erit in omnibus hujusmodi casibus litem, quantum fieri potest, amice componere, re etiam, si opus sit, ad consultores vel aedituos delata. In rebus vero ecclesiasticis, ex ipsa divina Ecclesiae constitutione, judicium non pertinet nisi ad jurisdictionem ecclesiasticam.

iudicem ecclesiasticum conveniri debent, nisi aliter pro locis particularibus legitime provisum fuerit.

§ 2. Patres Cardinales, Legati Sedis Apostolicae, Episcopi etiam titulares, Abbates vel Praelati *nullius*, supremi religionum iuris pontificii Superiores, Officiales maiores Romanae Curiae, ob negotia ad ipsorum munus pertinentia, apud iudicem laicum conveniri nequeunt sine venia Sedis Apostolicae; ceteri privilegio fori gaudentes, sine venia Ordinarii loci in quo causa peragitur; quam tamen licentiam Ordinarius, praesertim cum actor est laicus, ne deneget sine iusta et gravi causa, tum maxime cum controversiae inter partes componendae frustra operam dederit.

§ 3. Si nihilominus ab eo qui nullam praehabuerit veniam, conveniantur, possunt, ratione necessitatis, ad vitanda maiora mala comparere, certiore tamen facto Superiore a quo venia obtenta non fuit.

Canon 2341

Si quis contra praescriptum can. 120 ausus fuerit ad iudicem laicum trahere aliquem ex S. R. E. Cardinalibus vel Legatis Sedis Apostolicae, vel Officialibus maioribus Romanae Curiae ob negotia ad eorum munus pertinentia, vel Ordinarium proprium, contrahit ipso facto excommunicationem Sedi Apostolicae speciali modo reservatam; si alium Episcopum etiam mere titularem, aut Abbatem vel Praelatum *nullius*, vel aliquem ex supremis religionum iuris pontificii Superioribus, excommunicationem latae sententiae Sedi Apostolicae simpliciter reservatam; demum si, non obtenta ab Ordinario loci licentia, aliam personam privilegio fori fruentem, clericus quidem incurrit ipso facto in

suspensionem ab officio reservatam Ordinario, laicus autem congruis poenis pro gravitate culpae a proprio Ordinario puniatur.

The Second Plenary Council treats of the *privilegium fori* in numbers 155 and 156. In the first of these it lays down the general principle that clerics should not be hasty in going before a civil tribunal; that when difficulties arise even with laymen and in temporal affairs they should neither hail another before the secular court nor answer a summons there unless the matter cannot be settled otherwise. Number 156 is a repetition of a decree of the Third Provincial Council[17] and contains an exhortation to all the faithful to settle amicably their disputes concerning things or with persons ecclesiastical or at least to submit them to the judgment of the Bishop. It calls attention at the same time to the common law sanctions against ecclesiastics who hastily bring one another before the civil court in matters strictly pertaining to the Church.

The Third Plenary Council dealing with this subject in number 84 repeats the words of the Second as an exhortation and adds two strict prohibitions to clerics. By the first of these they are forbidden to bring laymen before the civil court for pew rent or other Church debt without the written permission of the Bishop. The second forbids them to institute civil proceedings against another cleric even in temporal matters without the written permission of the Bishop.

By expressly mentioning clerics only as forbidden to take the initiative in going before the secular tribunal without permission of the Bishop the Council implies that laymen may do so in matters temporal without consulting the Ordinary.

This interpretation seems to have gone unquestioned until 1911. On the occasion of the publication on October 9 of this year of the *Motu Proprio "Quantavis diligentia,"*[18] which treated of the *privilegium fori,* there was an outcry in our secular press. Catholic writers immediately took up the challenge, maintaining that these protests were unjustified; that the Church has no wish to deprive laymen of getting justice from the clergy; and that the liberty granted them through the Councils of Baltimore with the approval of the

[17] N. 6.

[18] *A. A. S.*, III (1911), 555.

Holy See was not being interfered with. They argued that, since the *Motu Proprio* made provision for such a custom as had existed in this country since before 1837, the laity of the United States continued to enjoy the immunity granted them by the Third Provincial Council of Baltimore.[19]

The Code treats of the *privilegium fori* in canons 120 and 2341. The first of these legislates that in all cases clerics are to be brought before the ecclesiastical court unless there be a legitimate local provision to the contrary. The canon further provides for the bringing of clerics before the civil court with the proper permission; which permission is to be obtained from the Holy See in the case of Cardinals, Legates, Bishops, Abbots and Prelates *nullius,* the supreme heads of religious orders of Pontifical right, and Officials of the Roman Curia; and from the local Ordinary in the case of all others enjoying the *privilegium fori.* Finally, the Ordinary is advised not to refuse such permission without just and serious reason, especially when the plaintiff is a layman and all efforts to effect an amicable settlement have failed. Canon 2341 determines the penalties to be meted out to those who would dare to act contrary to the prescription of canon 120; which penalties are excommunication, suspension or other punishments according to the dignity of the defendant and the quality of the plaintiff.

As will be seen from a detailed comparison, our local law on this point is either *secundum* or *praeter codicem* and therefore still binds. In the case of cleric *versus* cleric both laws agree in forbidding appeal to the civil court without the proper permission. The Council's requirement that the permission of the Ordinary be in writing seems something beyond, not opposed to the Code and so this formality should still be observed.

Since the Code makes no mention of a cleric taking action against a layman, the Council's prohibition against a cleric's suing a layman for pew rent or other Church debts before the civil court without the Ordinary's permission is *praeter codicem* and still in force.

In the case of layman *versus* cleric, as has been seen, the Council implies and the common interpretation has been[20] that no permis-

[19] *Conc. Prov. Balti. Habit.* pp. 140 and 142; *Eccl. Rev.*, XLVII (1912), 303, ff.

[20] Ayrinhac, *General Legislation*, p. 252; *Eccl. Rev.*, XLVII (1912), 313.

sion is needed. The Code, on the other hand, while requiring proper permission not only shows a certain leniency towards laymen in urging Ordinaries to grant this permission in the absence of serious reason to the contrary especially in their case,[21] but in the first part of canon 120 opens the way to our particular concession by the words *nisi aliter in locis particularibus legitime provisum fuerit.* Though this phrase refers directly to Concordats, it might be understood, as Vermeersch-Creusen seems to interpret it, to include a custom of one hundred years' standing.[22] Such a broad interpretation, however, is not necessary for us. In view of the fact that apparently for more than one hundred years before the promulgation of the Code the laity of this country had not been required to get permission to take action against a cleric in the civil court, we may appeal to canon 5 in support of the continuance of this liberty.

TITLE IV

The Right of the Clergy to Decent Support

THIRD PLENARY COUNCIL

71. Statuimus igitur ac decernimus, ut in singulis nostris dioecesibus Episcopi, inito prius cum clero suo consilio, quamprimum constituant motos mediaque opportuna, quibus subsidia ad decentem illorum sacerdotum sustentationem elargienda praesto habeantur. Quem in finem ab Episcopo aerarium vel gaza instituatur, imposita taxa singulis paroeciis, quae opportuna videbitur. Huic pecuniae juxta normas clare definitas administrandae commissio presbyterorum, ipso Episcopo praeside, praeponatur.

Si quis vero Episcopus, ob frequentes ad populum de pecunia appellationes, hanc novam taxam imponendam non esse judicaverit, ab aequitatis ac justitiae tramite alienum non erit, taxam annuam ipsismet dioecesis

CODE

CANON 981

§ 2. Ordinarius presbytero, quem promoverit titulo servitii ecclesiae vel missionis, debet beneficium vel officium vel subsidium, ad congruam eiusdem sustentationem sufficiens, conferre.

CANON 1484

Ordinarius ne admittat dimissionem beneficii a clerico in maioribus ordinibus constituto factam, nisi constet eum necessaria ad honestam sustentationem aliunde habere, et firmo praescripto can. 584.

CANON 2154

§ 1. Amoto parocho Ordinarius, examinatoribus vel parochis consultoribus, qui partem habuerunt in amotione decernenda, in consilium adscitis, pro viribus consulat sive

---

[21] Can. 120, 2.

[22] *Epitome Iuris Canonici,* I, 138.

sacerdotibus imponere, qua singuli pro rata salarii pecuniam contribuant.

Modus alius praedictae necessitati prospiciendi in eo est, ut societas mutui subsidii inter presbyteros constituatur, quae societas aerarii seu pecuniae congestae administrationem, item Episcopo praeside, curabit. Huic societati unusquisque sacerdos dioecesi adscriptus nomen dare urgeatur.

translatione ad aliam paroeciam vel assignatione alius officii aut beneficii, si ad haec idoneus sit, sive pensione, prout casus ferat et adiuncta permittant.

§ 2. Ceteris paribus, in provisione favendum magis renuntianti quam amoto.

In treating above of the diocesan clergy entering Religion the chief motive given was their constant sense of insecurity regarding sickness and old age. Since there were no benefices, our secular priests for the most part had a hand-to-mouth sort of existence and hence no chance to provide for the future. The Bishops were painfully aware of this situation and did what they could to remedy it.

The Fathers of the Third Provincial Council devoted to this matter their second decree. The Second Plenary Council in number 90 repeats this decree in which the Fathers having exhorted the Bishops to warn the faithful of their duty of supporting their priests add that, if because of sickness or for some other reason priests are no longer able to carry on their ministry, lest those already suffering be further afflicted, it is for their Bishop to see to it that what he judges they need will be furnished them by those whom they have served. If the congregation be so poor as not to be able to give this support Bishops are exhorted to seek it from the charity of the clergy and faithful. The Council further expresses the ardent desire that, as soon as possible, every Bishops with the advice and assistance of his priests will establish in his diocese a definite and stable method of providing for the aged and otherwise incapacitated. In the end the Fathers express their unwillingness that those priests who are unworthy, who oppose the authority of their Bishop or who refuse to contribute to the above-mentioned fund should profit by the provision of this decree.

The Fathers of the Third Plenary Council are even more authoritative and definite when in their seventy-first statute they say: "We decree and order that in every one of our dioceses, the Bishops as soon as possible having first taken council with their clergy determine upon suitable ways and means of having money from which they can readily contribute to the decent support of their priests. To which end the Bishop is to establish a fund or treasury by imposing on each parish a tax which seems to him fitting. This money is to be administered according to clearly defined rules by a commission of priests under the direction of the Bishop himself.

"If, however, any Bishop should judge that on account of the frequent appeals to the people for money this new tax ought not to be imposed, it will not be against justice or equity to impose on the diocesan clergy themselves an annual tax by which each priest will contribute according to the amount of his salary.

"Another way of providing for the above-mentioned necessity consists in the establishment among the priests of a society of mutual help; which society likewise under the direction of the Bishop will look after the administration of the fund or money collected. Every priest incardinated in the diocese is to be urged to join this society." [23]

There is no corresponding legislation in the Code, but the Baltimore decree is according to the spirit of the common law as reflected in canons 981, § 2, 1484 and 2154 which insist on the provision of support for the dioceasn clergy whether in active duty, resigned or even removed. The Council in determining the ways of fulfilling the common law is *praeter codicem* and still binding.

TITLE V

Obligations of Clerics

The Second Plenary Council after treating of Archbishops, Bishops and Pastors has a chapter *De Vita et Honestate Clericorum* which includes numbers 147 to 169. For the most part these decrees contain what was then the general legislation of the Church together with some ascetical and pastoral exhortations that are not law. Only on a few points does one find any statutes properly so called. The same must be said of the chapter of the Third Plenary Council which is devoted to this subject and comprises numbers 74 to 84.

[23] Nilles, *Commentaria*, Pars II, p. 111.

Article 1

Spiritual Exercises

Third Plenary Council

75. Statuimus itaque ut Episcopi clerum suarum dioecesium quotannis vel saltem singulis bienniis in sacrum istum secessum ducant, ut omnes mente cordeque renovati et ampliores adepti gratias divinas, ad munus sacri ministerii fructuosius peragendum redeant.

Code

Canon 126

Omnes sacerdotes saeculares debent tertio saltem quoque anno spiritualibus exercitiis, per tempus a proprio Ordinario determinandum, in pia aliqua religiosave domo ab eodem designata vacare; neque ab eis quisquam eximatur, nisi in casu particulari, iusta de causa ac de expressa eiusdem Ordinarii licentia.

The Second Council in numbers 147 and 163, as does the Code in canon 124, lays down the general principle of the necessity of personal holiness on the part of the clergy; and the Third Council in number 74 confirms this principle. The various means of acquiring priestly virtue are treated by both the particular and common laws. The Second Council does not go into detail, but in number 168 stresses the importance of a life of prayer for the clergy. The Third in number 75 after affirming the utility of the spiritual retreat decrees that every year or at least every two years Bishops must have one for their clergy.

The Code in canon 125 gives a list of the spiritual exercises which are the normal and morally necessary means of sustaining the priestly life. These are frequent confession and daily meditation, the daily visit to the Blessed Sacrament and the daily recitation of the rosary and examination of conscience. Canon 126 legislates the retreat which is to be made at least every three years.

Of all the spiritual exercises this last is the only one that forms common ground for a strict law on the part of both the Council and the Code. The latter admits a maximum of three years between retreats while the local law allows only two. There is, however, no opposition between the two laws. The use of the expression *tertio saltem quoque anno* by the Code implies the desire for more frequent retreats and leaves the way open for any particular legislation, as our, which orders them oftener. Our rule then requiring a diocesan retreat at least every other year is *praeter codicem* and still in force. As a matter of fact most of our Bishops have one every year.[24]

Article 2

Obedience to One's Bishop

Second Plenary Council

108. Nonnulla da Sacerdotibus Decreta in prioribus Baltimorensibus Conciliis lata confirmamus atque iterum promulgamus:

Quoniam saepius a quibusdam in dubium revocatum est, an competeret praesulibus Ecclesiae, in hisce Foederatis Provinciis, facultas sacerdotes in quamlibet dioeceseon suarum partem ad sacrum ministerium deputandi, eosque inde, prout in Domino judicaverint, revocandi; monemus omnes sacerdotes in hisce dioecesibus degentes, sive fuerint in iis ordinati, sive in easdem co-optati, ut memores promissionis in ordinatione emissae, non detrectent vacare cuilibet missioni ab episcopo designatae, si episcopus judicet sufficiens ad vitae decentem sustentationem subsidium illic haberi posse, idque munus viribus et valetudini sacerdotum ipsorum convenire. Hac autem declaratione nihil innovare volumus quoad illos qui parochialia obtinerent beneficia, quorum unum tantum, scilicet in civitate Neo-Aurelia adhuc noscitur in hisce Provinciis: neque ullatenus derogare intendimus privilegiis quae Religiosis fuerint a S. Sede concessa.

Code

Canon 127

Omnes clerici, praesertim vero presbyteri, speciali obligatione tenentur suo quisque Ordinario reverentiam et obedientiam exhibendi.

Canon 128

Quoties et quandiu id, iudicio proprii Ordinarii, exigat Ecclesiae necessitas, ac nisi legitimum impedimentum excuset, suscipiendum est clericis ac fideliter implendum munus quod ipsis fuerit ab Episcopo commissum.

The Second Plenary Council in number 108 repeating the first decree of the First Provincial Council reminds priests of their duty in virtue of their ordination promise to accept and persevere in the work assigned them by their Bishop.

[24] Ayrinhac, *General Legislation*, pp. 262 and 263.

The Code in canons 127 and 128 declares that all clerics and particularly priests have a special obligation of respect and obedience to their Ordinary; and that they must accept and faithfully discharge any work assigned them as often and as long as the Bishop judge the Church's need demands it and the cleric is not legitimately excused.

This law applies, as Ayrinhac points out,[25] even to those ordained with the title of patrimony though not in the same degree as to those having the title of service. The promise of the cleric is one not of vassalage, but of religion and links the clergyman to the legitimate power of the diocese.[26] According to the wording of the canon the extent of the obligation of the cleric is in direct proportion to the need of the Church. The conclusion logically is drawn that where there is no real need there is no strict obligation.[27]

The question now arises as to whether our priests are still bound by the above Baltimore law which is unconditional, making no mention of the Church's need, or may avail themselves of the greater liberty granted by the Code. Or practically can a priest whose services are not needed by his diocese and who is self-supporting retire? It would seem that on this point the canon of the Code has replaced our local statute since the restriction of the latter is opposed to the liberty given by the former. Such freedom is more in keeping with the age-old policy of the Church as evidenced by her general laws from the beginning. Nor does it seem that the Baltimore decree was intended in its spirit to be against this. But made, as it was, at a time and in a place where the necessity of the Church was always present, its Framers could not be expected to provide for a circumstance which they could not foresee would arise; and no doubt even before the Code had one of our priests sought retirement on the plea of not being needed his request, if well-founded, would have been granted.

Article 3

Studies

The Third Plenary Council devotes number 186 to the importance of a priest's continuing his studies after ordination and in the fol-

[25] *General Legislation*, p. 267.

[26] Augustine, *Commentary*, II, 73.

[27] *A. A. S.*, II (1910), 911; Vermeersch-Creusen, *op. cit.*, I, 143 and 144.

lowing numbers gives the means to this end. These are the examinations for the junior clergy and the theological conferences.

Section I—The Junior-Clergy Examinations

THIRD PLENARY COUNCIL

187. Ad praecavendum ne apud juniores de clero sacrae scientiae studium unquam obtorpescat aut defervescat, mandamus ut omnes et singuli sacerdotes quotannis per quinquennium saltem a die suscepti presbyteratus, coram Episcopo ejusve delegato et examinatoribus cleri dioecesani, districte examinentur super variis praestitutis ecclesiasticae scientiae partibus, Scripturae scilicet Sacrae, Theologiae Dogmaticae et Moralis, Juris Canonici, Historiae Ecclesiasticae, rei demum Liturgicae.

188. Si quis forsan quaestionibus propositis, uti par est, non satisfecerit, quinque annis elapsis, tot iteratis examinibus subjicietur, quot nulla vel insufficientia ab examinatoribus fuerint declarata. Idem statuimus quoad eos qui quacumque de causa, dispensatione non obtenta ab Episcopo, examen praescriptum non subierint.

De singulis autem examinatis scripto exaretur judicium in Episcopi archivo diligenter custodiendum. Inde fiet ut sacerdotum indoles ac doctrina superioribus ecclesiasticis magis magisque patescant, quod non parum proderit in assignandis missionibus.

CODE

CANON 130

§ 1. Expleto studiorum curriculo, sacerdotes omnes, etsi beneficium paroeciale aut canonicale consecuti, nisi ab Ordinario loci ob iustam causam fuerint exempti, examen singulis annis saltem per integrum triennium in diversis sacrarum scientiarum disciplinis, antea opportune designatis, subeant secundum modum ab eodem Ordinario determinandum.

§ 2. In collatione officiorum et beneficiorum ecclesiasticorum ratio habeatur eorum qui, ceteris paribus, in memoratis periculis magis praestiterunt.

Regarding the junior-clergy examinations the Council in numbers 187 and 188 orders that each and every priest for at least the first five years after his ordination be examined thoroughly before the Bishop or his delegate and the examiners of the diocesan clergy on the various prescribed parts of the ecclesiastical sciences; namely, Holy Scripture, Dogma, Moral, Canon Law, Church History and

Liturgy; and that should any one fail to answer the proposed questions satisfactorily, he must after five years, repeat as many of the examinations as have been declared null or insufficient by the examiners. The same applies to those who without being dispensed by the Bishop have for any reason whatsoever not stood these tests.

Each one's marks are to be preserved in writing in the diocesan archives.

The Code in canon 129 decrees the continuation of ecclesiastical studies after ordination and in canon 130 orders that all priests, unless excused for a good reason by the Ordinary, must every year for at least the first three years after ordination undergo according to the manner to be determined by the same Ordinary an examination in the different branches of the sacred sciences assigned a sufficient length of time ahead.

In appointments to ecclesiastical offices and benefices all things being equal those ought to be preferred who have excelled in these examinations.

The two laws on this point are practically identical save as regards the minimum number of years over which these examinations are to be continued; but even here there is no opposition for by the use of the expression *saltem per integrum triennium* the Code evidently favors a longer period and any legislation, as our own, requiring such continues to bind. In this country, then, the junior-clergy examinations should extend over a period of not less than five years.

Section II—The Theological Conferences

Third Plenary Council

190. Cum vero Episcopi invigilare teneantur, ne sacerdotum suorum imperitia populus sibi commissus detrimentum patiatur, ut tanto malo aditus praecludatur, volumus et edicimus, ut Ordinarii instituant perficiantque Collationes, seu coetus de rebus theologicis, "quae scientiae sacrae rudimenta in omnium mentibus conservent, praxim sanam ac uniformem pro animarum directione promoveant, intellectus inertiam depellant, ac abusus eliminandi opportunam praebeant occasionem."

Code

Canon 131

§ 1. In civitate episcopali et in singulis vicariatibus foraneis saepius in anno, diebus arbitrio Ordinarii loci praestituendis, conventus habeantur, quos *collationes* seu *conferentias* vocant, de re morali et liturgica; quibus addi possunt aliae exercitationes, quas Ordinarius opportunas iudicaverit ad scientiam et pietatem clericorum promovendam.

§ 2. Si conventus haberi difficile sit, resolutae quaestiones scriptae

mittantur, secundum normas ab Ordinario statuendas.

§ 3. Conventui interesse, aut, deficiente conventu, scriptam casuum solutionem mittere debent, nisi a loci Ordinario exemptionem antea expresse obtinuerint, tum omnes sacerdotes saeculares, tum religiosi licet exempti curam animarum habentes et etiam, si collatio in eorum domibus non habeatur, alii religiosi qui facultatem audiendi confessiones ab Ordinario obtinuerunt.

The Second Plenary Council in number 68 had already prescribed these conferences for the clergy in order to keep up their professional knowledge, promote uniformity of practice in the direction of souls and to correct abuses. These were ordered held, if possible, four times a year in cities, either on the Monday of the week preceding Ember week or on some other day definitely chosen by the Ordinary, and at least twice a year in rural districts.

The Third Council in numbers 189 to 193 treats the subject more fully. In number 190 it orders Bishops to institute theological conferences which all priests secular and religious who have the care of souls must attend. Those who frequently neglect to be present without a legitimate excuse and the permission of the Ordinary are to be punished.

The number is to be at least four a year in cities and two a year in the rural sections. The Bishops are yearly to propose a carefully prepared scheme of questions in doctrine and discipline. The solution of a case is to be prepared in writing by all who have the obligation of attending. Two whose names are drawn will read their solutions and discuss the case. The questions in Holy Scripture, Dogma, Canon Law and Liturgy will be treated by those appointed.

The Code treats of these conferences in canon 131 and orders them held often during the year in the episcopal city and each deanery. They are to deal with questions of Moral Theology and Sacred Liturgy to which the Ordinary may add whatever other exercises he thinks useful for the promotion of learning and piety among the clergy. Should the holding of a meeting be difficult the written answers are to be sent according to the directions of the Bishop.

Unless they have previously obtained from the Ordinary express exemption, all secular priests and all religious having the care of souls must attend these meetings or send their written solutions as the case may be. All other religious priests having from the Ordinary the faculty of hearing confessions are, likewise, bound if no conference is held in their own houses.

A study of the foregoing decrees shows that both the Code and Councils legislate on three phases of the theological conferences; namely, their number, their subject matter, and those who have the obligation of attendance. Regarding the number the Code is indefinite saying no more than *saepius in anno*. Our more definite local statute requiring at least each year four in cities gives a satisfactory interpretation and determination to the common law and continues to be our rule. As for the two a year allowed by the Council for rural districts the same can hardly be said. The Code makes no distinction between the city and the country and so the word *saepius* applies to both. Twice a year can hardly be considered often and so it would seem that this indulgence on the part of the Council is opposed to the Code and can no longer be availed of without the permission of the Holy See or the use of *epikeia.*

As for the subject-matter the Code mentions specifically only Moral Theology and Liturgy leaving the Bishop free to add questions from other branches. The Council on the other hand is more comprehensive requiring a case of conscience and various questions from all the other sacred sciences. Here again it seems the Council must yield to the Code. The greater restriction placed on the Bishop's choice by the former is opposed to the liberty which the common law grants.

Finally, as regards those obliged to attend the Code goes further than the Council by requiring the presence not only of priests having the care of souls, but also of all seculars and of all religious not having the care of souls, but who having faculties for confessions in the diocese have no conferences in their own houses.

Herein again the more exacting law of the Code prevails.

Article 4

Clerical Dress

Second Plenary Council

148. Itaque volumus, ut Ecclesiae legem servent, domique agentes vel in templo, veste talari, quae Clerico propria est, semper utantur. Cum foras prodeunt muneris vel animi recreandi causa, vel in itinere, breviori quadam indui liceat, quae tamen nigri coloris sit, et infra genua producatur. Venustiores quasdam et elegantiores vestium formas, quae novae in dies inveniuntur, aspernentur et respuant.

149. Duo hac de re praedecessorum nostrorum decreta adjicimus:

Sacerdotibus omnibus curandum est, ut veste talari et superpelliceo in omni sacro munere obeundo utantur. Iis etiam vehementer commendamus, ut vestem talarem constanter, quatenus fieri possit, gerant: quod si eam induere peculiaria rerum adjuncta non sinant, ipsis omnino injungimus, iis tantum uti vestibus quae suo congruant ordini, scilicet, quae nigri sint coloris, et omni inani ornatu careant, sintque ab omni mundana vanitate prorsus alienae.

150. Quoniam uniformitas etiam in rebus minimis maxime optanda Ecclesiae semper visa est, statuimus superpelliceum esse debere modestum, decorum, et sacris functionibus conveniens. Statuimus etiam, ut biretum, cum episcopis singulis visum fuerit morem illud gestandi in suas dioceses inducere, Romano bireto sit conforme.

Third Plenary Council

77. Volumus itaque et praecipimus, ut omnes Ecclesiae legem servent, domique agentes vel in templo veste talari, quae clerico propria est, semper utantur. Cum foras prodeunt muneris vel animi recreandi causa vel in itinere, breviori quadam veste indui licet, quae tamen nigri coloris sit et ad genua producatur, ita ut a laicis distingui possint. Elegantiores vestium formas et mundanas quae novae in dies inveniuntur respuant. Stricto praecepto sacerdotibus nostris injungimus, ut tam domiquam foris, sive in propria dioecesi degant sive extra eam, collare quod romanum vocatur gerant. Et quia ratio legis ecclesiasticae de vestitu clericorum non minus valet de regularibus quam saecularibus, sacerdotes quoque regulares tenentur lege utendi vel collari romano vel vestitu idoneo ad distinguendum clericos a laicis, quotiescumque seposito habitu sui ordinis proprio foras prodeunt.

Code

Canon 136

§ 1. Omnes clerici decentem habitum ecclesiasticum, secundum legitimas locorum consuetudines et Ordinarii loci praescripta, deferant, tonsuram seu coronam clericalem, nisi recepti populorum mores aliter ferant, gestent, et capillorum simplicem cultum abhibeant.

The Second Plenary Council treats of clerical dress in numbers 148, 149 and 150. The last two decrees are repetitions of the twenty-seventh and thirty-first statutes respectively of the First Provincial Council. Regarding the cassock, surplice and biretta are herein prescribed the following: The cassock and surplice are to be worn for all sacred functions; the surplice must be modest, decent and suited to the sacred ministry; the biretta is to conform to the Roman style.

As for the priest's general attire the Provincial Council urges that the cassock be worn as much as possible. Where this is not practical, it requires a black suit which is not to be unduly showy and worldly. The Second Plenary Council not only repeats these prescriptions but goes further and in number 148 after insisting on the necessity of a distinctly clerical garb declares that this in the church and the rectory is to be the cassock and elsewhere a black suit with a coat *infra genua.*

The Third Plenary Council in number 77 repeats verbatim this decree of the Second with the exception that in speaking of the length of the coat it substitutes the expression *ad genua* for the *infra genua* of its predecessor. It further orders that, both at home and outside whether in one's own diocese or away from it, the Roman collar is to be worn by priests.

The prescription of the Code on clerical dress is more general. In canon 134, § 1 it decrees that all clerics are bound to wear a becoming clerical costume according to legitimate local customs and the regulations of the Ordinary.

The detailed requirements of the Baltimore law are in no wise opposed to the Code, but on the contrary amply provided for by it and so remain in force.

In view of this a practical question naturally proposes itself. Are our clergy still obliged to wear the long coat in vogue at the time of the Councils and are the vast majority of our priests and seminarians guilty of a breach of law in adopting a shorter coat? With nothing but the word of the local law to argue from the answer must be in the affirmative. However, it seems possible to legalize the present practice by some deductions from what seems to have been the interpretation put upon this law from the beginning, from custom and from *epikeia.* From the very time of the Council our clergy seem to have interpreted this law rather broadly and while always as a general rule wearing a distinctive street-dress they have tended to conform somewhat to the style followed by the conservative layman. When our local statute went into force the long coat which it prescribed was being worn by men generally. As time went on even the more discriminating laymen began wearing shorter coats and the clergy did likewise.

This interpretation of the law became the foundation of our custom of wearing a shorter though plain coat. According to canon 27 the requirements were no more stringent before the Code,[28] such custom against the law to become acceptable must be reasonable, legitimate and of forty years' duration. Our custom seems to fulfill these conditions. It seems reasonable to adopt the shorter coat because of the inconvenience of the long one, its inadaptability to the marked change in our living conditions, its gradual fall into disuse as everyday apparel and its consequent conspicuousness. That our custom is legitimate appears from the fact that there has never been any pronouncement against it by either the Holy See or our Bishops collectively.[29] Finally, more than forty years have elapsed since the Third Council of Baltimore and so the time element necessary for our custom is supplied.

A third claim to justification for our present day clerical dress lies in *epikeia.* It is hardly probable that the Fathers of the Third Plenary Council meant to bind the clergy of this country permanently to a certain style of coat in spite of the exigencies of time and circumstances. It is not likely that, had they been able to foresee our present living conditions, they would notwithstanding have insisted on the observance of their decree to the letter. That on the other hand they were willing to cope with changes in dress is evident from the fact that, as mentioned above, they legislated a shortening of the coat from *infra genua* to *ad genua.*

Therefore, while the letter of our law on this point still stands, the present practice among our clergy seems justifiable. The foregoing canon, however, makes provision for any regulations of the local Ordinary on clerical dress. Hence any diocesan statutes regarding this matter are binding.

The Sacred Congregation of the Council on July 28, 1931, issued a decree on clerical dress. No new legislation is contained therein

[28] Smith, *Elements,* I, 47 and 48. [29] *Eccl. Rev.,* LV (1916), 87.

but the prescriptions of canons 136, § 1 and 811, § 1, which govern the priest's attire both outside of and during his sacred ministrations are reaffirmed.[30]

Article 5

Regarding the Hair and the Beard

Second Plenary Council

151. Comam et barbam studiose, aut laicorum more, ne nutriant. Comam alere saepius a Synodis vetitum est. Barbam Clericorum promissam nuper damnavit Pontifex Pius PP. IX. Ecclesiasticis omnibus hac in re morem Romanae Ecclesiae, tanquam normam sequendam, mandamus.

Code

Canon 136

§ 1. Omnes clerici decentem habitum ecclesiasticum, secundum legitimas locorum consuetudines et Ordinarii loci praescripta, deferant, tonsuram seu coronam clericalem, nisi recepti populorum mores aliter ferant, gestent, et capillorum simplicem cultum adhibeant.

The Second Plenary Council in number 151 legislated further in respect to the personal appearance of clerics. Herein it condemns any undue care of the hair and beard after the manner of the laity; calls attention to the prohibitions of Councils against too great care of the hair; mentions the condemnation by Pope Pius IX of the growing of the beard by clerics;[31] and finally commands that in all these things the custom of the Roman Church be followed.

Regarding the hair the Code in canon 136, § 1 after ordering the wearing of the tonsure, unless there be an accepted custom to the contrary, states, as our own Council, in a general way that the hair be dressed simply. As for the beard no mention whatsoever is made by the Code. This silence led some to believe that all former prohibitions had been withdrawn and that Bishops could no longer enforce them.[32] The Sacred Congregation of the Council, questioned on the soundness of this view by the Bishop of Breslau, replied on January 10, 1920, that it was unfounded and declared that the existing discipline remains unchanged.[33]

Our local statute, then, ordering clerics to practice simplicity in the care of the hair and forbidding them to grow the beard is in

[30] *A. A. S.*, XXIII (1931), 336.

[31] *Conc. Plen. Balti. II Acta et Decreta*, Appendix, p. 286.

[32] Ayrinhac, *General Legislation*, p. 293.

[33] *A. A. S.*, XII (1920), 43.

accord with the Code and the foregoing answer of the Sacred Congregation and hence still has the force of law.

Article 6

The Prohibition Against Engaging in Business

Third Plenary Council

274. Ad evitanda gravissima incommoda, quae facillime ob congestas undique pecunias oriri possent, nulli in posterum Episcopo, eoque minus rectori aut aliis personis ecclesiasticis, tam saecularibus quam regularibus, fas erit mensas argentarias tenere. Si quae adhuc existant, statuimus ut intra quinque annos a publicatis concilii nostri decretis dissolvantur, nisi longius tempus fuerit a S. Congregatione impetratum.

279. Reprobamus quoque ac damnamus eum, qui haud paucis in locis inolevit morem deponendi apud sacerdotes pecuniam ea lege, ut foenore aucta stato tempore recuperetur.

Code

Canon 142

Prohibentur clerici per se vel per alios negotiationem aut mercaturam exercere sive in propriam sive in aliorum utilitatem.

The Councils in treating the question of priests avoiding secular business and employments practically repeat the common law which in turn is but a somewhat detailed expression of the divine law. There is, therefore, very little of our local legislation that is special. One point, however, is strongly emphasized because of the dangers connected with it particularly in our country. This has to do with the carrying on of a kind of banking business by the clergy.

Fear of trusting their meagre savings to the keeping of laymen not infrequently led many of our Catholic immigrants to put their money in the care of some priest who out of pity would very often undertake its management. In view of the fact that this would prove a source not only of serious distraction but also of grave danger of scandal in case of loss, the Third Plenary Council in number 274 forbids ecclesiastics both secular and religious to carry on any kind of banking.

This absolute prohibition of the Council agrees with that of the Code contained in canon 142 by which clerics are forbidden either personally or through agents to engage in trading or business for the benefit of themselves or others and hence continues to bind.[34]

Very similar but more specific is the decree of number 159 of the Second Plenary Council incorporated in number 279 of the Third and which forbids the depositing of money with secular and religious Rectors of churches with a view to collecting interest at stated times.

This prohibition is in perfect accord with that of canon 142 quoted above and so remains in force.

Article 7

Unbecoming Recreations and Amusements

Second Plenary Council

153. Ludis scenicis, spectaculis, choreis ne intersint.

Third Plenary Council

79. Celebre inter SS. Patres axioma habet, multa quae fidelibus licent clericos dedecere. Itaque ut ecclesiastico ordini honor suus et decus servetur, mandamus ut sacerdotes a publicis equorum prorsus abstineant cursibus, a theatris et spectaculis.

Code

Canon 140

Spectaculis, choreis et pompis quae eos dedecent, vel quibus clericos interesse scandalo sit, praesertim in publicis theatris, ne intersint.

The Second Plenary Council in number 153 says very tersely that clerics are not to attend theatrical plays, spectacular entertainments or dances. The Third in number 79 contains a command that they abstain from horse races, theatres and spectacular entertainments. The Code in canon 140 decrees that clerics are not to attend, especially in public theatres, spectacular entertainments, dances and festivities that are unbecoming for them or their presence at which might give scandal.[35]

The Councils and the Code agree in substance but differ in details. As for the manner our local prohibition is without qualification while the common law forbids only such amusements as are unbecoming

[34] Even before the Code this practice had been condemned in a decree of the Sacred Congregation of The Consistory dated November 18, 1910.—*A. A. S.*, II (1910), 910.

[35] Vermeersch-Creuzen, *Epitome*, 1, 149; Woywod, *A Practical Commentary*, 1, 58; Ayrinhac, *General Legislation*, p. 305, ff.

or may prove a source of scandal. As far as the form of the Baltimore law is concerned its absolute prohibition is in no wise opposed to the Code and still stands. However, as canon 29 states, custom is the best interpreter of the law, and it seems that the American clergy have never strictly interpreted these decrees of the Councils, but have always understood them to mean practically the same as is now expressed in canon 140.

In comparing these two sources of law one finds regarding the specific amusements condemned that the words theatre and *spectacula* are common to all three; that dances are mentioned by the Second Council and the Code only; that the Third Council alone mentions horse racing; and that to the Code alone belongs the word pomps.

The Code, therefore, forbids by name everything that the Councils prohibit except horse racing. This Ayrinhac includes under *spectacula* [36] and undoubtedly with reason. But the question as to whether or not horse races are included under the forbidden *spectacula* of the Code, or as to whether or not custom may not have tempered the Baltimore law on this point seems no longer open to discussion. Though there has been no official publication of them, it is a matter of common knowledge that our Bishops have received documents from the Holy See urging the punishment of clerics who attend the races.

It is to be concluded then that these decrees of the Councils still bind with the prohibition against theatres to be understood, no doubt, as in the Code by reason of customary interpretation; and horse races absolutely forbidden because of the Holy See's special insistence that this phase of the local law be kept.

TITLE VI
Duties to the Holy Father

Second Plenary Council

48. Spectata demum inopia qua, ex sacrilega majoris et locupletioris partis Patrimonii sui spoliatione, laborat amatissimus Pater Pius Papa IX., aequum plane, dignum, justumque omnino esse reputamus, si Catholicus orbis universus, cujus bono spirituali totis viribus magnisque impensis die noctuque incumbit, illi in succursum perlubentissime veniat. Quapropter, ut etiam piae hac in parte fidelium Nobis commissorum erga Pontificem devotioni faciamus satis, statuimus, ut in singulis horum Statuum ecclesiis, ubicumque existant,

---

[36] *General Legislation*, p. 306.

omnibus annis, Dominica infra octavam festi SS. Petri et Pauli, sive alio opportuno tempore, mandantibus locorum Ordinariis, quorum mandatum Dominica antecedente populo perlegetur a Pastore, fiant Collectae in subsidium Confraternitatis Sancti Petri; quarum summae, et quidem ante festum Assumptae in coelum Beatissimae Virginis Mariae, ab Ordinariis respectivis locorum ad Metropolitas mittantur, qui illas quamprimum ad Pontificis manus pervenire satagant; aut si uni vel alteri Ordinario magis placuerit, directe mittantur ad Summum Pontificem. Hae autem Collectae fient singulis annis per omnes nostras Provincias; donec summus Pontifex in jura sua feliciter restitutus, vel alia ratione a divina Providentia sublevatus, amplius ejusmodi haud indigeat auxilio.

In the Councils the only law properly so called that treats of the Holy Father is that found in number 48 of the Second Plenary. This decree deals with the collection which we speak of familiarly as *Peter's Pence* and orders accordingly that in all our churches each year either on the Sunday within the octave of the feast of Sts. Peter and Paul or on some other suitable day according to the discretion of the Ordinary there be taken up a collection to aid the Confraternity of St. Peter. This collection is to be announced by the Pastor on the Sunday previous to its being taken up. The proceeds of each diocese are to be sent sometime before the feast of the Assumption by the Ordinary to the Metropolitan who in turn will see to it that this money comes as soon as possible into the hands of the Holy Father; or each Ordinary himself may forward the money directly to Rome. This annual collection is to continue in every province of the United States until the Holy Father has his rights restored or, otherwise helped by divine Providence, he has no further need of this kind of assistance.

The Fathers of the Council were prompted to enact this decree that, as they said, the American Church might show its filial devotion to the Holy Father by a generous effort to relieve the indigence of the Holy See caused by the recent spoliation of the larger and richer part of its territory.[37]

As the Code has no corresponding legislation, our local statute being clearly *praeter codicem* consequently remains in force and is faithfully observed in all our dioceses where each year this special collection is taken up.

[37] *Conc. Plen. Balti. II Acta et Decreta,* p. 39.

TITLE VII

Primates

Regarding the title of Primate the Fathers of the Seventh Provincial Council asked Rome that the Metropolitan See of Baltimore be granted the prerogative of the Primacy of honor,[38] but their request was not granted.[39]

The petition was repeated by the Fathers of the First Plenary and Eighth Provincial Councils of Baltimore and was finally granted by a decree of the Sacred Congregation of Propaganda dated August 15, 1858.[40] In virtue of this privilege the Archbishop of Baltimore in all councils, assemblies and meetings takes precedence over all the other Archbishops of the United States without regard to promotion or ordination. According to canon 4 of the Code acquired rights, privileges and indults which have been granted by the Holy See to individuals or organizations up to the present time, if still in use and not revoked, remain in force, unless explicitly repealed by the canons of the Code.

The Metropolitan of Baltimore, therefore, continues to enjoy the privilege of Primacy, whereby, though he has no more authority than other Metropolitans, he has, if a Cardinal, the right to the first place of honor or if an Archbishop to the first place after the Cardinals and the Apostolic Delegate.[41]

TITLE VIII

The Provincial Council

The Second Plenary Council

56. Quam sint Ecclesiae Catholicae proficua Concilia Provincialia, quinam illis debeant interesse, qui sint fines illis celebrandis praestituti, et qua ratione sint convocanda ac habenda, satis indicat Sacrosancta Synodus Tridentina, antiquam Ecclesiae legem et consuetudinem hac in parte renovans ac solemniter promulgans: "Provincialia Concilia, sicubi omissa sunt, pro moderandis moribus, corrigendis excessibus, controversiis componendis, aliisque ex sacris canonibus permissis, renoventur. Quare Metropolitani per seipsos,

---

[38] *Conc. Prov. Balti. Habita,* p. 269.

[39] *Conc. Prov. Balti. Habita,* pp. 287, ff.

[40] Shea, *Hist. of the Cath. Church in the U. S.,* II, 379 and 380; *Conc. Plen. Balti. II Acta et Decreta,* p. 343.

[41] Can. 239, § 1, 21°; can. 269, § 2; can. 280.

5

seu, illis legitime impeditis, Co-episcopus antiquior intra annum ad minus a fine praesentis Concilii, et deinde quolibet saltem triennio, post octavam Paschae Resurrectionis Domini Nostri Jesu Christi, seu alio commodiori tempore, pro more Provinciae, non praetermittat Synodum in Provincia sua cogere; quo Episcopi omnes, et alii qui de jure vel consuetudine interesse debent, exceptis iis quibus cum imminenti periculo transfretandum est, convenire omnino teneantur. * * * Itidem Episcopi, qui nulli Archiepiscopo subjiciuntur, aliquem vicinum Metropolitanum semel eligant, in cujus Synodo Provinciali cum aliis interesse debeant, et quae ibi ordinata fuerint, observent, ac observari faciant."

Code

Canon 283

In singulis provinciis ecclesiasticis celebretur provinciale Concilium vicesimo saltem quoque anno.

The Third Plenary Council makes no mention of Provincial Councils but the Second does in numbers 56 to 62.

In the first of these the Fathers merely state the Tridentine law, the common law of that time,[42] requiring a Provincial Council at least every three years.

The Code in canon 283 has made a change in the Tridentine law so that Provincial Councils need no longer be held every three years, but only every twenty years at least.

Since it is evident that it was the mind of the Fathers of the Second Plenary Council that we should follow the common law with regard to the Provincial Council, our present guidance in this matter is to be taken from the Code.

TITLE IX

Bishops

Article 1

The Election of Bishops

In the United States as elsewhere ecclesiastical discipline on the selection of candidates for the Episcopacy has changed with the growth of the Church. Up to the time of our Second Provincial

[42] Sess. XXIV, de Ref. cap. 2.

Council in 1833 we had no definite method of designating candidates for bishoprics. Bishop Carroll by special concession of the Holy See was nominated by the local clergy. Others were chosen at the suggestion of their Metropolitan and fellow suffragans and some had their names presented by individual Bishops.[43] The Fathers of the Second Provincial Council in their fourth enactment outlined a method which called forth from the Sacred Congregation of the Propaganda the Instruction of March 18, 1834.[44] This placed the presentation of candidates for the Episcopacy in the hands of the Metropolitan and Suffragans of our then only existing province. With the multiplication of provinces the above decree in the eyes of the Fathers of the Seventh Provincial Council needed amendment. This they made the subject of their third statute.[45] The Sacred Congregation granted the request in a decree dated August 10, 1850 which proposed that in the choice of candidates for whatever province a list be sent to all the Metropolitans who in turn must communicate their opinions to the Holy See.[46] Six years later an indult was granted to the Provinces of Baltimore, St. Louis, New Orleans and Cincinnati permitting the handling of this matter in a meeting of the provincial Hierarchy with the obligation of consulting the proper Ordinary in case their choice fell upon an extra-provincial candidate.[47] Another decree dated May 25, 1859 required in the selection of a candidate to rule or be coadjutor in a Metropolitan see the consulting of all the other Metropolitans.[48] Further amendments were made by the Sacred Congregation in a decree of January 21, 1861.[49] The most important of its requirements were, in the first place, that each Bishop send every three years a list of suitable candidates both to his Metropolitan and to the Sacred Congregation, and secondly, that for the immediate discussion of the candidates those concerned should convene in synod or special assembly.[50] The Second Plenary Council

[43] Smith, *Notes on the Second Plenary Council*, pp. 93 and 94.

[44] *Conc. Prov. Balti. Habita*, pp. 102 and 117.

[45] *Conc. Prov. Balti. Habita*, p. 278.

[46] *Conc. Prov. Balti. Habita*, p. 290.

[47] *Conc. Plen. Balti. II Acta Et Decreta*, p. 72.

[48] *Ibid.*

[49] *Conc. Plen. Balti. II Acta Et Decreta*, p. 73.

[50] *Ibid.*

devotes to this subject numbers 101 to 107, but without doing more than to repeat these various Instructions of the Holy See just referred to.

It remained for the Third Plenary Council in numbers 15 and 16 to effect the next big change in our method of choosing candidates for the Episcopacy. The chief innovation made by this body was to extend to the Diocesan Consultors and Irremovable Rectors the right to recommend candidates which right had previously been enjoyed by the Hierarchy only. According to the decree these priests prepared their own list of three names, *dignus, dignior, dignissimus,* copies of which were sent to the Bishops of the province and to the Sacred Congregation. With the exception of the special provision in the case of Bishop Carroll, never before had our priests any voice in the proposal of their Ordinaries. Nor was this present concession an empty one, for though the Bishops, whose meeting followed that of the Consultors and Irremovable Rectors, were free to disapprove of one or more of the three candidates presented by the priests, still they were bound to give their reasons for so doing to the Sacred Congregation. Thus all the names on the original list were sure to come before the Holy See. This presentation was neither election nor nomination, but merely recommendation; nevertheless, the Holy See nearly always appointed one of those suggested and usually the first one on the list if both the priests and the Bishops had made the same first choice.[51]

This method called *terna* remained in use for thirty years, but its inadequacy to the exigencies of the growing Church in America gradually became more apparent. It even occasioned strifes and intrigues as attested to by a letter from the Cardinal Prefect of the Sacred Congregation of Propaganda dated May 15, 1892,[52] and too frequently limited the choice to a diocese or province. Accordingly on July 25, 1916 the Consistorial Congregation issued a decree giving us our present method.[53] This briefly is as follows. Every other year at the beginning of Lent each Bishop is to indicate to his Metropolitan one or two priests whom he deems fit for the episcopal office, stating

[51] Smith, *Elements*, I, 155.

[52] *A. A. S.*, II (1910), 286; *Eccl. Rev.*, XLII (1910), 718; *A. S.S.*, XXIV (1891), 684; *Eccl. Rev.*, VII (1892), 63.

[53] *A. A. S.*, VIII (1916), 400; *Eccl. Rev.*, LVI (1917), 58.

the name, age, origin, residence and position of each. He may make his choice from any diocese or province, but he must know his candidates personally and very well. Before making his choice he must ask the advice of his Diocesan Consultors and Irremovable Rectors, not collectively but individually. He may consult other members of the clergy, secular or religious. In no case, however, is he bound to follow the advice given.

When the Metropolitan has received all these names, he adds his own and draws up a general list in alphabetical order. A copy of this he sends to each of his suffragans that they may make opportune investigations. All this is to be done prudently and cautiously so as not to break the strict secrecy of the proceedings. After Easter on a day and at a time fixed by the Archbishop, the Bishops meet, without any solemnity to avoid drawing attention, for a serious but moderate discussion of the candidates proposed. After this discussion the Bishops vote on each candidate in alphabetical order. No vote need be taken on the one or ones unanimously disqualified. For the voting three ballots are used, one white, one black and one colored, signifying respectively approbation, rejection and abstention from voting. The candidates are then listed in the order of merit. If several receive the same number of votes, the Bishops may by written ballot determine who is to be given the preference.

A report of the proceedings is to be sent to the Holy See with whatever information may help in the selection of the best fitted person. This a Bishop may do also by private letter to the Consistorial Congregation or to the Pope.

We continue to follow this method according to canon 330, which states that, before one is elevated to the Episcopate it must be ascertained according to the manner determined by the Holy See that he is qualified for the office.

Article 2

The Law of Residence for Bishops

Second Plenary Council

91. Monitos volumus praesules omnes qui aliqua ex causa e suis dioesesibus ad tempus recedunt, " legitimae absentiae causas, (juxta Tridentini Concilii Decretum, Sess. xxiii., Cap.

Code

Canon 338

§ 1. Etiamsi Episcopi Coadiutorem habeant, tenentur lege personalis in dioecesi residentiae.

§ 2. Praeterquam causa visitationis

1, de Ref.,) a beatissimo Romano Pontifice, aut a metropolitano, vel, eo absente, suffraganeo episcopo antiquiori residente, qui idem metropolitani absentiam probare debebit, in scriptis esse approbandas. Quoniam autem qui aliquantisper tantum absunt, ex veterum canonum sententia, non videntur abesse, quia statim reversuri sunt; illud absentiae spatium singulis annis, sive continuum, sive interruptum, nullo pacto debere duos aut ad summum tres menses excedere."

Sacrorum Liminum, Conciliorum, quibus interesse debent, vel civilis officii suis ecclesiis legitime adiuncti, abesse possunt aequa de causa non ultra duos vel ad summum tres menses intra annum, sive continuos sive intermissos, dummodo cautum sit ne ex ipsorum absentia dioecesis quidquam detrimenti capiat: quod tamen tempus coniungi nequit sive cum tempore sibi concesso occasione suae promotionis, vel visitationis Sacrorum Liminum, vel assistentiae Concilio, sive cum tempore vacationum anni subsequentis.

§ 3. Ab ecclesia cathedrali ne absint tempore Adventus et Quadragesimae, diebus Nativitatis, Resurrectionis Domini, Pentecostes et Corporis Christi, nisi ex gravi et urgenti causa.

§ 4. Si ultra sex menses e dioecesi illegitime abfuerint, Episcopum Metropolita, ad normam can. 274, n. 4, Metropolitam antiquior Suffraganeus residens Sedi Apostolicae denuntiet.

The law of residence for Bishops is one to be made normally by the Holy See and not by the members of the Hierarchy themselves. Accordingly one does not expect to nor does one actually find any local statute on this point. The Third Plenary Council makes no mention of it whatsoever, but in number 91 of the Second, the Fathers say that they wish to warn all Ordinaries who for any reason leave their dioceses for an appreciable length of time that according to the Council of Trent[54] the cause of their legitimate absence is to be approved in writing by the Holy Father or the Metropolitan, and in his absence or in his case by the senior suffragan. Those absent for only a short time are not to be considered as having been away. Absence from the diocese whether continuous or interrupted is in no case to extend two or at the most three months of the year.

Here, as in the case of the Provincial Council, the Fathers evidently wish to do no more than to inculcate the common law of the time.

[54] Sess. XXIII, de Ref., cap. 1.

Pope Urban VIII by his Constitution, "*Sancta Synodus,*" of December 12, 1634 [55] amended the Council of Trent on this point and decreed that the Roman Pontiff alone could grant the requisite permission, but Smith quoting Father Konings [56] says that since the Council of Baltimore did not mention this Constitution, it never applied to us. It did, however, later when in 1908 we came under the common law.

The Code has modified the former common law. In canon 338 it provides for certain absences without special permission. One of these is a three month's vacation either continuous or interrupted on condition that this does not militate against the interests of the diocese; others are for the visit *ad limina,* attendance at councils and the performance of any civil duties legitimately attached to the Bishop's office. The vacation period is not to be added to any of these enforced absences, or to the four months of grace granted the Bishop by canon 333 before taking possession of his see, nor are the vacations of two years to be joined.

The only authority given to the Metropolitan or senior suffragan—and it is not merely authority but obligation—is that of reporting an Ordinary who would unlawfully prolong his absence beyond six months.

Since repeating the Tridentine Law in question the Fathers of the Second Plenary Council did not give it added local enforcement, it affects us only in the measure of its present binding force. Whether or not the Constitution, "*Sancta Synodus,*" of Pope Urban VIII ever applied to us and made the Holy See our Bishops' only source for dispensation from the law of residence is of no further consequence now. Since the Code is silent regarding the Metropolitans or senior Suffragans dispensing from the law of residence, any former statute granting that power is opposed to it and so is abrogated in accordance with the canon 6, § 1.[57]

We continue to follow the common law in this respect which, as has been shown, is that of canon 338 of the Code. For any prolonged absences outside of those enumerated herein as also for any

[55] *Fontes,* 215.

[56] *Elements,* I, 311, No. 549; cf. also Konings, *op. cit.,* p. 436, No. 1134.

[57] Cf. also can. 6, §§ 3 and 6.

other exceptions to this law of residence dispensation must come from the law maker, the Holy See, if time permits. Otherwise, the Bishop has only to presume permission.

Article 3

The Visit ad Limina

Third Plenary Council

13. Canonicis institutis sapienter inductus fuit mos, quo Episcopi statis temporibus ad sacra Apostolorum Limina accedunt, ut obsequium et obedientiam suam Pontifici praestent, eidemque de pastorali ipsorum munere rationem reddant, deque ecclesiarum suarum statu ceterisque omnibus referant, quae summum Ecclesiae Rectorem scire opportunum et utile est. Et hoc quidem Episcoporum officium ab antiquissimis Patribus tanquam ex intimis Primatus juribus derivatum commendatur, laudaturque quasi tessera unitatis ac communionis, quam omnes qui sunt undique fideles per praesules suos habere debent cum maxima et antiquissima omnium Ecclesia et gloriosissima B. Petri Sede. Episcopis et Vicariis Apostolicis nostris indultum fuit ut hanc sacrorum Liminum visitationem intra decennium peragerent. Unde vero initium hujus decennii computandum sit, nulli dubium esse potest qui Congregationis de Propaganda Fide declarationes hac in re perlegerit. Diserte enim edicunt, decennia ita esse computanda, ut initio sumpto a die quo Sixti V. Constitutio *Romanus Pontifex* edita fuit, nimirum a die 20 Decembris anni 1585, perpetuo et sine ulla interruptione pro omnibus successoribus Episcopis decurrant. Neque alia est computandi ratio, etiam si agatur de sedibus recenter erectis. Harum ergo sedium Episcopi, sicut in aliis dis-

Code

Canon 340

§ 1. Omnes Episcopi tenentur singulis quinquenniis relationem Summo Pontifici facere super statu dioecesis sibi commissae secundum formulam ab Apostolica Sede datam.

§ 2. Quinquennia sunt fixa et communia, atque computantur a die 1 Ianuarii 1911; in primo quinquennii anno relationem exhibere debent Episcopi Italiae, insularum Corsicae, Sardiniae, Siciliae, Melitae, et aliarum minorum adiacentium; in altero, Episcopi Hispaniae, Portugalliae, Galliae, Belgii, Hollandiae, Angliae, Scotiae et Hiberniae, cum insulis adiacentibus; in tertio, ceteri Europae Episcopi, cum insulis adiacentibus; in quarto, Episcopi totius Americae et insularum adiacentium; in quinto, Episcopi Africae, Asiae, Australiae et insularum his orbis partibus adiacentium.

§ 3. Si annus pro exhibenda relatione assignatus inciderit ex toto vel ex parte in primum biennium ab inito dioecesis regimine, Episcopus pro ea vice a conficienda et exhibenda relatione abstinere potest.

Canon 341

§ 1. Omnes et singuli Episcopi eo anno quo relationem exhibere tenentur, ad Urbem, Beatorum Apostolorum Petri et Pauli sepulcra veneraturi, accedant et Romano Pontifici se sistant.

positionibus, etiam in hac constitutioni Sixtinae adhaerere debent. (Ita respondit S. Congregatio de Propaganda Fide in Comitiis generalibus die 3 Maji 1875 habitis, ut refertur in Instructione ejusdem S. Congregationis super Visitatione SS. Liminum.) Episcopus, qui non potest per se, tenetur per procuratorem visitare.

§ 2. Sed Episcopis qui extra Europam sunt, permittitur ut alternis quinquenniis, idest singulis decenniis, Urbem petant.

As for the law on residence, so, and even more especially for that governing the *ad limina* visit is one to look to the Holy See rather than to any locally enacted statute. Nor does one look in vain for special instructions for our Bishops. The Second Plenary Council is silent on this matter, but the Third in number 13 gives the substance of an Instruction of the Sacred Congregation of the Propagation of the Faith which is printed in the Appendix to the Council.[58] This Instruction was based on the regulations set forth in the Constitution of Pope Sixtus V, "*Romanus Pontifex*," dated December 20, 1585.[59] Accordingly our Bishops along with those of other countries especially remote from Rome were to make their visit *ad limina* and report on the state of their diocese only every ten years, while for the rest of the Bishops the period ranged from every three to every five years in proportion to their distance from the Holy See. The date from which these periods were to be computed was that of the above mentioned Constitution, December 20, 1585. Though the common law has remained substantially the same on this subject, there have been modifications from time to time.[60] Of these the most recent before the Code was the decree of the Consistorial Congregation of December 31, 1909.[61] This abrogated the existing law on the time of both the visit and the report to the Holy See. It required from all Bishops throughout the world without exception a report on the state of their dioceses every five years instead of every three, five or ten years according to their previously assigned times of visitation. It further fixed January 1, 1911 as the new date from which these five

[58] Pp. 197 to 202.

[59] *Fontes*, 156.

[60] Ayrinhac, *Constitution of the Church*, p. 170.

[61] *A. A. S.*, II (1910), 13.

year periods were to be computed and subdivided the *quinquennia* into five units of one year during each of which the Bishops of certain countries were to report. Our Bishops were allotted the fourth year of each *quinquennium.* Finally, it was decreed that all European Bishops should make their *ad limina* visit sometime during the year in which their report was due, while all others, which of course included those of America, were required to go to Rome only at the recurrence of each alternate *quinquennium,* or every ten years.

The Code in canons 340 and 341 has incorporated this legislation without any alterations and so our Bishops continue to send a report on their dioceses during the fourth of every five year period from 1911, that is, 1914, 1919, 1924, 1929, 1934 and so forth, and to make their *ad limina* visits only during every other of these periods, that is 1919, 1929, 1939 and so on.

On November 4, 1918 the Consistorial Congregation published a new formula to be followed in making the quinquennial report.[62] This formula which corresponds more completely to the order and prescriptions of the Code was to be followed from the beginning of the first year of the third quinquennial period, that is from January 1, 1921. Divided into twelve chapters this *schema* after some preliminary remarks deals successively with the administration of temporalities, inventories, archives, faith and divine worship, the Ordinary, the diocesan Curia, the seminary, the clergy in general, Chapters, Vicars Forane, religious and the faithful. In the end it calls for a summary appreciation of the state of the diocese by the Ordinary.

Article 4

The Visitation of the Diocese

Second Plenary Council

86. Meminerint Episcopi se Dioeceses suas frequenter ac regulariter visitare districte teneri, non solum ut Confirmationis Sacramentum statutis temporibus administrent, verum etiam ut gregem sibi creditum bene cognoscant, eaque omnia, quae spirituale ejus bonum promoveant, melius pro-

Code

Canon 343

§ 1. Ad sanam et orthodoxam doctrinam conservandam, bonos mores tuendos, pravos corrigendos, pacem, innocentiam, pietatem et disciplinam in populo et clero promovendam ceteraque pro ratione adiunctorum ad bonum religionis constituenda, tenen-

[62] *A. A. S.*, X (1918), 487.

videre possint. Quod si ob locorum distantiam et ecclesiarum numerum, quotannis haud possint omnes visitare ecclesias, visitent saltem principaliores et quae sint urbi Episcopali propiores, eaque ratione visitationem ordinent, ut omni biennio, juxta Tridentini praescriptum, vel si id fieri nequeat, omni saltem triennio singulas dioeceseos perlustrent partes. Gravissimum vero hoc munus episcopale haud praepropere vel perfunctorie, sed omni adhibita diligentia, ac zelo animarum ducti, perficiant; de iis omnibus solerter et de plano inquirentes quae in Pontificali Romano praescribuntur.

THIRD PLENARY COUNCIL

14. Quum boni pastoris sit, exemplo Christi Domini oves suas nosse et ab iisdem cognosci, Visitatio dioecesis cum pastorali Episcoporum officio tam arcte conjuncta est ut nullo modo omitti aut negligi possit. Unusquisque igitur Episcopus saltem unoquoque triennio totam dioecesim perlustrare teneatur, non solum ut gregem suum cognoscat eaque omnia quae ad spirituale eorum bonum necessaria sunt suis ipse oculis perspiciat, sed etiam ut fideles tot amitendae fidei in hac regione periculis expositos Sacramento Confirmationis munire possit. Quod si per se ipse facere nequeat, id per alios idoneos viros praestet, adhibito etiam pro Sacramento Confirmationis alicujus inter viciniores Episcopos ministerio. Quum vero, inter cetera, in temporalem Ecclesiarum administrationem accurate inquirere maximi intersit, si fieri potest secum ducat duos convisitatores, vel saltem unum, hosque eligat ex praestantioribus inter presbyteros, et praesertim ex iis qui in bonis temporalibus Ecclesiae administrandis tur Episcopi obligatione visitandae quotannis dioecesis vel ex toto vel ex parte, ita ut saltem singulis quinquenniis universam vel ipsi per se vel, si fuerint legitime impediti, per Vicarium Generalem aliumve lustrent.

§ 2. Fas est Episcopo clericos duos etiam e Capitulo sive cathedrali sive collegiali sibi adsciscere visitationis comites atque adiutores; eosque, quos maluerit, eligere, reprobato quocunque contrario privilegio vel consuetudine.

§ 3. Si obligationi de qua in § 1, Episcopus graviter defuerit, servetur praescriptum can. 274, nn. 4, 5.

CANON 344

§ 1. Ordinariae episcopali visitationi obnoxiae sunt personae, res ac loca pia, quamvis exempta, quae intra dioecesis ambitum continentur, nisi probari possit specialem a visitatione exemptionem fuisse ipsis ab Apostolica Sede concessam.

§ 2. Religiosos autem exemptos Episcopus visitare potest in casibus tantum in iure expressis.

CANON 345

Visitator, in iis quae obiectum et finem visitationis respiciunt, debet paterna forma procedere, et ab eius praeceptis ac decretis datur recursus in devolutivo tantum; in aliis vero causis, etiam tempore visitationis, Episcopus ad normam iuris procedat necesse est.

CANON 346

Studeant Episcopi debita cum diligentia, sine inutilibus tamen moris, pastoralem visitationem absolvere: caveant, ne superfluis sumptibus cuiquam graves onerosive sint, neve ratione visitationis ipsi aut quisquam suorum pro se suisve dona quodvis genus petant aut accipiant, reprobata quavis contraria consuetudine; circa

scientia et experientia excellere noscuntur. In visitatione peragenda, praeter caeremonias praescriptas, serventur quae in jure praecipiuntur. (Vide Caeremoniale Baltimorae anno 1883 editum.) Neque omittat Episcopus prae oculis habere quaesita a S. Congregatione proposita, quo accuratiorem de Statu Dioecesis Relationem ad Sanctam Sedem juxta morem hujus S. Congregationis singulis quinquenniis transmittat. De expensis Episcopi eorumque quos secum ducit providebitur in Synodo Dioecesana. Denique accuratam visitationis relationem in scriptis fieri curet Episcopus in archivio dioecesano asservandam.

vero victualia sibi suisque ministranda vel procurationes et expensas itineris, servetur legitima locorum consuetudo.

On this subject of the visitation of the diocese the Second Plenary Council in number 86 reminds the Bishop of his strict obligation to visit his diocese frequently and regularly not merely to administer the Sacrament of Confirmation, but that he may know his flock well and may the better provide for its spiritual good. If on account of great distances and the number of churches he cannot visit them all every year, he is to visit the larger parishes and those nearer the episcopal city. This visitation is to be so regulated that the entire diocese will be visited every two years as the Council of Trent prescribed,[63] or if this be not possible then at the very least every three years.

The Third Plenary Council in number 14 is more detailed in its requirements. As regards the purpose of the visit after repeating the spiritual motives given by the Second it stresses the need of an accurate inquiry into the temporal administration of churches and requires if possible two, or at least one co-visitor to be chosen from among the priests excelling in knowledge and experience as administrators.

Like the Second Council the Third requires that the visitation be completed within at least every three years. The method of defraying the expenses is to be determined by diocesan synod. Finally, it is

[63] Sess. XXIV, de Ref., cap. 3.

decreed that an accurately written account of each visitation be kept in the diocesan archives.

The Code devotes four canons, 343 to 346, to this matter and is much more detailed even than the Third Plenary Council. Regarding the spiritual purpose the Code is more minute, but does not mention the administration of Confirmation in connection with the visit. It makes no specific mention of the temporalities though these may be considered included under the phrase *ceteraque pro ratione adjunctorum ad bonum religionis constituenda.*[64] Again it permits but does not require co-visitors.[65] In the third place it requires that the diocese be visited every year in whole or in part, so that a complete visitation will have been made at least every five years. Fourthly, it leaves the method of defraying the expenses of the visitation to legitimate local customs. Finally, the Code makes no mention of a written report to be kept in the diocesan archives. In view of these differences the question now arises as to what remains and what has been abrogated of our conciliar law on this subject. In the first place the inquiry into the temporalities is still obligatory since this not only is not opposed to the Code but rather a particular measure interpretative of its phrase *ceteraque pro ratione adjunctorum ad bonum religionis constituenda.*

Secondly, as regards the period of time within which the visitation must be completed, the three year limit of the Council is still our rule since the *saltem singulis quinquennis* of the Code leaves the way open to the stricter particular law.

Thirdly, as to the expenses the Code by allowing local customs to determine the method of their settlement leaves the way open to the Baltimore provision that diocesan synods fix the responsibility for these. The common custom in this country seems to be that the Bishop pays for the visitation from his cathedraticum.

Fourthly, the co-visitors are no longer compulsory since the obligation of the Council is opposed to the freedom granted in the respect to the Bishop by the Code.

[64] Can. 343, § 1.
[65] Can. 343, § 2.

TITLE X

The Diocesan Synod

SECOND PLENARY COUNCIL

67. Quod si, ob locorum distantiam aliaque peculiaria rerum adjuncta, magno foret incommodo Synodum quotannis celebrare, curent Episcopi, ut saltem post habitum ac a Sancta Sede recognitum Concilium Provinciale sive Plenarium, quam levissima interposita mora, Synodum convocent Dioecesanam, in qua Statuta Provincialia seu Plenaria omnibus promulgentur, atque executioni dentur.

CODE

CANON 356

§ 1. In singulis dioecesibus celebranda est decimo saltem quoque anno dioecesana Synodus, in qua de iis tantum agendum quae ad particulares cleri populique dioecesis necessitates vel utilitates referuntur.

The Second Plenary Council devoted its entire fourth chapter, numbers 63 to 69, to the diocesan synod; the Third, however, has no *ex professo* treatment of this matter, but just mentions it in connection with other subjects as the visitation of the diocese,[66] the Diocesan Consultors,[67] Synodal Examiners,[68] salaries,[69] stole fees,[70] and so forth.

The only local law on the Synod is that found in number 67 of the Second Council and leading with the frequency of these meetings. They are to be held at least after provincial and plenary councils for the promulgation and carrying out of their decrees.

According to the Code in canon 356, § 1 each diocese is to hold a Synod at least every ten years.

Since the Code nowhere makes the plenary council a necessity and requires a Provincial one only every twenty years at the least,[71] the Diocesan Synod according to the Baltimore law would be obligatory no more frequently.

This makes the local statute opposed to the stricter law of the Code and hence abrogated.

[66] No. 14.

[67] No. 20.

[68] No. 25.

[69] No. 273.

[70] No. 294.

[71] Can. 283.

TITLE XI

The Vicar General

SECOND PLENARY COUNCIL

72. Vicarius Generalis, ab Episcopo designatus, eandem cum eo moralem gerit personam, eandemque ecclesiasticam constituit curiam; atque cum sit Archipresbyter, omnes alios in Dioecesi Presbyteros et dignitates praecellit. Nihil tamen potest sine Episcopi delegata potestate; nec, juxta Sanctae Sedis Instructionem ultimam, potest uti facultatibus extraordinariis, nisi per unum integrum diem Ordinarius absens sit futurus.

CODE

CANON 368

§ 1. Vicario Generali, vi officii, ea competit in universa dioecesi iurisdictio in spiritualibus ac temporalibus, quae ad Episcopum iure ordinario pertinet, exceptis iis quae Episcopus sibi reservaverit, vel quae ex iure requirant speciale Episcopi mandatum.

§ 2. Nisi aliud expresse cautum fuerit, Vicarius Generalis exsequi potest rescripta apostolica quae Episcopo vel praecedenti rectori dioecesis remissa sint, ac generatim ad ipsum quoque pertinent facultates habituales Ordinario loci a Sencta Sede concessae, ad normam can. 66.

There is practically no direct particular legislation in the Councils of Baltimore touching the Vicar General and the Chancellor. In number 72 of the Second Plenary, however, there is a reference to an Instruction of the Holy See relative to the use of a Bishop's extraordinary faculties by his Vicar General. This states that the latter cannot use these special faculties unless the Bishop has been absent for a day. This prohibition is now set aside by the Code in canon 368. According to this canon the Vicar General by virtue of his office enjoys throughout the diocese both in spiritual and in temporal matters the ordinary powers belonging to the Bishop by the common law except those which the Bishop may have reserved to himself or those which by law require the special mandate of the Bishop.

The canon further provides that, unless it is otherwise expressly stated, the Vicar General has the faculties which are habitually granted to the Ordinary of the place by the Holy See according to canon 66.

TITLE XII
The Synodal Examiners

SECOND PLENARY COUNCIL

76. Juxta Tridentini Concilii praescriptum, " Examinatores singulis annis in Dioecesana Synodo ab Episcopo, vel ejus Vicario, ad minus sex proponantur, qui Synodo satisfaciant, et ab ea probentur." Quamvis autem Examinatorum munus ad ea quae Parochiales Concursus respiciunt, qui hisce in Provinciis haud adhuc obtinent, praecise spectet, tamen ad examina etiam, quae sacrorum Ordinum collationem facultatumque confessiones excipiendi concessionem debeant praecedere, jure merito extendi poterit, necnon et ad Literas Testimoniales exarandas quae Episcopo sint praevie tradendae. Hinc nominandos esse ejusmodi Examinatores in Dioecesanis Synodis vel cleri Conventibus consulimus. Ob sacerdotum vero hisce in Provinciis inopiam, poterunt etiam inter Consultores Episcopi numerari, de quibus in Decreto superiori erat mentio.

THIRD PLENARY COUNCIL

24. Ut igitur mentem Sacrosanctae Synodi sequamur, quamdiu paroeciae canonice erectae non sint, constituant singuli Episcopi examinatores cleri dioecesani pro concursibus ad missiones, in quibus rectori privilegium tributum est inamovibilitatis, ad instar examinatorum synodalium vel prosynodalium; et eorumdem examinatorum opera utilius et securius utentur etiam sive pro approbandis confessariis, sive pro ordinandorum scrutinio, sive pro examine juniorum sacerdotum, sive pro examinandis alumnis qui in seminarium majus admitti volunt. Ad examinatorum

CODE

CANON 385

§ 1. In quavis dioecesi habeantur examinatores synodales et parochi consultores qui omnes in Synodo constituantur, propositi ab Episcopo, a Synodo approbati.

§ 2. Tot eligantur quot Episcopus prudenti suo iudicio necessarios iudicaverit, non tamen infra quatuor, nec ultra duodecim.

CANON 386

§ 1. Examinatoribus et parochis consultoribus medio tempore inter unam et aliam Synodum demortuis vel alia ratione a munere cessantibus, alios pro-synodales Episcopus substituat de consilio Capituli cathedralis.

§ 2. Quae regula servetur quoque in examinatoribus et parochis consultoribus constituendis quoties Synodus non habeatur.

CANON 387

§ 1. Examinatores et parochi consultores, sive in Synodo sive extra Synodum constituti, post decennium ab incepto munere vel etiam prius, adveniente nova Synodo, officio cadunt; possunt tamen negotium iam coeptum ad exitum perducere et, servatis de iure servandis, denuo constitui.

§ 2. Qui loco examinatorum ac parochorum consultorum deficientium constituantur, in officio persistunt dumtaxat quousque perstitissent ii quibus substituti fuerunt.

CANON 388

Removeri ab Episcopo nequeunt, nisi ex gravi causa et de consilio Capituli cathedralis.

munus assumantur viri ecclesiastici morum probitate maxime commendabiles et, quantum fieri possit, in sacris disciplinis et jure canonico apprime versati.

25. Hi examinatores, in quantum fieri potest, sint ad minus sex. Obtenta facultate S. Sedis, Episcopus poterit eligere Examinatores extra synodum, auditis tamen consultoribus. Quod si morte, aut renuntiatione, aut alia causa praescriptus examinatorum numerus deficiat, Episcopus, de consilio consultorum, alios subrogabit.

26. Electi examinatores juramentum praestent de munere suo sincere adimplendo ac de donis non recipiendis intuitu examinis. Quod juramentum in ipsa synodo erit emittendum, si examinatores in synodo eligantur et electi synodo adsint; sin minus coram Episcopo aut ejus vicario. (Bened. XIV., l. c., n. 6.)

Canon 389

§ 1. Examinatores synodales operam suam diligenter navent praesertim experimentis habendis ad provisionem paroeciarum nec non processibus de quibus in can. 2147 seqq.

§ 2. Pro experimentis vero habendis ad clericorum ordinationem et approbationem sacerdotum qui petunt facultatem excipiendi sacramentales confessiones aut sacras conciones habendi, et pro examinibus de quibus in can. 130, integrum est Episcopo vel examinatorum synodalium vel aliorum opera uti.

Canon 390

Idem potest esse examinator et parochus consultor, non autem in eadem causa.

The Second Plenary Council in number 76 advises Bishops to appoint Examiners not for their chief common-law purpose of examining candidates for parishes since canonical parishes did not exist in this country at that time, but to examine candidates for orders and priests for faculties. It further advises that, if these be appointed, their appointment take place in a diocesan synod or meeting of the clergy.

The Third Plenary Council has a much more elaborate treatment of this subject to which it devotes numbers 23 to 26. Herein the Fathers expressing their wish to adhere to the mind of the Council of Trent prescribe the appointment of Examiners after the manner of the Synodal or pro-Synodal Examiners of the common law and for the kindred purpose of examining candidates for the irremovable missions. It is also suggested that the services of these Examiners be employed in approving priests for faculties and in examining aspirants to Orders, the junior clergy and those seeking admission to the major seminary.

The Examiners are to be men of approved character and, as far as possible, skilled in the Sacred Sciences. Their number, if possible, is not to be less than six. They are to be appointed in synod; but with the permission of the Holy See and the advice of the Diocesan Consultors they may be appointed outside of synod. Vacancies, likewise, may be filled outside of synod with the advice of the Diocesan Consultors.[72]

They are to take the oath of office in synod if appointed there, or before the Bishop or his delegate if their appointment takes place outside of synod.

The Code treats of Synodal Examiners in canons 385 to 390. The only strict law of the Council that is in disagreement with the Code is that regarding the number of Examiners. The Council fixes a minimum of six and gives no maximum, while according to the Code the number may range from four to twelve.

The common law must now be followed since an indefinite maximum is opposed to the fixed limit of the Code and a minimum of six is opposed to the greater freedom which the Code gives in allowing a minimum of four.

TITLE XIII

The Diocesan Consultors

From the beginning it has always been the policy of the Church that those in authority have an advisory board. For centuries the proper advisory board or senate of Bishops has been the Cathedral Chapter. In countries where this ideal has been found impracticable, there has gradually developed a substitute in the Diocesan Consultors. In this country as early as the First Plenary Council the Bishops were

[72] By requiring only the advice of the Consultors for the appointment of Examiners outside of synod our particular law differed from the then existing common law which demanded their consent. (Benedict XIV, *de Synod. Dioeces.*, 1, IV, c. 7, N. 7.) The decree "*Maxima Cura*" of August 20, 1910 (*A. A. S.*, II (1910), 636) again promulgated the common law on this point. This decree, officially declared on March 13, 1911 (*A. A. S.*, III (1911), 313) to apply to the United States abrogated the above Baltimore statute. The Code while assimilating substantially the decree, "*Maxima Cura*," nevertheless, made some changes. One of these is to be found in canon 386 which requires only the advice, not the consent, of the Diocesan Consultors in appointing an Examiner outside of synod.

exhorted where possible to have a body of Consultors.[73] The Fathers of the Second Plenary Council in number 71 repeated this wish of their Predecessors. Only, however, by the Third Plenary Council were the Diocesan Consultors made of obligation. This Council devoted to these Consultors numbers 17 to 22 which perhaps comprise the most original piece of our local legislation and undoubtedly were the foundation of the present common law on the subject.

The Holy See in an effort to bring the American Church more in conformity with the General law had thought of establishing here a modified form of Chapter such as exists in England, Ireland, Holland and Canada. The Archbishops who met in Rome in 1883 to prepare for the Third Plenary Council of Baltimore represented to the Sacred Congregation of Propaganda that the time was not ripe for this and so the Diocesan Consultors became a happy compromise.[74]

The present common law deals *ex professo* with the subject in canons 423 to 428, but there are other references to the Consultors scattered throughout the Code especially as to the Bishop's need of their advice and regarding those things they have in common with Cathedral Chapters.

The various points of contact between the particular and general laws will be taken up separately.

Article 1

The Number of Diocesan Consultors

Third Plenary Council	Code
18. Ejusmodi consultores numero debent esse sex vel saltem quatuor; ubi vero nullo modo tot haberi poterunt, sint saltem duo.	Canon 425 § 1. Consultores dioecesani numero sint saltem sex; in dioecesibus ubi pauci sint sacerdotes, saltem quatuor; iidemque omnes in civitate episcopali vel in locis viciniorибus commorentur.

The Third Council in number 18 decrees there must be six or at least four Diocesan Consultors; but allows a minimum of two where no more can be had. The Code in canon 425, § 1 requires normally

[73] *Conc. Plen. Balti. Habit. 1852*, No. 6.

[74] Ayrinhac, *Constitution of the Church*, p. 258; Smith, *Elements*, I, 466, footnote 5.

at least six, but tolerates four in dioceses where there is a scarcity of priests. The minimum of four established without qualification by the Code makes the allowing of a smaller number a case of opposition. In so far, then, as it premits so few as two Consultors the Council is abrogated by the Code.[75]

Article 2

The Appointment of the Diocesan Consultors

Third Plenary Council

19. Eligendi erunt consultores ab Episcopo, ea tamen ratione, ut dimidiam eorum partem eligat ex sese, alteram vero partem nonnisi post propositionem cleri. Propositio autem ex parte cleri fiet hoc modo: singuli sacerdotes qui in dioecesi sacro ministerio funguntur, Episcopo exhibebunt nomina eorum scripta, quos pro munere consultorum idoneos putaverint, quin taxative aliquos designent. Pro unoquoque seligendo consultore tria nomina proponi debent; ex his vero Episcopus eos eliget, quos ipse in Domino aptiores judicaverit.

21. Casu quo triennium exspirare contigerit tempore vacationis sedis episcopalis, consultores in officio manebunt usque ad accessum novi Episcopi, qui intra sex menses a consecratione sua ad novam consultorum electionem instituendam tenetur.

Code

Canon 424

Consultores nominat Episcopus, firmo praescripto can. 426.

Canon 426

§ 1. Officium consultorum est ad triennium.

§ 2. Exacto triennio, Episcopus vel alios in eorum locum substituat, vel eosdem ad aliud triennium confirmet, quod idem servetur singulis trienniis.

§ 3. Deficiente, quavis de causa, aliquo consultore intra triennium, Episcopus alium de consilio ceterorum consultorum substituat, isque in officio maneat usque ad expletum idem triennium.

§ 4. Cum vero triennium excidisse contigerit vacante sede episcopali, consultores in officio maneant usque ad accessum novi Episcopi, qui intra sex menses ab inita possessione providere debet ad normam huius canonis.

§5. Si, sede vacante, aliquis consultor moriatur vel renuntiet, Vicarius Capitularis, de consensu aliorum consultorum, alium nominet, qui tamen, ut munere, sede plena, fungatur, indiget novi Episcopi confirmatione.

As to the method of choosing the body of Consultors the Council in number 19 legislates that the Bishop choose the Consultors but

[75] Klekotka, *op. cit.*, p. 72; Augustine, *Commentary*, II, 466.

in this manner that half the number be taken from names proposed by the clergy and the other half, as it implies, freely. The Code in canon 424 decrees that the Bishop chooses the Consultors with due regard to canon 426 which in turn provides that every three years the Consultors be reappointed or new ones substituted and that should a vacancy occur during the three year term, the Bishop with the advice of the remaining Consultors fill it. The Code clearly shows, especially in requiring merely the advice of the Consultors and that only when supplying a vacancy in their body, that it wants the Bishop to be free in the choice of his advisors.[76] In so far, then, as the Council by giving the right of proposal to the clergy curtails the liberty granted to the Bishop by the common law, it is opposed to the latter and, therefore, abrogated. Inasmuch, however, as the Code does not specify the manner of making the selection the Bishop is still free to borrow what he wishes from the conciliar method.[77]

In the third place the Council and Code differ in regard to the initial date of the six-month period of grace which a new Bishop has before reappointing or replacing Consultors whose term of office has expired during the vacancy. According to the Council in number 21 this period dates from the Bishop's consecration while according to canon 426, § 4 of the Code it dates from the time of his taking canonical possession. Such a contradiction, of course, makes the two laws incompatible in which case the Council must yield and is abrogated.

Article 3

The Advice of the Diocesan Consultors

Third Plenary Council

20. Ad Consultorum attributiones quod pertinet, Patres de his convenerunt: 1° Consilium consultorum exquiret Episcopus pro synodo dioecesana indicenda et publicanda. 2° Si contingat ut missio seu parochia aliqua sit dismembranda, exquirendum erit consilium consultorum, necnon et rectoris dismembrandae missionis. 3° Consultorum item requiretur consilium, quando id agetur, ut missio seu parochia tradatur alicui familiae religiosae; quo in casu necessaria erit etiam venia S. Sedis. 4° Consultorum consilium exquiretur in constituendis deputatis pro seminariis dioecesanis. 5° Item consultorum consilium necessarium erit in eligendo novo consultore et in eligendis examinatoribus qui sint

[76] Ayrinhac, *Constitution of the Church*, p. 260.

[77] Augustine, *ibid.;* Klekotka, *op. cit.*, p. 52.

loco synodalium. 6° Quando agitur de bonis et fundis dioecesis vel missionum permutandis aliisque agendis, quae speciem alienationis prae se ferunt, ubi summa pecuniae non excedat valorem quinque millium scutatorum, Episcopi liberi erunt; ubi vero negotium eam summam superat, tunc requiritur consilium consultorum, eoque praehabito, necessaria est S. Sedis permissio. Verum quum peculiares circumstantiae in quibus Ecclesia in Statibus Foederatis impraesentiarum versatur, non permittant habere in singulis casibus recursum ad S. Sedem, Sanctissimus D. N. Leo XIII. ad preces Patrum benigne indulget, ut interim per S. Congregationem de Propaganda Fide speciales et extraordinariae facultates hac super re tribuantur.

Item, praehabito consilio consultorum, necessarius erit recursus ad S. Sedem in singulis casibus, in quibus agatur de imponenda nova taxa pro Episcopo quae excedat limites a canonibus constitutos.

179. Statuunt igitur Patres in hac synodo coadunati, ut pro unoquoque seminario, sive minori, sive majori, duo saltem constituantur deputati, unus pro spiritualibus, uti est institutio, disciplina et mores clericorum, alter pro temporalibus. Ejusmodi deputati eligendi erunt pro seminariis dioecesanis ab Episcopo de consilio consultorum, pro provincialibus ab Episcopis provinciae collegialiter.

Code

Canon 357

§ 1. Synodum dioecesanam convocat eique praeest Episcopus, non autem Vicarius Generalis sine mandato speciali nec Vicarius Capitularis.

Canon 362

Unicus est in Synodo legislator Episcopus, ceteris votum tantum consultivum habentibus; unus ipse subscribit synodalibus constitutionibus; quae, si in Synodo promulgentur, eo ipso obligare incipiunt, nisi aliud expresse caveatur.

Canon 386

§ 1. Examinatoribus et parochis consultoribus medio tempore inter unam et aliam Synodum demortuis vel alia ratione a munere cessantibus, alios prosynodales Episcopus substituat de consilio Capituli cathedralis.

Canon 426

§ 3. Deficiente, quavis de causa, aliquo consultore intra triennium, Episcopus alium de consilio ceterorum consultorum substituat, isque in officio maneat usque ad expletum idem triennium.

§ 5. Si, sede vacante, aliquis consultor moriatur vel renuntiet, Vicarius Capitularis, de consensu aliorum consultorum, alium nominet, qui tamen, ut munere, sede plena, fungatur, indiget novi Episcopi confirmatione.

Canon 452

§ 1. Sine Apostolicae Sedis indulto paroecia nequit personae morali pleno iure uniri, ita nempe ut ipsamet persona moralis sit parochus, ad normam can. 1423, § 2.

§ 2. Persona moralis, cui paroecia sit pleno iure unita, habitualem tantum curam animarum retinere potest, servato, quod ad actualem spectat, praescripto can. 471.

CANON 1359

§ 1. Diocesanis Seminariis bini constituantur coetus deputatorum, alter pro disciplina, alter pro administratione bonorum temporalium.

§ 2. Utrumque deputatorum coetum constituunt bini sacerdotes, ab Episcopo, audito Capitulo, electi; sed excluduntur Vicarius Generalis, familiares Episcopi, rector Seminarii, oeconomus, et confessarii ordinarii.

CANON 1423

§ 1. Ordinarii locorum, non autem Vicarius Capitularis, nec Vicarius Generalis sine mandato speciali, possunt, ob Ecclesiae necessitatem vel magnam et evidentem utilitatem, aeque aut minus principaliter unire quaslibet paroeciales ecclesias inter se aut cum beneficio non curato, ita tamen ut altero in casu, si unio fiat minus principalis, beneficium non curatum sit accessorium.

§ 2. Nequeunt vero paroeciam unire cum mensa capitulari vel episcopali, cum monasteriis, ecclesiis religiosorum aut alia persona morali, neque cum dignitatibus et beneficiis ecclesiae cathedralis vel collegiatae; sed possunt eam cum ecclesia cathedrali aut collegiali, quae in territorio paroeciae sita sit, ita unire ut reditus paroeciae cedant in commodum ipsius ecclesiae, relicta parocho vel vicario congrua portione.

§ 3. Unio beneficiorum a locorum Ordinariis fieri non potest, nisi in perpetuum.

CANON 1428

§ 1. Locorum Ordinarii uniones, translationes, divisiones, dismembrationes beneficiorum ne faciant nisi per authenticam scripturam, auditis Capitulo cathedrali et iis, si qui sint, quorum intersit, praesertim rectoribus ecclesiarum.

§ 2. Unio, translatio, divisio, dismembratio facta sine canonica causa irrita est.

§ 3. Adversus decretum Ordinarii unientis, transferentis, dividentis aut dismembrantis beneficia, datur in devolutivo tantum recursus ad Sanctam Sedem.

CANON 1442

Beneficia saecularia nonnisi clericis e clero saeculari conferenda sunt; religiosa sodalibus illius religionis, ad quam beneficia pertinent.

CANON 1532

§ 1. Legitimus Superior de quo in can. 1530, § 1, n. 3, est Sedes Apostolica, si agatur:

1.° De rebus pretiosis;

2.° De rebus quae valorem excedunt triginta millium libellarum seu francorum.

§ 2. Si vero agatur de rebus quae valorem non excedunt mille libellarum seu francorum, est loci Ordinarius, audito administrationis Consilio, nisi res minimi momenti sit, et cum eorum consensu quorum interest.

§ 3. Si denique de rebus quarum pretium continetur intra mille libellas et triginta millia libellarum seu francorum, est loci Ordinarius, dummodo accesserit consensus tum Capituli cathedralis, tum Consilii administrationis, tum eorum quorum interest.

§ 4. Si agatur de alienanda re divisibili, in petenda licentia aut consensu pro alienatione exprimi debent partes antea alienatae; secus licentia irrita est.

Canon 2347

Firma nullitate actus et obligatione, etiam per censuram urgenda, restituendi bona illegitime acquisita ac reparandi damna forte illata, qui bona ecclesiastica alienare praesumpserit aut in iis alienandis consensum praebere contra praescripta can. 534, § 1, et can. 1532:

1.° Si agatur de re cuius pretium non excedit mille libellas, congruis poenis a legitimo Superiore ecclesiastico puniatur;

2.° Si agatur de re cuius pretium sit supra mille, sed infra triginta millia libellarum, privetur patronus iure patronatus; administrator, munere administratoris; Superior vel oeconomus religiosus, proprio officio et habilitate ad cetera officia, praeter alias congruas poenas a Superioribus infligendas; Ordinarius vero aliique clerici, officium, beneficium, dignitatem, munus in Ecclesia obtinentes, solvant duplum favore ecclesiae vel piae causae laesae; ceteri clerici suspendantur ad tempus ab Ordinario definiendum;

3.° Quod si beneplacitum apostolicum, in memoratis canonibus praescriptum, fuerit scienter praetermissum, omnes quovis modo reos sive dando sive recipiendo sive consensum praebendo, manet praeterea excommunicatio latae sententiae nemini reservata.

The Council nowhere requires the consent of the Diocesan Consultors. In number 20, however, it enumerates seven instances in which their advice must be asked by the Bishop. Since these are not dealt with collectively by the Code, each individual instance must be sought there under its proper subject. Since in four of these instances the Council and Code are in agreement no discussion is necessary and they need be hardly more than listed.

In the first of these the Council requires the advice of the Consultors for the division of a mission, there being no canonically erected parishes in this country at the time. The Code in canon 1428 has the same requirement for parishes.

In the second case the Council both in number 20 and in number 179 requires the advice of the Consultors in the appointment of the deputies whose duty is the spiritual and temporal management of the seminary. The Code makes this same demand in canon 1359.

In the third instance the Council orders the Bishop to ask his Consultor's advice both in filling a vacancy in their body and in choosing Examiners outside of synod.[78] The Code has the same legislation for these two appointments in canons 386, § 1 and 426, § 3 respectively.

It might be mentioned here that the Council makes no provision for the appointment of a new Consultor while the see is vacant; whereas the Code does make such provision in canon 426, § 5 wherein it empowers the Administrator to appoint a new Consultor but with the consent, not merely the advice, of the others.

The fourth and last case in which the two laws agree is that concerning the giving of a mission or parish to the care of a religious community. The Code deals with this matter in four canons, namely, 452, 1423, 1428 and 1442. Herein one finds that the mind of the Church is that secular benefices are for the secular clergy and religious ones for the religious. When it is a question of any transfer of a secular benefice, such as our parishes are now considered to be, the Bishop is to ask the advice of his Consultors; and when that transfer of a secular benefice is to be *pleno jure* to a moral body, such as is a religious community, then also the permission of the Holy See is to be obtained.[79]

Of the cases in which the Council and Code differ regarding the advice of the Consultors the first is that of the diocesan synod. The Council requires the Bishop to seek the advice of his Consultors before calling a synod and promulgating its decrees. The Code in canons 357, § 1 and 362 states simply that the Bishop calls a synod, presides over it and is its only law maker, and nowhere makes mention of his asking the Consultors' advice in the matter.

The two laws are evidently contradictory. The Council in denying to the Bishop the freedom which the Code now gives him is opposed to the latter and, therefore, abrogated. The Consultors' advice, then, may still be sought in this regard, but it is no longer of obligation. Klekotka [80] considers the Council as practically *praeter codicem* on

[78] *Supra*, p. 61, footnote 72.

[79] Augustine, *Commentary*, II, 515, 520, 525; Klekotka, *op. cit.*, pp. 123, ff.

[80] *Op. cit.*, p. 112, ff.

this point. But in this he seems not only wrong, but inconsistent. For as he previously [81] judges the Bishop free in the choice of all his Consultors by reason of the Code's not mentioning any right of the clergy in this regard, so by the same token he should consider the Bishop free in the matter of calling the synod by reason of the Code's not giving the Diocesan Consultors any rights in this connection.

The second difference between the local particular law and the common law regarding the advice of Consultors concerns the alienation of Church property. According to the Council the Bishops are free in this matter for sums up to $5000; while for transaction in excess of this amount they needed the advice of their Consultors and the permission of the Holy See. In answer to a petition of the Fathers of the Council the Sacred Congregation of the Propagation of the Faith on September 25, 1885 granted our Bishops for ten years an indult which went into effect with the Council.[82] This indult dispensed our Bishops from the formalities of the law and required of them simply the advice of the Consultors and a triennial report on the number and amount of their expenditures together with an account of the financial status of the missions in the interest of which the transactions had taken place. This favor was renewed every ten years up to and including 1916, and so was in effect when the Code was promulgated.[83] The formality of the law from which it released our Bishops was the obligation of obtaining the permission of the Holy See in every particular case of alienation of sums in excess of the amount of $5,000 as fixed by the Council.[84] So up to the coming of the Code our Bishops were free to spend sums up to $5,000 and for larger amounts needed only the advice of their Consultors.

The Code in canon 1532 prescribes the following regarding the alienation of property:

For precious goods and sums over 30,000 lire or francs (about $6,000 when the Code was promulgated) the permission of the Holy See is necessary.

For sums between 1,000 and 30,000 lire or francs (about $200 to $6,000) the permission of the Ordinary of the place and the consent

[81] *Op. cit.*, p. 52.

[82] *Conc. Plen. Balti, III Acta et Decreta*, p. ciii.

[83] Klekotka, *op. cit.*, p. 140.

[84] Smith, *Elements*, I, 489.

of the Diocesan Consultors, of the Board of Administration and of the interested parties is needed.

For amounts less than 1,000 lire or francs it requires the permission of the Ordinary of the place, the consent of the interested parties and, unless the sum is very small, the advice of the Board of Administration.[85]

It further provides in Canon 2347 that one who presumes to alienate ecclesiastical goods or consents thereto in violation of the above canon shall be punished with appropriate penalties by the legitimate ecclesiastical superior if the sum does not exceed 1,000 francs (about $200); if the sum be between 1,000 and 30,000 francs ($200 and $6,000) a patron who is guilty of illegal alienation shall be deprived of the right of patronage; an Administrator is to be deprived of his office; a religious Superior or religious *economus* of his office and of eligibility to acquire any other office, in addition to other appropriate penalties to be imposed by the Superiors; an Ordinary or other cleric having an office, benefice, dignity or position in the Church shall pay double the amount to the church or pious institute that has been injured; while all other clerics are to be suspended for a time the length of which is to be determined by the Ordinary; finally, if the permission of the Holy See is required and has been knowingly neglected, all guilty parties, whether giving, receiving or consenting, incur over and above the other penalties mentioned an *ipso facto* excommunication that is not reserved.

A reconciling of the two laws brings about a rather anomalous situation. In the first place, it would seem, and there is no direct difficulty herein, that after the coming of the Code the sum in excess of which the permission of the Holy See is needed is $6,000 instead of the $5,000 limit fixed by the Third Plenary Council, the superior law being given the preference in any case of conflict. In virtue of our indult which dispensed from this permission and which by canon 4 continued in force, our Bishops after May 19, 1918 for transactions involving values above $6,000 needed only the advice of their Consultors; their only obligation to the Holy See being the triennial report.[86]

[85] Augustine, *Commentary*, III, 183, ff.

[86] Klekotka, *op. cit.*, 139 and 141.

In the second place, and herein lies the incongruity, for amounts less than $6,000 our Bishops needed not merely advice but consent. For sums between $200 and $6,000 that consent was to be obtained from the Consultors, the Board and the interested parties; while for sums below $200 the consent of the interested parties was required and moreover the advice of the Board unless the amount was very small.

By reason of our indult there was a much greater check upon sums below $6,000 than on those above that amount, whereas the opposite is the tenor of the common law in requiring the judgment of the Holy See for the bigger transaction.[87]

This situation together with the fact that our local business transactions are so frequently in excess of $6,000 showed the need of new indults better adapted to the mind of the Code and our local conditions. These have since been obtained by our Bishops collectively and individually.[88]

Among the faculties issued to the Bishops of the United States by the Sacred Congregation of the Council is that of permitting the alienation of ecclesiastical goods to the sum of $10,000.[89]

By a rescript dated November 18, 1924 the Sacred Congregation of the Council granted to our Bishops for ten years the faculty of permitting, when any real necessity should arise, negotiations of loans up to $50,000.[90]

The last of these instances in which the Council orders the advice of the Consultors is before the Bishop has the required recourse to the Holy See itself before the approval of the decrees.[91] The himself of a new tax which exceeds the limits established by the canons.

The meaning of this law seems never to have been clear. This may be explained by the fact that the statute in question was not included in the original draft of the Council submitted to the Sacred Congregation of the Propagation of the Faith, but was inserted by the Holy See itself before the approval of the decrees.[91] The

[87] Klekotka, *op. cit.*, pp. 134, ff.

[88] Ayrinhac, *Administrative Legislation*, p. 446.

[89] Vermeersch-Creusen, *Epitome*, II, Appendix, p. 502; Woywod, *A Practical Commentary*, II, Appendix V, p. 649.

[90] From a copy of the rescript in the author's possession.

[91] Smith, *Elements*, I, 490.

doubt centers about the expression *nova taxa pro Episcopo quae excedat limites a canonibus constitutos.* Neither Dr. Smith nor Father Nilles, S. J. gives more than a hint at the possible meaning when they repeat in connection with this decree the common law requiring the Consultor's consent for new taxes.[92] The former explains his reluctance to express an opinion when he writes, ". . . owing to the general terms in which these phrases are couched, and the consequent difference of opinions as to their meaning, it is desirable that an authentic explanation of them be given by the Holy See; especially as the phrases were inserted by the Holy See itself when the acts and decrees of the Third Plenary Council of Baltimore were submitted to the Sacred Congregation of the Propagation of the Faith for revision. Until such an authentic explanation is given it would appear unsafe, or at least unsatisfactory, to attempt to give any private or doctrinal explanation that would commend itself to the approval of others." [93]

Such authentic explanation evidently never was given for Klekotka writing rather exhaustively on this decree as late as 1920 makes no mention of it.

What then is to be said of its present status from a legal standpoint? Because of the persevering doubt about its meaning, it is impossible to institute any other than a purely speculative comparison between this law and the Code. This Klekotka [94] has done thoroughly by comparison with the Code all the taxes that the above decree might be expected to apply to and his conclusion is that this local statute is abrogated by reason of its opposition to canons 1504 to 1507.

In connection with only one of all the expenses named and provided for by the Code, and that is the determining of funeral offerings in canon 1234, is the Bishop required to consult his Diocesan Consultors. This tax, of course, cannot be included among those referred to by the Council since it is neither extraordinary nor for the Bishop. Nor can the *cathedraticum* although for the Bishop be included in these taxes since it is neither new nor extraordinary.[95]

[92] Smith, *Elements*, I, 363; Nilles, *op. cit.*, p. 63.

[93] Smith, *op. cit.*, I, 490.

[94] *Op. cit.*, pp. 143-148.

[95] Klekotka, *op. cit.*, p. 148; Smith, *Elements*, I, 187.

Article 4

Meetings of the Diocesan Consultors

Third Plenary Council

21. Consilium consultorum praestabitur collegialiter, et quoties eis ita videbitur, secretis suffragiis, ideoque Episcopus eos quater in anno statutis temporibus convocabit, vel, ubi id fieri non potest, saltem bis in anno; alias vero quoties ad pertractanda negotia erit necessarium.

Code

Canon 411

§ 1. Stato tempore ac loco conveniat canonicorum coetus de suae ecclesiae et Capituli negotiis acturus; alii praeterea conventus haberi poterunt, quoties id aut Episcopo aut Capituli praesidi aut maiori canonicorum parti expedire videatur.

According to number 21 of the Third Plenary Council the Bishop is to summon the Diocesan Consultors four times a year at stated times and, where this is impossible, at least twice a year and, of course, at any other time there is business to be transacted. In the common law on Consultors there is no reference to regular meetings.

Since there is nothing in the Code against regular meetings of the Diocesan Consultors and, whereas, according to canon 411 their prototype, the Cathedral Chapter, is to convene regularly at a fixed time and place,[96] the prescription of the Baltimore law seems in no wise opposed to the Code, but rather something *praeter codicem* and hence still in force, so that our Bishops continue under the obligation of having four or at least two regular meetings of their Consultors every year.[97]

TITLE XIV

The Administrator of a Vacant Diocese

Article 1

The Appointment of The Administrator

Second Plenary Council

96. Unusquisque Episcopus acceptas a Sancta Sede facultates idoneis sacerdotibus, qui in eorum dioecesibus laboraverint, communicare potest; et praesertim tempore sui obitus, ut sede

Code

Canon 427

Coetus consultorum dioecesanorum vices Capituli cathedralis, qua Episcopi senatus, supplet; quare quae canones ad gubernationem dioecesis,

[96] Vermeersch-Creusen, *Epitome*, I, 267.

[97] Klekotka, *op. cit.*, p. 106.

vacante sit qui possit Episcopi defuncti vices supplere, donec Apostolica sedes certior facta, quod quamprimum fieri debebit, alio modo provideat.

97. Quod si Archiepiscopo aut Episcopo obeunte, nemo adsit qui praedictarum facultatum communicationem rite ab eodem obtinuerit, seu aliter quam per Antistitis obitum dioecesim vacare contigerit, Metropolitanus Antistes, vel in ipsius defectu aut si de ipsa Metropolitana ecclesia agatur, senior ex suffraganeis idoneum virum ecclesiasticum designet, qui dioecesis regimen gerat, cum usu facultatum, quae in prima formula recensentur, donec Apostolica Sedes certior facta secus de re non disposuerit.

98. Sanctae Sedi vero supplicandum duximus, ob plurima incommoda, quibus aliter provideri vix potest, ut in supradictis casibus Episcopus, aut, prout casus feret, Metropolita vel senior Episcopus, possit Presbytero sedis vacantis Administratori tribuere eas omnes facultates, tam ordinarias quam extraordinarias, quibus gaudent Episcopi ex Sanctae Sedis concessione.

sive sede plena sive ea impedita aut vacante, Capitulo cathedrali tribuunt, ea de coetu quoque consultorum dioecesanorum intelligenda sunt.

Canon 431

§ 1. Sede vacante, nisi adfuerit Administrator Apostolicus vel aliter a Sancta Sede provisum fuerit, ad Capitulum ecclesiae cathedralis regimen dioecesis devolvitur.

§ 2. Sicubi ex speciali Sanctae Sedis dispositione Archiepiscopus aliusve Episcopus Administratorem dioecesis vacantis designet, hic omnes et solas facultates habet quae Vicario Capitulari competunt, eisdem obligationibus ac poenis obnoxius.

Canon 432

§ 1. Capitulum ecclesiae cathedralis, sede vacante, intra octo dies ab accepta notitia vacationis, debet Vicarium Capitularem qui loco sui dioecesim regat et, si fructuum percipiendorum ei munus incumbat, oeconomum unum vel plures fideles ac diligentes constituere.

§ 2. Si Capitulum intra praescriptum tempus Vicarium aut oeconomum, quavis de causa, nullum deputaverit, deputatio ad Metropolitam devolvitur; si autem ecclesia ipsa metropolitana fuerit vacans vel metropolitana simul et suffraganea, ad antiquiorem ex Episcopis suffraganeis.

§ 3. Etiam vacante dioecesi aut abbatia vel praelatura de quibus in can. 285, si Capitulum intra octiduum Vicarium vel oeconomum non nominaverit, hunc Metropolita qui fuit legitime electus ad normam citati canonis, constituat, nisi in abbatia vel praelatura *nullius* religiosa aliter ad normam constitutionum provideatur.

§ 4. Capitulum quantocius de morte

Episcopi et deinde electus in Vicarium Capitularem de sua electione Sedem Apostolicam certiorem faciant.

CANON 438

Vicarius Capitularis, edita fidei professione de qua in can. 1406-1408, statim iurisdictionem obtinet, quin necessaria sit ullius confirmatio.

By common law for centuries the Administrator of a vacant diocese was elected by the Cathedral Chapter and had with some restriction the power of jurisdiction of the Bishop. In missionary countries without Chapters various methods obtained. In some places the administration of the diocese passed automatically to the Vicar General or to one appointed by the Bishop before his death. In others the Administrator was appointed by the Metropolitan or senior suffragan. For us the Second Plenary Council in numbers 96 to 98 decreed that every Bishop should make provision for the administration of the diocese in the event of his death by designating a priest who would govern in virtue of his appointment until the Holy See either confirmed him or appointed another. If the Bishop failed to make this provision, the Metropolitan or senior suffragan was to make the appointment. The Administrator was to enjoy not only the ordinary jurisdiction but also all the extraordinary faculties granted the Bishop by indults.

The Third Plenary Council says nothing about this and so the law of the Second Council remained in force until the promulgation of the Code. This latter in canon 427 lays down the principle that the Consultors take the place of the Chapter and that therefore what the canons grant the Chapter in the government of the diocese *sede plena* or *sede impedita aut vacante* is granted, likewise, to the Diocesan Consultors. Now canon 432 decrees that the Cathedral Chapter and, therefore, our body of Consultors is bound to elect an Administrator within eight days after they learn that the see has become vacant. Should the Consultors fail for any reason to make this appointment, the right passes to the Metropolitan or if his see be vacant, to the senior suffragan. It seems clear that the Code sets aside the law of Baltimore and gives the right and duty of appointing the Administrator to the Diocesan Consultors. At the time of the publication of Code, however, a doubt arose concerning this. Some argued that the Council of Baltimore having been approved by the Holy See fell under the exception made by the Code in canon 431 which states that in the case of vacancy the government of the diocese devolves on the Cathedral Chapter or Diocesan Consultors unless the Holy See has appointed an Apostolic Administrator, or made other provision. This opinion, however, was set aside by a decision of the Commission for the Authentic Interpretation of the Code dated February 22, 1919 [98] in which it was replied that on this point the Council of Baltimore had been abrogated by the Code and that henceforth we were to observe the prescriptions of canon 427. An exception was made, however, for three years for dioceses in which there were not at least five Consultors. In these the Archbishop or senior suffragan was authorized to provide with the ratification of the Apostolic Delegate. This rule was extended to the dioceses of Canada and Newfoundland on May 8, 1919.[99]

This answer was to be expected because according to the general principle laid down in canon 6, §1 all particular laws opposed to the Code are abrogated and there is evident opposition in this case.

It is true that canon 431 does make allowance for other methods but these must have been provided by the Holy See and where such exist they continue in force. The method of the Council of Baltimore was provided by the American Bishops and received the approbation of the Holy See; but such approbation does not constitute special Apostolic provision.

It is to be noted that the Code in abrogating this local statute has done away with the need our Administrators previously had of papal confirmation; for canon 438 decrees that the Administrator having made the profession of faith receives his jurisdiction immediately without the confirmation of anyone. It is required, however, by canon 432, §4 that the Diocesan Consultors acquaint the Holy See with the fact of the Administrator's election.

[98] *A. A. S.*, XI (1919), 75.

[99] *A. A. S.*, XI (1919), 233.

ARTICLE 2

The Power of the Administrator

SECOND PLENARY COUNCIL

98. Sanctae Sedi vero supplicandum duximus, ob plurima incommoda, quibus aliter provideri vix potest, ut in supradictis casibus Episcopus, aut, prout casus feret, Metropolita vel senior Episcopus, possit Presbytero sedis vacantis Administratori tribuere eas omnes facultates, tam ordinarias quam extraordinarias, quibus gaudent Episcopi ex Sanctae Sedis concessione.

CODE

CANON 435

§ 1. Sicut ad Capitulum ante deputationem Vicarii Capitularis, ita deinde ad Vicarium Capitularem transit ordinaria Episcopi iurisdictio in spiritualibus et temporalibus, exceptis iis quae in iure expresse sunt eidem prohibita.

§ 2. Quare Capitulum et postea Vicarius Capitularis omnia possunt quae enumerata sunt can. 368, § 2; item facultate pollent exercitium pontificalium in dioecesi cuilibet Episcopo permittendi, imo, si Vicarius Capitularis sit Episcopus, potest ipse eadem exercere, excluso tamen usu throni cum baldachino.

§ 3. Vicario Capitulari et Capitulo non licet agere quidpiam quod vel dioecesi vel episcopalibus iuribus praeiudicium aliquod afferre possit; nominatim vero Vicarius Capitularis aliique sive de Capitulo sive extranei, clerici aut laici, per se vel per alium prohibentur Curiae episcopalis documenta quaelibet subtrahere vel destruere vel celare vel immutare.

The Second Plenary Council in number 98 decreed that a petition should be sent to Rome to have the Administrators of our vacant sees granted all the faculties ordinary and extraordinary which our Bishops enjoyed from the Holy See.

The faculties referred to had been granted our Bishops by the Sacred Congregation of the Propagation of the Faith. The terms "ordinary" and "extraordinary" are significant. All propaganda faculties are so divided. Drawn up into lists called *Forms* the ordinary faculties are designated by Roman numerals and their grant varies with different countries, while the extraordinary ones are distinguished by capital letters and are given according to need.[100] In this country *Form* 1 and *Forms* C, D and E obtained. Since permission to confer upon Administrators the ordinary faculties of *Form* 1 not requiring the Episcopal Order had already been granted,[101] the above petition was concerned actually with only the extraordinary faculties of *Forms* C, D and E. The request having gone unanswered by Rome[102] was repeated in 1869 by the Tenth Provincial Council of Baltimore.[103] This time the Holy See granted the petition except for the extraordinary faculties which require the Episcopal character.[104]

This concession asked by and made to the Province of Baltimore only, which at the time of the grant included the present Province of Philadelphia, was not intended for the whole United States;[105] nor was this privilege ever generally extended to the whole country.

The Code now provides the Vicar-Capitular or the Administrator, as he is called in this country, with ample faculties to govern the vacant see. In canon 435 it gives to the Consultors and in turn after his election to the Administrator all the Bishop's ordinary jurisdiction in both spiritual and temporal affairs except wherein that jurisdiction is expressly denied by law. The following are those exceptions: The Administrator may not convoke diocesan synods (can. 357, §1); appoint honorary Canons (can. 406, §1); give permanency to removable parishes (can. 454, § 1); establish religious Congregations (can. 492, § 1); erect pious associations or give his consent for the same (can. 686, § 4); reserve cases to himself (can. 893, § 1); allow poor churches to demand a compensation for the privilege of saying Mass (can. 1303, §3); unite parishes (can. 1423, § 1); permit permutation of benefices (can. 1487, § 1); remove the *Promotor Justitiae* or *Defensor Vinculi* (can. 1590).[106]

[100] Taunton, *op. cit.*, p. 521.
[101] *Conc. Plen. Balti. II Acta et Decreta*, N. 97.
[102] Smith, *Elements*, I, 399.
[103] *Collectio Lacensis*, T, III, p. 596.
[104] *Collectio Lacensis*, T, III, p. 599; Smith, *Elements*, I, 399.
[105] Smith, *op. cit.*, p. 400, footnote 1.
[106] Cf. Ayrinhac, *Constitution of the Church*, p. 277.

TITLE XV

Pastors

Article 1

The Appointment and Removal of Pastors

Second Plenary Council

123. Quum olim jure optimo, ut ait Tridentinum Concilium, "distinctae fuerint dioeceses et parochiae, ac unicuique gregi proprii attributi pastores et inferiorum Ecclesiarum rectores, qui suarum quisque ovium curam habeant," optandum omnino esset, ut juxta Ecclesiae universae consuetudinem, parochi proprie dicti, quemadmodum in Catholicis regionibus existunt, in nostrarum quoque provinciarum ecclesiis constituerentur. Verum ea sunt nostra rerum tempora, quae id fieri nondum patiantur. Patrum tamen hujus Concilii Plenarii mens est, ut paullatim, et quatenus per adjuncta liceat, disciplina nostra hac in re Ecclesiae universae disciplinae conformetur.

124. Volumus igitur, ut per omnes hasce Provincias, praesertim majoribus in urbibus, ubi plures sunt Ecclesiae, districtus quidam, paroeciae instar, descriptis accurate limitibus, unicuique ecclesiae assignetur; ejusque rectori jura parochialia, vel quasi-parochialia, tribuantur.

125. Parochialis juris, paroeciae, et parochi nomina usurpando, nullatenus intendimus Ecclesiae cujuslibet rectori jus, ut ajunt, *inamovibilitatis* tribuere; aut potestatem illam tollere seu ullo modo imminuere, quam ex recepta in his provinciis disciplina habet Episcopus quem vis sacerdotem munere privandi aut alio transferendi. Monemus autem et hortamur, ne Episcopi hoc jure suo, nisi graves ob causas et habita meritorum ratione, uti velint.

126. Quum animarum saluti maxime expediat a dignis atque idoneis parochis regi, Tridentina lege cautum est, ne quis ad parochialis ecclesiae regimen assumatur, nisi prius, per concursum coram Episcopo et tribus saltem examinatoribus, idoneus probetur ac dignus qui id muneris suscipiat. Quod apud nos, etiam si veri nominis parochos haberemus, servari vix posset. Ut tamen mentem Ecclesiae haec praecipientis, quantum licet, sequamur; neminem parochiali Ecclesiae praeponendum censemus, quin examen coram Episcopo et duobus presbyteris ab Episcopo designandis antea subierit. Neque ullus ad hoc examen admittatur, qui in dioecesi, ubi parochia sita est, sacris missionibus per quinquennium saltem operam non dederit. Quod si sacerdos ad parochialis ecclesiae curam assumatur, qui nondum in dioecesi quinque annos in sacris missionibus insumserit, tanquam paroeciae administrator tantum habeatur; neque, nisi expleto quinquennio, factoque ut supra examine, parochi nomen et jura obtineat: quod quidem Regulares, qui quinque annos in his Provinciis vixerint, non attingat.

Third Plenary Council

33. Ex quo superius Concilium Plenarium celebratum fuit, nostrarum rerum status profecto non adeo est immutatus, ut ad literam servari possint omnia et singula, quae sacris canonibus, et praesertim Concilii Tridentini decretis de instituendis paroeciis sapientissime provisa sunt. Verum ut disciplina nostra hac in re ad normam sanctionum canonicarum in tantum redigatur, in quantum locorum circumstantiae sinunt, haec statuenda censuimus:

In singulis dioecesibus, auctoritate Episcopi, de consultorum suorum consilio seligantur certae missiones quae magis aptae videntur ut paroeciarum instar haberi possint, atque a rectoribus missionariis permanenter institutis seu inamovibilibus sicut in Anglia regantur. Ejusmodi missio, cui praeficiendus erit rector inamovibilis, omnino instructa esse debet ecclesia congrua, schola pro utroque sexu, domo sacerdotis usui accommodata, et proventibus sufficientibus et satis certis ad sacerdotis, ecclesiae et scholae necessariam sustentationem.

34. Missio cujus Rector semel inamovibilis est constitutus, in posterum semper habebit Rectorem inamovibilem, licet aliqua territorii parte juxta normam in n. 20 discriptam minuatur. Novarum autem paroeciarum ex dismembratione efformatarum rectores non erunt inamovibiles, nisi Episcopi auctoritate tales constituti feurint. Paroeciae eadem dismembratione efformatae independentes tamen constituentur ab ecclesia matrice.

35. *Pro nunc* instituantur in singulis dioecesibus rectores missionarii inamovibiles tali numero, ut inter omnes dioeceseos rectores missionarios decimus quisque sit inamovibilis, dummodo conditiones requisitae adsint tum ex parte missionis, cum ex parte rectoris eligendi. Quae proportio (unus inter decem) ne inconsulte excedatur intra viginti primos annos post concilium promulgatum. Institutio autem rectorum inamovibilium, ut praescripta, ultra triennium a promulgatione concilii computandum non erit differenda. Inter rectores inamovibiles tamen rector ecclesiae cathedralis non est ponendus; et quando nova dioecesis erigitur, rector ecclesiae quam Episcopus in cathedralem eligit, ipso facto erit amovibilis.

36. Ad conditiones quod spectat, quae ex parte eligendorum ad missiones inamovibilitatis privilegio insignitas requiruntur, ut quis sacerdos ejusmodi missioni praefici valeat, opus erit: I. ut per decem saltem annos in dioecesi sacrum ministerium laudabiliter exercuerit; II. ut intra idem temporis spatium sese habilem probaverit ad parochiam administrandam et in temporalibus et in spiritualibus; III. ut concursum faciat juxta normam infra statuendam. Inter eos qui hisce conditionibus satisfecerint, electio dignioris relinquitur judicio et conscientiae Episcopi, salva appellatione juxta constitutionem s. m. Benedicti XIV., *Cum illud,* diei 14 Dec. 1742.

37. Volumus tamen, ut Episcopi facultate gaudeant, pro *prima vice,* omisso concursu Rectores inamovibiles designandi quos magis dignos et idoneos coram Deo judicaverint, praehabito consilio Consultorum suorum.

38. Rector missionarius permanenter institutus seu inamovibilis, a sua missione definitive removeri non poterit, nisi ob causam canonicam, et tam in remediis praeventivis quam repressivis servata forma procedendi juxta normam Instructionis S. Congregationis de Propaganda Fide de cognoscendis et definiendis causis criminalibus et disciplinaribus clericorum, quae incipit "*Cum Magnopere*," nuperrime ad Episcopos Foederatorum Statuum Americae Septentrionalis directae.

39. Pro gradu quo rectores inamovibilitatis titulo condecorati aliis praeeunt sacerdotibus, eo strictiori filialis obsequii vinculo cum Episcopo constringantur oportet. Ita fiet, ut a Christo, summo animarum Pastore, uberrimas gratias consequantur ad suum tam grave munus digne ac prospere obeundum, necnon a populo Christiano obedientiam ac observantiam suae auctoritati debitam.

40. Concilium Tridentinum perpendens, maxime saluti animarum expedire ut Dominici gregis regimen nonnisi dignis atque idoneis parochis concredatur, decrevit in conferendis paroeciis adhibendam esse formam concursus, quo fieret, ut non solum indigni arcerentur, sed digniores eligerentur. Summus Pontifex Benedictus XIV. in Const. *Cum illud* supra n. 36 cit., deinde formam statuit seu methodum pro examine in consursu eligendorum ad ecclesias parochiales servandam. Ut igitur hisce in provinciis, in concursu promovendorum ad missiones inamovibilitatis dote insignitas, methodus adhibeatur, quae hinc, quoad substantialia saltem, ad tramitem memoratae constitutionis sit redacta, inde vero rerum nostrarum statui accommodata, praesens Synodus haec servanda decrevit:

41. Examen seu concursus ad missiones inamovibilitatis privilegio gaudentes institui debet coram Episcopo vel ejus vicario generali a tribus saltem ex dioecesanis examinatoribus loco synodalium vel prosynodalium, constitutis, quos Episcopus designavit. (Conc. Trid., Sess. xxiv., de Ref. c. 18.) Pauciores quam tres adhibere non licebit, nisi tot examinatores ob sacerdotum paucitatem nequaquam haberi possunt.

42. Vacante missione, quae sit per concursum conferenda, Episcopus idoneum vicarium in ea constituat; vacationem exinde annuntiabit clero dioecesis concursum indicendo; et dies decem assignabit ad concurrentes adscribendos; hunc vero terminum prorogare poterit ad viginti dies. Non ultra autem sex menses ex quo missionem suo rectore orbatam cognoverit, differet novi rectoris nominationem. Opportunum etiam erit, ut Episcopi a S. Pontifice facultatem implorent pro dicto termino dierum decem ad dies triginta prorogando.

43. Ad subeundum examen admittentur tantum sacerdotes fide ac moribus integri, qui per decennium saltem sacrum ministerium laudabiliter exercuerint in dioecesi, et intra idem temporis spatium per tres saltem annos alicujus ecclesiae curam habuerint tanquam simplices rectores, aut aliter specimen dederint suae habilitatis ad missionem administrandam, tam in spiritualibus quam in temporalibus. Qui igitur admitti cupient, statuto tempore ab Episcopo licentiam petent, cujus erit de eorum admissione judicare.

44. In scientiae periculo subeundo respondendum erit tum voce tum scripto. Quaestiones ab examinatoribus proponendae depromantur e theologicis disciplinis, praesertim e Theologia Morali, Dogmatica et Liturgica Jureque Canonico; nec versentur nisi circa ea quorum scientia ad munus pastorale rite obeundum requiritur; in his etiam ea potissimum deligantur, quorum notitia prompta ac parata semper habeatur oportet, eo quod solutio dilationem communiter non patitur. Singulis etiam assignetur ex catechismo una alteraque quaestio catechetice exponenda, ut uniuscujusque patescat methodus ac peritia in explicanda illustrandaque doctrina Christiana, plane ac lucide et accommodate ad captum parvulorum ac rudium. Proponatur demum textus Evangelii super quo singuli concurrentes concionandi facultatem probaturi scribant. (Const. cit., § 7.)

Code

Canon 216

§ 1. Territorium cuiuslibet dioecesis dividatur in distinctas partes territoriales; unicuique autem parti sua peculiaris ecclesia cum populo determinato est assignanda, suusque peculiaris rector, tanquam proprius eiusdem pastor, est praeficiendus pro necessaria animarum cura.

§ 2. Pari modo vicariatus apostolicus et praefectura apostolica, ubi commode fieri possit, dividantur.

§ 3. Partes dioecesis de quibus in § 1, sunt *paroeciae*; partes vicariatus apostolici ac praefecturae apostolicae, si peculiaris rector eisdem fuerit assignatus, appellantur *quasi-paroeciae.*

§ 4. Non possunt sine speciali apostolico indulto constitui paroeciae pro diversitate sermonis seu nationis fidelium in eadem civitate vel territorio degentium, nec paroeciae mere familiares aut personales; ad constitutas autem quod attinet, nihil innovandum, inconsulta Apostolica Sede.

Canon 454

§ 2. At non omnes parochi eandem obtinent stabilitatem; qui maiore gaudent, inamovibiles; qui minore, amovibiles appellari solent.

§ 3. Paroeciae inamovibiles nequeunt amovibiles reddi sine beneplacito apostolico; amovibiles possunt ab Episcopo, non autem a Vicario Capitulari, de Capituli cathedralis consilio, inamovibiles declarari; novae quae erigantur, sint inamovibiles, nisi Episcopus, prudenti suo arbitrio, attentis peculiaribus locorum ac personarum adiunctis, audito Capitulo, amovibilitatem magis expedire decreverit.

Canon 459

§ 4. In regionibus in quibus paroeciarum provisio fit per concursum sive specialem ad normam const. Benedicti XIV *Cum illud,* 14 Dec. 1742, sive generalem, haec forma retineatur, donec Sedes Apostolica aliud decreverit.

During the missionary period before the appointment of Bishop

Carroll the priests in this country, regular and secular, were missionaries. There were no canonically erected parishes and consequently no canonical pastors except in New Orleans and San Francisco.[107] Gradually as the clergy and faithful became more numerous, dioceses were established, limits were drawn between the various missions and the priest in charge was given most of the rights and duties of a canonical pastor. But all our National Councils, even the decrees of the Third Plenary Council as late as 1884, repeatedly asserted that there are no canonical parishes and no pastors but rectors of missions in the United States.

The chief reason for this was that in most dioceses there were no priests prepared to form a Curia to carry on regular trials such as the law required for the removal of pastors and the Bishops felt they must safeguard their freedom to remove them, whenever the good of souls required it, without the formalities of a regular trial.

Parallel to this and equally clear is the expression of their desire and feeling of real obligation of gradually preparing to conform to the general law as the Holy See constantly urged and especially at the time of the preparation and approval of our Plenary Councils.

In number 123 of the Second Plenary Council the Fathers state that it would be desirable, yet not practical, to have canonical pastors in this country. They decided, however, in number 124 to prepare the way by having as near an approach as possible to canonical parishes with the priest in charge enjoying parochial or quasi-parochial rights. It is expressly stated in the following number, 125, that irremovability is not included among these. Though in number 126 the time is said to be not ripe for the *concursus* still it is decreed that the newly appointed rectors must pass an examination.

The Third Council practically quoting in numbers 31 and 32 the decrees of the Second Council goes on to say in number 33 that conditions have not changed sufficiently to adopt here in its fullness the general legislation of the Church on parishes and pastors; but in numbers 33 to 39 it makes laws to bring us nearer to the common discipline by decreeing a certain number of irremovable rectorships[108]

[107] *Cath. Encycl.*, II, 474.

[108] One out of every ten rectors was to be irremovable provided a sufficient number could be found eligible to maintain that proportion which was not

and giving minute regulations about the conditions of their establishment, appointment to and removal from them. In proceeding against clerics the Instruction of the Congregation of the Propagation of the Faith "*Cum Magnopere*" [109] was to be followed. The Fathers devoted an entire chapter, numbers 40 to 59, to the *concursus* for these irremovable rectorships and herein they practically adopted the rules given on the subject by Benedict XIV.[110]

On this point of the *concursus* the law of Baltimore continued in force until recently, since the Code in canon 459, §4 requires that where this mode of appointment to irremovable rectorships has been in vogue, it is to continue in use until the Holy See shall provide otherwise. Such provision was made by a decree of the Sacred Congregation of the Council of June 24, 1931. During the annual meeting of our Bishops in November 1930 His Eminence Cardinal O'Connell was authorized by the Assembly to petition the Holy See "that the special legislation of the Third Council of Baltimore with regard to the appointment of irremovable rectors give way to the legislation of the present Code of Canon law," which petition the Sacred Congregation of the Council graciously granted.[111]

The Decree "*Maxima Cura*" of August 20, 1910,[112] officially declared to apply to us on March 13, 1911,[113] replaced the Council procedure on the removal of irremovable pastors. That it did not apply to removable ones also was made certain by a decree of the Sacred Congregation of the Consistory, dated June 28, 1915,[114] which Congregation in answer to a query on this point replied that removable pastors could still be removed *ad nutum Episcopi,* but the Bishop should not use this right without grave reason and due regard for the worth of the pastor in question, as the Fathers of the Second Plenary Council of Baltimore in number 125 had advised and urged.

The Code in canon 216 prescribes the division of a diocese into

inadvisedly to be increased within twenty years from the promulgation of the Council.

[109] 1883, *Coll. de Prop. Fide.*, 1586.

[110] "*Cum Illud*" of Dec. 14, 1742—*Fontes*, 333.

[111] *Eccl. Rev.*, LXXXV (1931), 383.

[112] *A. A. S.*, II (1910), 636.

[113] *A. A. S.*, III (1911), 313.

[114] *A. A. S.*, VII (1915), 378.

parishes each of which has its own pastor. Canon 454, §2 distinguishes, as the Baltimore law does, between removable and irremovable pastors. Again in canon 454, § 3 it decrees that irremovable parishes cannot be made removable without the permission of the Holy See; that removable ones can be made irremovable by the Bishop with the advice of his Consultors; and that all new parishes are irremovable unless the Bishop having prudently considered the special circumstances of place and people and having sought the advice of his Consultors decrees removability. Finally, after treating of the regular procedure for trials, the Code gives the rules for the administrative removal of both irremovable and removable pastors in canons 2142 to 2161. It is in these and the following canons that our Bishops now find the rules of procedure in taking action against their clerics; and herein it will be seen that the common law is well adapted to the exigencies that formerly made the American Hierarchy reluctant to have canonically erected parishes.

Article 2

Stole Fees

Section I—Determining the Stole Fees

Second Plenary Council

221. Quum, jubente Christo Domino, dona spiritualia gratis accepta gratis danda sint, quumque, teste Apostolo, avaritia sit quaedam "idolorum servitus," quae quidem in homine Christiano gravis noxa, in veri autem Dei Sacrorum ministro turpissimum facinus est; edicimus, ne quid pro Sacramentorum administratione exigere, petere, aut pacisci quisquam audeat. Ea vero, quae pietatis studio post collatum Baptisma vel Matrimonium, eleemosynae nomine, a fidelibus sponte offeruntur, Sacerdos, si velit, accipiat. Hoc enim apud nos consuetudo tolerat, neque Ecclesia improbat.

Code

Canon 1234

§ 1. Locorum Ordinarii indicem funeralium taxarum seu eleemosynarum, si non exsistat, pro suo territorio, de consilio Capituli cathedralis, ac, si opportunum duxerint, vicariorum foraneorum dioecesis et parochorum civitatis episcopalis, conficiant, attentis legitimis consuetudinibus particularibus et omnibus personarum et locorum circumstantiis; in eoque pro diversis casibus iura singulorum moderate determinent, ita ut quaelibet contentionum et scandali removeatur occasio.

§ 2. Si in indice plures classes enumerentur, liberum est iis quorum interest classem eligere.

THIRD PLENARY COUNCIL

294. In immensa hac regione, atque inter gentes ex variis Europae populis aut advenientes aut oriundas, ideoque indole ac moribus tam diversas, vix fieri potest, ut leges disciplinares uniformes sint pro omnibus provinciis aut dioecesibus. Itaque quod spectat ad jura stolae et taxam pro ministeriis ecclesiasticis determinandam, unusquisque Episcopus agat in synodo dioecesana, vel extra synodum auditis consultoribus eas leges ferat, quae clero ac populo suo magis convenire videantur. Meminerit autem (idque expresse in synodo commemoretur) ministeria ecclesiastica pauperibus esse gratis praestanda. Taxam quoque, si qua in synodo constituatur, Romam mittat, ut Sanctae Sedis approbationi subjiciatur.

CANON 1507

§ 1. Salvo praescripto can. 1056 et can. 1234, praefinire taxas pro variis actibus iurisdictionis voluntariae vel pro exsecutione rescriptorum Sedis Apostolicae vel occasione ministrationis Sacramentorum vel Sacramentalium, in tota ecclesiastica provincia solvendas, est Concilii provincialis aut conventus Episcoporum provinciae; sed nulla vi praefinitio eiusmodi pollet, nisi prius a Sede Apostolica approbata fuerit.

The Second Plenary Council in number 221 forbids exacting, asking or stipulating anything for the administration of the Sacraments, but sanctions the acceptance of such free will offerings as the faithful may make on the occasions of baptisms or marriages.

The Third Council indirectly sets aside this prohibition when in number 294 it decrees that each Bishop in synod or outside of synod with the advice of his Consultors is to determine stole fees that will be suited both to the clergy and the faithful. These regulations were to be sent to Rome for approval.

The Code in canon 1234 prescribes that the stole fees for funerals are to be determined by the Bishop with the advice of his Consultors and, if convenient, also of the Vicars Forane and of the Pastors of the episcopal city. It is further prescribed in canon 1507, §1 that the fees for the administration of the Sacraments be determined for the whole province by the Bishops, either in council or in one of their meetings and submitted for approval to the Holy See.

Since the two methods are not in harmony, that of the Code prevails and that of the Council is abrogated. Strictly speaking, however, the Council may still well be followed in the method of determining the funeral fees; for by dealing with this matter in synod the Bishop may the more easily consult those mentioned by the Code.[115]

Of course, in accordance with canon 5 any immemorial custom not expressly disapproved by the Code may be tolerated if the Ordinary judges that because of the circumstances of place and people it cannot prudently be abolished.

Section II—Dividing the Stole Fees

Second Plenary Council

94. Ne turpis lucri cupido sacerdotalem inficiat ordinem, vel aliqua oriatur inter sacerdotes simul commorantes dissensio, propter eleemosynas quas fideles occasione sacramentorum baptismi vel matrimonii administrationis sponte conferunt, monemus Episcopos ut in prima sua synodo dioecesana, vel alias, prout illis in Domino visum fuerit, consilio sacerdotum etiam adhibito, justam statuant rationem qua inter sacerdotes simul ita commorantes distribuantur, potioris juris et graviorum onerum pastoris non neglecta consideratione.

Code

Canon 463

§ 1. Ius est parocho ad praestationes quas ei tribuit vel probata consuetudo vel legitima taxatio ad normam can. 1507, § 1.

§ 2. Potiores exigens, ad restitutionem tenetur.

§ 3. Licet paroeciale aliquod officium ab alio fuerit expletum, praestationes tamen parocho cedunt, nisi de contraria offerentium voluntate certo constet circa summam quae taxam excedit.

§ 4. Gratuitum ministerium ne deneget parochus iis qui solvendo pares non sunt.

The Second Plenary Council in number 94 merely warns the Bishops to determine in their first synod the manner in which are to be divided among the parish clergy the offerings that the faithful freely make at the time of baptisms and marriages. In this apportionment due consideration is to be given to the prior right and greater responsibility of the Pastor.

The Code in canon 463 decrees that to the Pastors belong the perquisites which legitimate custom or the prescription of canon 1507, §1 quoted above has determined and this even when the ministry has been performed by another. Technically the two laws legislate about different things, the Council treating of free-will offerings

[115] Canons 358 and 1234, § 1.

while the Code deals with fixed taxes. In practice, however, there is hardly any difference especially since, as has been seen above, the Third Council recognized set fees.

The question then arises about the legality of the practices of dividing the perquisites among the parish clergy or of diverting all or part of them to the general parish fund where these practices have come about by custom or synodal legislation. In that all such practices deprive the Pastor of his right to the full amount of the perquisites, they are *in se* opposed to the Code and, therefore, illegal and abrogated.[116]

There is, of course, free renunciation on the part of the Pastor, and according to canon 5, immemorial custom to be appealed to. Then, too, there is the question of the assistant's salary about which the Code in canon 476, §1 says no more than that it should be *congrua remuneratio* and there seems to be nothing in the present common law to prevent the Bishop's decreeing that a percentage of the stole fees should be used in part payment of this.[117] Likewise, wherever there exists the practice of diverting a portion of the perquisites from the pastor there is such salary compensation as to make the net result the same and the consent of the Pastors to this arrangement makes it licit.

It is interesting to note that before the Code this same question was a mooted one. The old common law like the new made the stole fees the exclusive property of Pastors.[118] Those who held that there would be no division of the perquisites based their argument on this right of Pastors and on the fact that according to the more probable opinion these fees do not belong to the *fructus beneficii parochialis* nor to the *reditus Ecclesiae* from which alone Bishops could provide for the suitable sustenance of assistance. Those holding that there should be a division argued from the Council of Trent[119] which said of curates "*partemque fructum eisdem pro sufficienti victu assignare vel aliter providere possint.*" They urged that this latter clause empowered Bishops to draw on other emoluments than the parish rev-

[116] Augustine, *Commentary*, II, 542.
[117] Ayrinhac, *Constitution*, p. 364.
[118] Bouix, *De Episcopo*, II, 328.
[119] Sess. XXI, de Ref., cap. VI.

enues for assistants' salaries and hence on the stole fees of Pastors.[120] The conclusion was that, though the former or negative side was the more probable, the affiirmative did not lack probability and hence the decisions of Bishops who had assigned a portion of these fees to assistants must stand.[121]

Bouix[122] relates that in 1848 on the occasion of a decree of Archbishop Affre of Paris requiring the division of the perquisites among the priests of the parish the Pastors appealed to Rome, but the decision of the Sacred Congregation of the Council was never published.

Article 3

The Mass for the People

Code

Canon 466

§ 1. Applicandae Missae pro populo obligatione tenetur parochus ad normam can. 339, quasi-parochus ad normam can. 306.

§ 2. Parochus qui plures forte paroecias aeque principaliter unitas regat aut, praeter propriam paroeciam, aliam vel alias in administrationem habeat, unam tantum debet Missam pro populis sibi commissis diebus praescriptis applicare.

§ 3. Ordinarius loci iusta de causa permittere potest ut parochus Missam pro populo alia die applicet ab ea qua iure adstringitur.

§ 4. Parochus Missam pro populo applicandam celebret in ecclesia paroeciali, nisi rerum adiuncta Missam alibi celebrandam exigant aut suadeant.

§ 5. Legitime absens parochus potest Missam pro populo applicare vel ipse per se in loco in quo degit, vel per sacerdotem qui eius vices gerat in paroecia.

Among the decrees of the Sacred Congregation of the Propagation of the Faith published with the Second Council,[123] there is one declaring that where there are no canonical parishes the rectors are not bound to the *Missa pro populo* but that it is fitting to say it from motives of charity.

The Code in canon 466 decrees this obligation for canonical Pastors.

After the Code went into effect the foregoing exemption ceased to

[120] Craisson, *op. cit.*, I, Nos. 1061 and 1062.

[121] *Ibid.*

[122] *De Episcopo*, II, 329.

[123] P. cxlviii.

apply because of the canonical status of our parishes.[124] Where an indult has been granted to Bishops to dispense Pastors from this obligation where the income is insufficient for their support it continues in force in virtue of canon 4. It is understood that such an indult was granted to our Bishops through the late Cardinal Gibbons.

Article 4

The Pastor's Salary

Third Plenary Council

273. Ne tamen rectus justitiae ordo turbetur, nec integram suspicio lucri minuat famam, decernimus ut Episcopi pro singulis suis dioecesibus in synodo, vel extra synodum e consultorum consilio, fixam ratamque definiant summam quae ab ecclesiarum rectoribus congruae seu salarii nomine percipi possit. Minori tamen summa contenti sint oportet sacerdotes casu quo eorum missio vel missiones per reditus suos annuos statutam congruam suppeditare nequeant, cujus rei judex erit Ordinarius, audito Consultorum consilio.

281. Ob gravia secus oritura incommoda monemus sacerdotes ut congruam suam seu salarium, nisi id ecclesiae donare velint, opportuno tempore exigere et percipere non negligant. Ideo statuimus eos qui pecuniam ea ratione sibi debitam infra annum a termino quo solvenda erat, percipere omiserint, aut saltem non exegerint per scriptum ab Ordinario vel ejus cancellario probatum, eo ipso renuntiasse juri suo, eosque nullo titulo postea summam istam repetere posse.

The Third Plenary Council in number 273 orders Bishops with the advice of their Consultors to determine either in or out of synod the amount of the Pastor's salary. The same Council in number 281 declares that priests who within a year from the time their salary is due neglect to take it or at least to ask the Ordinary or Chancellor in writing for it thereby renounce all right to it and henceforth cannot seek it under any title.

The Code does not explicitly provide a method for fixing the salary of Pastors nor does it legislate the forfeiting of any salaries for failure of collection within a prescribed time.

These two local statutes, therefore, continue in force as something outside the common law.

[124] From a reply of Cardinal Gasparri, head of the Commission on Interpretation, to the Apostolic Delegate on September 26, 1921, concerning parishes it is clear that ours are to be considered ecclesiastical benefices.—*Hom. Rev.*, XXIII (1922-23), 409.

TITLE XVI

Religious

Article 1

The Relations Between Religious and Bishops

Second Plenary Council

406. Ut tamen optimi hi fructus colligantur, hoc omnino requiritur, ut stabiles ac permanentes fiant fundationes, quae in qualibet dioecesi a communitate Religiosa instituantur. Jampridem enim conquestus fuit Summus Pontifex, Bonifacius VIII., Religiosos Ordines, qui tunc temporis existebant, "domos vel loca de novo suscipere, vel olim suscepta dimittere, se ibidem ad alia transferentes"; idque omnino fieri Apostolica auctoritate vetuit. In eamdem sententiam Patres Concilii Cincinnatensis Provincialis I., quod a Sancta Sede recognitum est, caverunt ne Religiosi a conventionibus cum Episcopis factis resilirent; et ne pastores et rectores Religiosi ab ecclesiis et locis quibus praepositi fuerant, ab ipsorum superioribus amoverentur, nisi alii societatum sodales, cum .consensu Ordinarii, subrogarentur. Et sane maxime tum dioecesibus, tum Ordinibus ipsis in bonum cederet, si haec regula omnino servetur.

407. Quum vero ea sint apud nos rerum adjuncta, ut non semper canonice vel permanenter erigi possint domus Religiosae, seu monasteria, id interdum nolentibus ipsius communitatis superioribus; ut in talibus casibus omnis disputationibus et querelis locus auferatur, duxerunt Patres hujus Plenarii Concilii, hoc conditionis instar contractui Ordinarium inter et Religiosam communitatem appositae habendum, istam scilicet nullum collegium, paroeciam, congregationem, scholam, aliudve opus pium deserere posse, Ordinario invito, nisi sex saltem menses elapsi fuerint a tempore, quo de intentione ita agendi illum certiorem fecerit. Hoc enim temporis spatium requiri ad minimum videtur, ut Episcopus alios idoneos operarios sufficere possit, et sic opera, vel necessaria, vel certe maxime utilia continuare. Haec vero de iis tantum communitatibus intellecta volumus, quae regenda assumunt opera proprie dicta dioecesana, sive ea quae per pecunias aliaque media ex dioecesi desumpta sustentantur, et ad tempus tantum, nulla perpetuo permanendi suscepta obligatione. Neque quidquam per ea, quae dicta sunt, ullo modo iis derogari censendum est, quae de monasterii canonice erecti bonis non alienandis, permutandis, vel relinquendis, per venerandas SS. Pontificum Constitutiones sancita jamdudum fuerint. Salva etiam jura tertii volumus, praesertim vero eorum benefactorum, qui bona vel mobilia vel immobilia donaverint, ut in specie opus aliquod bonum in aliquo determinato loco, vel aliis praestitutis conditionibus, institueretur vel foveretur.

408. Curent tamen Episcopi, ut juxta canonicas sanctiones omnia jura ac privilegia Regularium, sive Congregationum Religiosarum, intra limites suae jurisdictionis existtentium tueantur, et cum iis ea ratione agant, ut nulla illis nedum discedendi nequidem conquerendi justa occasio suppeditetur. Quod efficacius fiet, si quo tempore in Dioecesi considunt, omnia quoad tam spiritualia quam temporalia Episcopum inter et illorum superiores accurate intelligantur, scriptoque instrumento consignentur. Tunc enim, si unquam ex Dioecesi discedant, quid bonorum ad illos, quid vero ad Diocesim, ex justitia vel aequitate pertineat intelligetur, adeoque insignis causa querelarum tolletur.

THIRD PLENARY COUNCIL

86. Gaudenti et grato animo testamur et alte proclamamus, sanctam hanc concordiam, pia omnium moderatione ac temperantia, hactenus in hac qua late patet regione illaesam servatam fuisse inter clerum saecularem et plures illos ac benedictione divina crescentes ordines religiosos, tam egregie laborantes pro ecclesiis nostris in ministerio animarum et in juventutis educatione; atque fraternum hoc foedus ac voluntatum consensionem perpetuam fore merito confidimus ac praesagimus. Ne tamen, quod Deus avertat, pax isthaec unquam humana fragilitate turbetur, haud parum opportunum fore arbitramur, si constitutio sapientissima *Romanos Pontifices* recenter a SS. D. N. Leone XIII. pro Anglia et Scotia edita, ad has etiam provincias extendatur. Id autem se rogantibus Nobis libenter praestituram significavit jam Sedes Apostolica.

87. Tria autem decernit haec constitutio circa relationes regularium cum Episcoporum auctoritate. Primo quidem explicat et decernit ea quae pertinent ad familiarum religiosarum exemptionem ab Episcopali jurisdictione; dehinc ea quae ministeria respiciunt, quae a regularibus missionariis exercentur, ac demum quaestiones de bonis temporalibus regularium, deque usu in quem illa oportet converti.

88. Ad regularium exemptionem quod attinet, declarat constitutio: "Regulares, qui in residentiis missionum commorantur, exemptos esse ab Ordinarii jurisdictione, non secus ac regulares intra claustra viventes, praeterquam in casibus a jure nominatim expressis, et generatim in iis, quae concernunt curam animarum et sacramentorum administrationem." Propter quas exceptiones, ut consequenter deducit Pontifex, cleri collationibus adesse debent omnes ex regularibus missionum rectores, vicarii quoque et generatim alii religiosi viri missionariis facultatibus concedi solitis instructi. Ad synodum pariter dioecesanam: "exempti omnes, qui alias, cessante exemptione, interesse deberent, nec capitulis generalibus subduntur, accedere tenentur," maxime qui curam gerunt "parochialium aut aliarum saecularium ecclesiarum, etiam adnexarum," atque decretis synodalibus pareant oportet "in iis quae ad curam animarum et sacramentorum administrationem referuntur, ceterisque in rebus, in quibus eos Episcoporum jurisdictioni subesse canonica praecipiunt instituta." Ab Episcopi interpretatione decretorum synodalium licet ipsis appellare *in devolutivo* tantum quoad decreta quae de jure communi sive ordinario sive delegato regulares etiam afficiunt; quoad reliqua vero decreta *in suspensivo.*

89. Quod deinde ministeria spectat per regulares exercita, edicit constitutio "licere Episcopis (eorum) missiones dividere" "ad formam Synodi I. Provin-

8

cialis Westmonasteriensis" audito tamen ordinis praefecto et salvo jure appellandi *in devolutivo;* atque Episcopo liberum esse novae missioni praeficere quem maluerit sacerdotem, sive saecularem sive regularem. Decernit etiam Summus Pontifex quaenam coemeteria et pia loca intra fines missionum regularibus commissarum sita, Episcopi visitationi sint subjecta, declaratque Episcopos jus habere quoad omnia visitandi scholas parochiales in missionibus et paroeciis regularibus aeque ac in saecularibus, ac demum, firmis remanentibus privilegiis regularium quoad ceteras jam erectas scholas et collegia, in quibus religiosi viri secundum ordinis sui praescripta juventuti catholicae erudiendae operam dare solent, "sodalibus religiosis novas sibi sedes constituere, erigendo novas ecclesias, aperiendove coenobia, collegia, scholas, nisi obtenta prius expressa licentia ordinarii loci et Sedis Apostolicae, non licere."

90. Denique tertio loco de temporalibus missionum bonis haec decernit constitutio: "I. Missionarii regulares bonorum temporalium, ad ipsos *qua regulares* spectantium, rationem Episcopis reddere non tenentur. II. Eorum tamen bonorum quae missioni vel regularibus *intuitu missionis* tributa fuerunt, Episcopi jus habent ab iisdem missionariis regularibus aeque ac a parochis cleri saecularis rationem exigendi." Atque juxta leges Westmonasteriensis Synodi II. definit quae pecuniae, quaeque res viris religiosis oblatae intuitu missionum sint intelligendae, simul indicans Episcopis inesse potestatem imperandi pecuniae collationes, decernendique quo tempore et qua de causa conferri oporteat.

99. Inter viros religiosos qui pluribus in locis apud nos, quemadmodum in Europa aliisque orbis regionibus, piam et sedulam juventuti christianae instituendae navant operam, egregiam laudem merentur Fratres qui a scholis Christianis nomen trahunt. Horum progressibus ac stabilitati quo melius consuleret, Benedictus XIII. (in Bulla approbationis *In Apostolicae dignitatis*) edixit, ut "nullus ex fratribus instituti hujusmodi, absque expresso consensu superiorum generalium ipsius instituti, etiam praetextu arctiorem religionem amplectendi e praedicto instituto egredi . . . valeat." Itaque Patres hujus Concilii, cupientes aliquam benevolentiae significationem praeclari hujus instituti religiosis exhibere, ipsorum regulas et constitutiones pro viribus tuendo, et simul menti S. Sedis, ne ad sacerdotium aspirent praecipientis obsecundare, decernunt neminem qui in hac congregatione prima vota emiserit, et deinde quacumque de causa congregationi valedixerit, in provinciarum nostrarum seminaria tanquam sacrorum ordinum candidatum sine dispensatione S. Congregationis admitti posse. Idem statuunt de Fratribus Xaverianis, Franciscalibus aliisque quibus lege sua sacerdotium ambire vetitum est, quo diligentius ac constantius Christianae puerorum institutioni unice incumbant.

Code

Canon 1427

§ 1. Possunt etiam Ordinarii ex iusta et canonica causa paroecias quaslibet, invitis quoque earum rectoribus et sine populi consensu, dividere, vicariam

perpetuam vel novam paroeciam erigentes, aut earum territorium dismembrare.

In the early days of the American Church Religious as well as diocesan priests were missionaries equally engaged in the care of souls. The fundamental and general principle of law that Religious are exempt from episcopal authority had to be modified here much more than elsewhere by the other great principle that they are subject to the Bishop in all that pertains to the care of souls; also by the principle that exemption is restricted when Religious do not live in religious houses. Gradually, as our missions were organized into parishes and religious houses as monasteries, novitiates, colleges and so forth were established, various questions arose especially on the relations between Bishops and Religious. The Second Plenary Council of Baltimore has a chapter including numbers 405 to 414 on religious Orders of them and one including numbers 415 to 422 *De Monialibus.* The Bishops require in numbers 406 and 407 that religious should not leave places where they are doing diocesan work without giving six months' notice and in number 408 the Fathers further require that, when Religious undertake diocesan work, a contract be drawn up between them and the Bishop so that when they are leaving there might be no difficulty in determining what belongs to them and what to the diocese. In the following numbers the Bishops insist on the common law principle that Religious are subject to the Ordinaries of the place in what pertains to the care of souls.

A few years later difficulties between the Bishops and Religious in England where conditions were very much the same as here, it being a missionary country like our own, brought about the Constitution of Pope Leo XIII, "*Romanos Pontifices*" of May 8, 1881.[125] At the request of the Fathers of the Third Plenary Council in number 86 this was extended to the United States.[126] This Constitution is given in full in the Appendix to this Council[127] and a summary of it is embodied in its decrees in numbers 87 to 90. In brief it provides, first, that Religious enjoy the privileges of exemption on missions or parishes as well as in their religious houses; secondly, those of them

[125] *Fontes,* 582.

[126] *Conc. Plen. Balti. III Acta et Decreta,* p. cv.

[127] Pp. 212 to 230.

having the care of souls are subject to the Bishop in all that pertains to such, the Bishop having the right to divide missions entrusted to Regulars and to give the new mission to diocesan priests or to a different religious Order; [128] thirdly, with regard to their temporal goods they do not have to give an account to the Bishop of that given them as Religious, but they must account for that given for the mission.[129] The Fathers in number 90 adopt a decree of the Second Provincial Council of Westminster which applies this principle in detail.[130]

The Code of course has a much fuller treatment of the question of Religious than our Councils and on careful comparison one finds that the decrees of Baltimore contain nothing *contra codicem,* so nothing of it is set aside by the Code. There are very few points that are *praeter codicem.* Consequently whatever may be their historical interest, they are of little practical value now. The Code gives us ample law on this subject.

Certainly *praeter codicem* are the following: first, the decree of the Second Plenary Council in number 408 which requires a written agreement between the Bishop and the Religious when the latter take up diocesan work; secondly, that in number 407 of the same Council which requires that the Religious give the Bishop six months' warning before giving up any diocesan work they have undertaken; thirdly, that of the Third Plenary Council in number 89 wherein the Fathers making their own the words of the First Synod of Westminster [131] decree that Bishops having consulted the superior of the Order, who has the right to appeal *in devolutivo,* may divide missions entrusted to Religious and put the new mission in charge of either secular or religious priests; fourthly and lastly, that of the same Council in number 99 which prohibits the admission into ecclesiastical seminaries without the permission of the Holy See of men who have made vows, whether dispensed or expired, in Orders of Brothers whose Constitutions forbid them to aspire to the priesthood.

The first two and the last of these four decrees, continue in force

[128] No. 89.

[129] No. 90.

[130] *Conc. Plen. Balti. III Acta Et Decreta,* p. 231.

[131] *Conc. Plen. Balti. III Acta Et Decreta,* p. 230.

since they are not opposed to but go beyond the Code. The third is now replaced by canon 1427, § 1 with which it agrees.

Article 2

Ownership of Church Property

Second Plenary Council

195. De Bonis Ecclesiasticis, Patres Concilii septimi hoc statuerunt generale principium:

Statuerunt Patres ecclesias omnes, ceteraque bona ecclesiastica, quae vel dono, vel fidelium oblationibus acquisita, in charitatis vel religionis operibus sunt impendenda, ad Ordinarium pertinere; nisi appareat, scriptoque constet, illa Ordini alicui regulari, vel sacerdotum Congregationi, in ipsorum usum tradita fuisse.

Code

Canon 630

§ 4. Non obstante voto paupertatis, eidem licet eleemosynas in bonum paroecianorum, vel pro scholis catholicis aut locis piis paroeciae coniunctis, quovis modo oblatas accipere aut colligere, et acceptas sive collectas administrare, itemque, servata offerentium voluntate, pro prudenti suo arbitrio, erogare, salva semper vigilantia sui Superioris; sed eleemosynas pro ecclesia paroeciali aedificanda, conservanda, in stauranda, exornanda accipere, apud se retinere, colligere aut administrare pertinet ad Superiores, si ecclesia sit communitatis religiosae; secus ad loci Ordinarium.

Canon 1519

§ 1. Loci Ordinarii est sedulo advigilare administrationi omnium bonorum ecclesiasticorum quae in suo territorio sint nec ex eius iurisdictione fuerint subducta, salvis legitimis praescriptionibus, quae eidem potiora iura tribuant.

§ 2. Habita ratione iurium, legitimarum consuetudinum et circumstantiarum, Ordinarii, opportune editis peculiaribus instructionibus intra fines iuris communis, universum administrationis bonorum ecclesiasticorum negotium ordinandum curent.

Canon 1536

§ 1. Nisi contrarium probetur, praesumendum ea quae donantur rectoribus ecclesiarum, etiam religiosorum, esse ecclesiae donata.

§ 2. Donatio facta ecclesiae, ab eius rectore seu Superiore repudiari nequit sine licentia Ordinarii.

§ 3. Repudiata illegitime donatione, ob damna quae inde obvenerint actio datur restitutionis in integrum vel indemnitatis.

§ 4. Donatio ecclesiae facta et ab eadem legitime acceptata, propter ingratum Praelati vel rectoris animum revocari nequit.

The Fathers of the Second Plenary Council in number 195 lay it down as a general principle that all churches and other Church property acquired either by gift or through the contributions of the faithful and which are to be used in charitable or religious work are to pertain to the Ordinary unless it appears and has been set down in writing that these are to be regulated by that Order or Congregation of priests for whose use they have been given.

There is no exact duplicate of this statute in the Code. It is, however, in accord wtih the general tenor of the common law as set forth particularly in canons 630, § 4, 1519 and 1536. By the first of these all gifts and contributions to a church are placed under the jurisdiction of the Ordinary of the place unless the church belongs to a religious community. In the second the local Ordinary is declared to be the supervisor of all ecclesiastical goods in his territory except such as have been withdrawn from his jurisdiction. The third legislates that, unless the contrary is proved, it is to be presumed that donations given to rectors of churches even those in charge of religious communities are given to the church.

The documentary proof required by the Council seems to be *praeter codicem* and, therefore, still of obligation.

Article 3

Religious Seeking Alms

Third Plenary Council

295. Sed nec minores nec minus fundatae querimoniae ex parte tam laicorum quam ecclesiasticorum virorum audiri solent de nimia et importuna multitudine sacerdotum, sive saecularium sive regularium, qui ex alienis regionibus huc variis de causis mendicaturi adveniunt. Ex istis enim non pauci, non petita venia Ordinariorum aut rectorum, imo utrorumque non raro spreta prohibitione, cum nostratum scandalo et causarum loci piarum detrimento, de domo in domum transeunt, aut operariorum in officinis vel ad opera publica congregatorum nummos audacter emendicant, qui plerumque templis aliisque aedificiis minime necessariis destinantur. Huic ergo malo nullum aliud remedium nacti, volumus et edicimus ut in posterum nullis qui ad colligendum venisse sciuntur, venia detur a rectoribus vel unica vice celebrandi missam (quod tamen de regularibus in monasteriis proprii ordinis privatim celebrantibus intelligi nolumus) donec ab Ordinario ipso hanc veniam acceperint; utque nullis hujusmodi quaestoribus colligendi concedatur licentia, nisi eorum Ordinarius vel Ordinis Praefectus ipsi per litteras praevias eam

proiisdem obtinuerint ab Episcopis in quorum dioecesibus eleemosynas rogare desiderant. Praeterea continuo exposcatur ab eorum Episcopo vel Superiori, ut eos revocent; qui si id facere noluerint vel neglexerint, ad S. Congregationem de Prop. Fide sine mora abusus corrigendus deferatur.

CODE

CANON 1503

Salvis praescriptis can. 621-624, vetantur privati tam clerici quam laici sine Sedis Apostolicae aut proprii Ordinarii et Ordinarii loci licentia, in scriptis data, stipem cogere pro quolibet pio aut ecclesiastico instituto vel fine.

The Third Plenary Council in number 295 treats of Religious who come into a parish to collect. Herein it is decreed that they are not to be given permission to beg alms unless they have obtained through their Superior written authorization to do so from the Ordinary of the place. If they are without such organization their recall is to be asked of their Superior at once; which if he is unwilling or neglects to do, the abuse is to be referred to the Holy See without delay for correction.

The Code in canon 1503 decrees that private persons whether cleric or lay are forbidden to collect alms for any charitable or Church institution or purpose without the written permission of the Apostolic See or of their own and the local Ordinary. The canon further provides for the safeguarding of the regulations governing the collection of alms by religious organizations as set forth in canons 621 to 624. The relevant point of these canons is the special provisions made for Mendicants whereby in the diocese of their religious house they need only the permission of their Superiors to collect alms, while in other dioceses they must have also that of the local Ordinary.

The meaning of the term Mendicant as used in these canons has been defined by the Commission for the Authentic Interpretation of The Code in a response of October 16, 1919.[182]

[182] **Utrum canon 621, § 1, intelligendus sit tantum de religiosis mendicantibus strictu sensu dictis; an etiam de illis, qui latiori sensu tales appellantur, uti sunt Fratres Ordinis Praedicatorum.**

Et quatenus affirmative ad primam partem:

An dicti mendicantes indigeant Ordinarii licentia, si velint stipem petere in dioecesi pro aedificatione, ornatu, etc., suarum ecclesiarum.

Resp.: Affirmative ad primam partem, negative ad secundam; quod vero

In so far as our local statute makes no exception for Mendicants and others privileged by the Holy See, it is opposed to the Code. In other respects it is in agreement with the common law and continues to bind to that extent.

Article 4

Moniales

Second Plenary Council

422. Demum, quum omnino deceat ut Moniales, sint vel non sint claustratae, in conventibus suis, quantum fieri possit, permaneant, atque in sancta solitudine spiritualibus exercitiis et operibus pietatis et charitatis secundum earum institutum sese devoveant, prorsus reprobamus morem illum, seu verius abusum, qui nuper invectus est, juxta quem nonnullae ex istis piis foeminis huc illuc circumcursant, et saepe ad loca ab earum Monasteriis remota divertunt, causa pecuniae colligendae pro novis domibus fundandis, vel ab aere alieno iis quae jam sunt fundatae liberandis. Ordinarios vero locorum in Domino hortamur, atque enixe obsecramus, ne permittant, ne quidem tolerent istam consuetudinem, quae tum verae status religiosi indoli repugnat, tum gravibus periculis et publicis nonnunquam scandalis obnoxia est.

Third Plenary Council

95. Non tantum passiva haec clausura, sed etiam *activa* quantum fieri potest, servanda est; ideoque denuo severe reprobamus illum abusum, quo moniales nonnullae ad colligendas eleemosynas aliquando circumcursant et saepe ad loca divertunt ab earum monasteriis remota, non sine scandali et vocationis religiosae perdendae

Code

Canon 621

§ 1. Regulares, qui ex instituto mendicantes vocatur et sunt, eleemosynas in dioecesi, ubi eorum religiosa domus est constituta, quaerere valent de sola Superiorum suorum licentia; extra dioecesim vero indigent praeterea licentia scripto data ab Ordinario loci in quo eleemosynas colligere cupiunt.

§ 2. Hanc licentiam Ordinarii locorum, praecipue dioecesium finitimarum, nisi gravibus et urgentibus de causis, ne denegent neve revocent, si religiosa domus ex mendicatione in sola dioecesi, in qua est constituta, vivere nullo modo possit.

Canon 622

§ 1. Alii omnes religiosi Congregationum iuris pontificii, sine peculiari Sanctae Sedis privilegio, stipem petere prohibentur; quibus, si hoc privilegium impetraverint, opus erit praeterea licentia scripto data ab Ordinario loci, nisi aliter in ipso privilegio cautum fuerit.

§ 2. Religiosi Congregationum iuris dioecesani stipem quaeritare nequaquam possunt sine licentia scripto data tum ab Ordinario loci in quo sita est eorum domus, tum ab Ordinario loci in quo stipem quaerere cupiunt.

attinet ad licentiam ab Ordinario obtinendam provisum in cit. can. 621, § 1.—*A. A. S.*, XI (1919), 478.

periculo. Ordinarios hortamur, ut id non permittant sine necessariis et prudentibus praecautionibus, uti sunt praesertim, ne unquam solae, nec juniores, nec post solis occasum, eleemosynas colligere permittantur, et ita ut, ubi fieri potest, in domo sororum suae vel alterius congregationis pernoctent. Hae vero praecautiones accurate serventur a sororibus quarum regula eleemosynarum collectionem vel praecipit vel saltem in certis rerum adjunctis concedere censetur, quibus scil. tantum sororibus collectae permittantur. In alienam vero dioecesim nunquam iis stipem collecturis transeundi dent licentiam, nisi prius obtenta in scriptis venia Ordinarii loci.

Quodsi Sorores vel etiam laici Fratres alicujus congregationis simplicium votorum non dioecesanae, sed sub superiore generali constitutae, absque hujusmodi inter Ordinarios conventione stipem colligentes in aliena dioecesi deprehendantur, Episcopus vel ipse vel facta relatione ad Ordinarium dioecesis unde venerunt, efficiet, ut statim per suae congregationis superiores revocentur. Si remedium efficax congruo tempore allatum non fuerit, res renuntietur S. Congregationi de Prop. Fide.

§ 3. Religiosis, de quibus in §§ 1 et 2 huius canonis, Ordinarii locorum licentiam quaeritandae stipis ne concedant, praesertim ubi sunt conventus regularium nomine et re mendicantium, nisi sibi constet de vera domus vel pii operis necessitate, cui alio modo occurri nequeat; quod si necessitati provideri possit stipe quaerenda intra locum seu districtum vel dioecesim in qua iidem commorantur, ampliorem licentiam ne largiantur.

§ 4. Sine authentico et recenti rescripto Sacrae Congregationis pro Ecclesia Orientali, Ordinarii latini nec sinant orientalem ullum cuiusvis ordinis et dignitatis in proprio territorio pecuniam colligere, nec suum subditum in orientales dioeceses ad eundem finem mittant.

The Second Plenary Council in number 419 relates that on account of special circumstances in this country doubts and controversies have arisen as to whether nuns who in Europe had solemn vows have here solemn or simple vows. The matter was referred to the Holy See and the Fathers embody the answer made on September 1, 1864, namely, that the vows of all nuns in the United States are simple except those made in the convents of the Visitation of Georgetown, Mobile, St. Louis (Kaskaskia) and Baltimore.[133]

[133] *A. S. S.*, 1 (1865-66), 708.

This is *contra codicem* as set forth in canons 488 and the following which declare that Religious make solemn or simple vows according to their Constitutions. But this concession apparently partaking of the nature of a privilege remains unaffected by the Code in accordance with canon 4.[134]

On the question of religious women going around collecting money, the Second Plenary Council in number 422 condemns the practice. The Third Council in number 95 qualifies the Second by allowing this to be done with the permission of the Ordinary and proper precautions, namely, that the Religious is not too young, does not go unaccompanied nor remains out after sundown.

The Code in canons 621 and 622 decrees that Regulars who by their Constitutions are Mendicants need the permission of their Superiors only to beg in the diocese of their houses, while outside their diocese they need also the written permission of the Ordinary of the place; that the members of religious Congregations of Pontifical right need the permission of the Holy See and also that of the local Ordinary in writing unless their privilege exempts them from the latter permission; finally, that the members of the religious Congregations of diocesan right need the written permission of the Ordinary of the place of their house and of the Ordinary of the place in which they wish to seek alms.

The Baltimore statute is limited to women while the common law is unqualified. In that the former makes no exceptions to the need of the Ordinary's permission, while the latter does for Mendicants in their own dioceses and for some Congregations of pontifical right enjoying a privilege of exemption on this score, it is opposed to the Code. Otherwise, the two laws agree.

TITLE XVII

The Laity

Article 1

Confraternities and Other Catholic Societies

Third Plenary Council

256. Ad has igitur utilitates nostris fidelibus in societatibus honestis pro-

[134] *A. A. S.*, XI (1919), p. 240.

curandas decernimus, ubicumque fieri potest Episcoporum auspiciis patrocinioque, opificum aliorumque civium Catholicorum societates instituendas et promovendas esse, quae quamvis finem sibi proponant temporalem et materialem, consilia tamen et directionem cleri sequantur.

257. Pro juvenibus, quia majoribus periculis objiciuntur, majorem curam impendi volumus; proinde statuimus, ut in omni paroecia vel missione, ubi numerus eorum sufficiens invenitur, societates speciales pro ipsis a rectore instituantur et omni opera foveantur.

259. Omnibus denique vehementer commendamus Lugdunensem Propagationis Fidei Societatem quam inde ab ejus ortu Romani Pontifices summis laudibus et amplissimis pontificalis gratiae privilegiis prosecuti sunt; quamque sedulo fovendam et promovendam recentioribus diebus Leo XIII. fel. reg. in Encycl. *Sancta Dei Civitas*, 3 Dec. 1880, iterum Episcopos ardenter commonuit. Mentem S. Sedis, et praedecessorum in superioribus Conciliis Plenariis exemplum sequentes statuimus, ut per omnes nostras dioeceses societas illa praeclara, sicubi forte nondum vigeat, instituatur ac promoveatur.

Both the Second Plenary Council in numbers 477 to 482 and the Third Plenary Council in numbers 244 to 263 treat this subject at some length. Their treatment, however, is more along the lines of pastoral theology and direction than of strict law. It is interesting to note that in the long list of approved confraternities given by the Fathers of the Second Council in number 478, one for the conversion of the non-Catholics of America is given special consideration.

The Third Council contains three positive decrees on this subject. In numbers 256 it orders that where possible all societies whether of workmen or other Catholic citizens be instituted under the auspices and patronage of the Bishops even though their purpose be temporal and material.

In number 257 it decrees that in every parish or mission, where there is a sufficient number of young people, the Rector establish and in every way foster special societies for them. Finally, in number 259 it prescribes the establishment of the Society of the Propagation of the Faith in every diocese where it does not yet exist.

The Code in its lengthy treatise on associations and confraternities in canons 684 to 725 has nothing about such societies and so these three decrees of the Council are *praeter codicem* and so in force.

On May 3, 1922, the Holy See ordered the establishment of the Society of the Propagation of the Faith in every diocese [135] which

[135] *A. A. S.*, XIV (1922), 321, ff.

decree supersedes that of the Council making a like obligation for this country.

Article 2

Forbidden Societies

Second Plenary Council

513. Propter gravissimas rationes vetuerunt SS. Pontifices, ne fideles Secretas Societates quovis nomine nuncupatas ineant, jurejurando sese adstringentes ad arcana servanda. Nam foedera hujusmodi clanculum inita, mali suspicionem et periculum prae se ferunt, et jusjurandum temere adhibetur. Idcirco monemus sacerdotes omnes, neminem posse absolutione sacramentali donari, nisi ab hujusmodi Societatibus prorsus recedat. Hortamur autem, et in Domino obsecramus fideles omnes, ut occulta illa foedera omnino declinent, mente revolventes se Christi membra esse, et Ecclesiae quae mater nostra est mandatis teneri, eosque ut filios lucis debere ambulare, juxta sanctissima et divina illa documenta quae Christus Dominus tradidit.

Third Plenary Council

253. Demum, hic opportunum ducimus in mentem fidelium revocare monita salutaria, quae Patres superioris Concilii Plenarii titulo *De Societatibus Secretis*, No. 519, dederunt circa societates quasdam de quarum liceitate quaestio aliquando mota fuit. "Quibus accurate perpensis, Nobis quidem nulla apparet ratio, ob quam prohibitio Ecclesiae adversus Massonicam aliasque occultas sectas, ad illas extendatur operariorum sodalitates, quas non constat aliud sibi proponere quam sociorum in propria arte exercenda mutuam tutelam ac juvamen. Cavendum tamen, ne sub hoc praetextu quidpiam admittatur, quod sectis damnatis faveat; neve operarii qui his societatibus nomen dant, pravis subdolisque malorum hominum artibus inducantur, ut contra justitiae leges laborem ab ipsis debitum subtrahant, vel alio quovis modo eorum, quibus subjiciuntur, jura laedant. * * * Illic etiam coetus prorsus illiciti sunt, in quibus ita arcto foedere in mutuam defensionem conjunguntur socii, ut exinde oriatur turbarum vel caedium periculum."

254. "Nolumus enim," sicut jam decretum fuit in eodem Concilio, No. 520, "ut in posterum ullus in hisce provinciis, in quavis ecclesiastica dignitate constitutus, nominatim societatem damnet, nisi certo et praeter omne dubium constet, eam ex eis esse, quae Constitutionibus Pontificiis [aut aliis documentis Sedis Apostolicae], comprehenduntur. Si vero eae fuerint circumstantiae, ut ultiorem expositionem doctrinae jam traditae postulare videantur, pro ea 'omnibus ad amussim expositis rerum adjunctis' recurrendum esse monemus ad Sanctam Sedem, cujus sapientissimo judicio omnes pleno animo ac corde morem geremus."

255. Ad praecavendum praeterea, ne confusio disciplinae habeatur, dum cum magno fidelium scandalo et auctoritatis ecclesiasticae detrimento, eadem societas in una dioecesi damnatur, et in alia toleratur, nolumus ullam socie-

tatem, uti cadentem sub una ex classibus indicatis, nominatim damnari, antequam Ordinarius rem retulerit ad Commissionem, quam pro hujusmodi causis judicandis nunc constituimus, et quae constabit ex omnibus Archiepiscopis harum provinciarum. Quod si societas damnanda omnibus visa non fuerit, recurrendum erit ad Sanctam Sedem, ut judicium certum accipiatur, et disciplina in nostris provinciis uniformis servetur.

The Second Plenary Council devotes to the consideration of Secret Societies numbers 511 to 523 and the Third Council numbers 244 to 255. The Second Council in numbers 511 and 512 reviews the Papal condemnations of the Masons, Carbonari and similar organizations and in number 513 repeats the seventh decree of the Fourth Provincial Council which warns priests not to give absolution to the members of any secret society until they have handed in their resignations.

It further records in number 514 that because of some doubt about the condemnation of the Odd Fellows, the Sons of Temperance and other such societies, the Right Reverend Patrick Kenrick while Bishop of Philadelphia consulted the Holy See.[136] The answer of the Sacred Congregation of the Inquisition on August 21, 1850 was that these societies are comprehended in the Pontifical Constitution.[137] This response, as Quigley says,[138] obscured the issue. The matter was later settled for four secret societies by the nominal condemnation of the Independent Order of Good Templars on August 3, 1893,[139] and of the Old Fellows, the Knights of Pythias and the Sons of Temperance on August 20, 1894.[140]

The question of Labor Unions and whether or not they were to be considered condemned societies was taken up in numbers 515 to 519. The Fathers after a consideration of the Apostolic Constitution, "*Providas*" of Benedict XIV [141] and the Response of the Holy Office of August 26, 1846 [142] decided that Labor Unions are not to be included among the societies forbidden by the Church. This decision the Third Council upheld in number 253.

In number 520 the Second Council wisely objects to the nominal

[136] Bishop Kenrick wrote twice to the Holy See before obtaining an answer. His first letter was written on February 26, 1848; and the second on May 24, 1848 (Cf. *Conc. Plen. Balti. II Acta Et Decreta*, Appendix, pp. 335 and 336.).

[137] *Ibid.*

[138] *Condemned Societies*, p. 25.

[139] *Fontes*, 1167.

[140] *Fontes*, 1171.

[141] May 18, 1751.—*Fontes*, 412.

[142] *A. S. S.*, I (1865-66), 290.

condemnation of any society by a cleric, no matter what his dignity, unless it be certain beyond all doubt that it is among those included in the Pontifical Constitution. This policy the Fathers of the Third Council reiterate in numbers 254 and 255 wherein they further declare that when there is question of the nominal condemnation of a society the Bishop is to institute a thorough investigation to ascertain whether for certain it comes under those condemned by the Holy See and, if so, whether or not it is included among those sanctioned with excommunication. After this investigation the matter is to be placed before a Commission composed of all the Archbishops of the Country. If this body cannot come to an unanimous agreement, the matter is to be referred to the Holy See.

Finally, in number 522 of the Second Council the faithful are warned and exhorted to avoid all condemned societies, even those questionable ones that do not seem to be included in the strict censures of the Church.

The Third Council in numbers 244 and 245 comments on the many ways the hostility of Secret Societies to the Church was demonstrated and commands that the Pontifical decrees against these societies be proclaimed and executed; that there are societies other than the Freemasons and Carbonari, and differing from them in name, ritual, form and origin which also come under the declaration of the Holy See since they are in the same class with those condemned nominally and under censure. The norms by which a society could be distinguished as condemned or not condemned and the justice of the condemnation are also shown. Certain *ipso facto* censures to be incurred by the members of societies that are heretical or schismatical, though not anti-social, were pointed out as were those contained in the Constitution "*Apostolicae Sedis,*"[143] against the Masons, Carbonari and other societies of this kind.

The whole tenor of the Councils regarding forbidden societies is the carrying out of the common law. This now is the Code and the kindred sources. The only piece of particular legislation is that which leaves the final judgment about the application of the general principles of condemnation and censures of any local society that may spring up to the Commission of Archbishops. This is in no wise opposed to the common law and should still be followed.

[143] Oct. 12, 1869.—*Fontes*, 552.

CHAPTER IV

THE SACRAMENTS

Second Plenary Council

210. Quanto vero diligentiâ praedecessores nostri adlaborarint, ut Rituale Romanum accurate et ubique apud nos servaretur, et quanto studio caverint, ne ritus novi aut a S. Romanae Ecclesiae consuetudine alieni inducerentur, patet ex pluribus eorum decretis, quae hic adjicimus, atque, quatenus opus sit, iterum confirmamus:

211. Cum vehementer optemus, ut, quatenus fieri poterit, per totam nostram provinciam accurate serventur quae salubriter in Rituali Romano praescripta sunt, ut pote quae venerandae antiquitatis exemplo, et Apostolicae Sedis nituntur auctoritate; et ut tollantur abusus seu suppleantur omissiones ortae ex priorum temporum difficultatibus; injungimus omnibus sacerdotibus in hac provincia degentibus ut studeant Ritualis regulas accurate servare.

212. Revmis. Episcopis S. Ludovici et Bostoniensi munus a Patribus demandatum est concinnandi, et hujus concilii nomine et auctoritate in lucem edendi Ritualis Romani accuratam editionem, necnon ejusdem breve exemplar in usum missionariorum; atque utrisque editionibus, in modum appendicis, adjungendi modificationes, hucusque a S. Sede concessas, una cum versione, vernacula lingua, eorum quae predictis praesulibus vertenda esse visa fuerint.

213. Placuit ut Rituale edatur Romano conforme, adjectis in appendice quae ad aedificationem fidelium conducere visa fuerint, quod Baltimorae edatur, auctoritate Revmi. Archiepiscopi, et ubique per Foederatas Provincias servetur. Ne autem peculiares ritus cujusque arbitrio inducantur, districte vetamus, ne sacerdotes a forma sibi in Rituali praescripta, consuetudinis obtentu vel alio quocumque praetextu, discedant.

214. Statuimus, Juxta Ritualis Romani praescriptum, in Sacramentis administrandis, et in defunctorum sepultura, sacerdotes omnino teneri ad adhibendam linguam Latinam: et si censuerint expedire, explicationis causa, eorum quae recitant adjungere versionem lingua vernacula, eam tantum versionem adhibendam esse, quae fuerit ab Ordinario sancita. Ubicumque autem consuetudo aliqua invaluerit huic decreto adversa, eam quamprimum abrogandam statuimus.

The Second Plenary Council has a very lengthy treatise on the Sacraments. It devotes a chapter to the Sacraments in general and one to each of the Sacraments in particular comprising in all numbers 205 to 340.

The Third Council has little to add to the work of its predecessor and so its treatment in numbers 120 to 134 is brief and confines itself to considerations on the baptism of converts and the Sacrament of Matrimony.

Legislation on a subject of this kind belongs chiefly to the general law, so the Councils are taken up particularly with ascetic and pastoral theology, meditation, sermon matter and directions. Bishop Stang has made extensive and good use of the decrees of the Second Council in his standard work on Pastoral Theology.

There are only two positive laws on the Sacraments in general. The first of these, found in numbers 210 to 213 of the Second Council, insists on the use of the Roman Ritual, reprobates customs contrary to it and provides for a correct edition of the same. The second law given in number 214 of the same Council insists on the use of Latin in the administration of the Sacraments and the burial of the dead, as prescribed by the Roman Ritual. It allows, however, repetitions in the vernacular from versions approved by the Ordinary.

These two laws have no exact correspondents in the Code. The first, however, is in keeping with canon 2 which sanctions the use of all books of liturgy that have been approved and are up to date. The second is a kind of corollary to the first in that it requires the use of the Latin language in the sacred rites as does the Roman Ritual.

As regards repetitions in the vernacular our local permission has been generally, if not universally, availed of. The publication in the *Ecclesiastical Review* of January, 1932 [1] of a rescript of the Sacred Congregation of Rites addressed to the Bishop of Rochester disapproving the custom of adding in the vernacular any part of the liturgical prayers of the *absolutio ad tumulum,* even when the corpse is present,[2] raised the question of the lawfulness of this practice for

[1] LXXXVI, 64.

[2] Hodiernus Magister Caeremoniarum Ecclesiae Cathedralis Roffensis in America Septentrionali Sacrae Rituum Congregationi pro opportuna solutione, sequentia dubia discutienda proposuit:

I. Utrum quaedam lingua vernacula, sicut mos est hisce in regionibus, addere liceat absolutioni, praesente cadavere, post Missam de Requie peractae?

II. Si affirmative, utrum translatio in linguam vernaculam dumtaxat partium liturgicarum, id est: Non intres in judicium—Libera me Domine—et

the future in this country. It would seem, however, that the Council of Baltimore may continue to be followed. In the first place, the Sacred Congregation merely disapproved of a custom, but did not abrogate our particular law. Secondly, the rescript itself is particular and, therefore, does not apply outside of the diocese of Rochester. This is in accordance with canon 17, § 3 which states than an interpretation of the law given by way of a judicial sentence or by a rescript in a particular matter has no force of law and binds only the persons and affects the things for which it is given. Thirdly, this response has never been given official publication, and so it hardly can be considered as replacing our particular statute authoritatively approved by the Holy See and in vogue since 1868.

TITLE I

Baptism

SECOND PLENARY COUNCIL

236. De more, qui olim in hac regione invaluerat, neque adhuc omni ex parte sublatus est, Baptismum in privatis domibus conferendi, haec in supra commemorato Baltimorensi Concilio habentur:

Ex praeteritorum temporum difficultate, invaluit in his regionibus consuetudo Baptismum privatis in domibus administrandi. Cum igitur magnae gravitatis sit generalem legem

CODE

CANON 17

§ 3. Data autem per modum sententiae iudicialis aut rescripti in re peculiari, vim legis non habet et ligat tantum personas atquē afficit res pro quibus data est.

CANON 773

Proprius baptismi sollemnis administrandi locus est baptisterium in ecclesia vel oratorio publico.

Orationis Deus cui proprium est etc. an et etiam alia, v. g. Epistola et Evangelium de Missa in die obitus permittantur?

III. Si affirmative, utrum has preces in lingua vernacula inserere liceat inter orationem Deus cui proprium est misereri etc. et antiphonam In Paradisum?

IV. Si negative ad tertium, ubinam dicendae erunt hae preces? Et Sacra eadem Congregatio, audito Specialis Commissionis suffragio ad praepositas quaestiones respondendum censuit:

Ad I Negative et ad mentem. Nimirum servatis omnibus quoad ordinem exequiarum in Rituali Romano praescriptis, funebris oratio haberi potest vel post Missam solemnem et ante absolutionem ad castrum doloris vel expletis exsequiis cum psalmo De Profundis et adnexis precibus juxta Decretum S. R. Cong. N. 3790:

Ad II et III Negative. Ad IV Provisum.

Atque ita rescripsit ac declaravit. Die 29 Aprilis, 1931.

in istis regionibus servandam statim ferre, cui contraria est consuetudo; etsi censemus curandum esse, quoad fieri potest, ut hoc sacramentum in ecclesia conferatur, tamen episcoporum et missionariorum judicio relinquimus, ut statuant quando sint urgendi fideles ut infantes ad ecclesiam deferant, ut baptismus iis conferatur.

CANON 776

§ 1. In domibus autem privatis baptismus sollemnis administrari non debet, nisi hisce in adiunctis:

1.° Si baptizandi sint filii aut nepotes eorum qui supremum actu tenent populorum principatum vel ius habent succedendi in thronum, quoties isti id rite poposcerint;

2.° Si loci Ordinarius, pro suo prudenti arbitrio et conscientia, iusta ac rationabili de causa, in casu aliquo extraordinario id concedendum censuerit.

The Fathers of the Second Plenary Council in number 236 wherein they repeat the sixteenth decree of the First Provincial Council and in number 237 refer to the custom which prevailed in the early days of the American Church of baptizing children even outside the danger of death in private houses with all the ceremonies. This, they insist, should not be done where the church is easy of access. They allow it, however, in those cases in which bad weather, bad roads, the poverty of the parents or some other grave reason makes it practically impossible to bring the children to the church.

The Code in canon 773 decrees that the proper place for the administration of solemn Baptism is the baptistry of a church or public oratory. Canon 776, § 1 provides for exceptions allowing solemn Baptism in private houses if the Ordinary prudently and conscientiously judges there is a just and reasonable cause for it in an extraordinary case.

The tenor of the two laws is the same. But inasmuch as the Council gives a general permission while the Code requires the permission of the Ordinary in each case, the former is abrogated. The common law seems amply adequate to conditions as generally prevailing in our country today. Where it is not, an indult should be obtained as is frequently done in missionary countries.

TITLE II
Confirmation

SECOND PLENARY COUNCIL

252. Decreta duo in prioribus Conciliis Baltimorae habitis hic referre placet, atque iterum confirmare:

Statuimus confirmationis sacramentum administrandum esse nemini minori septennio, nisi ob peculiares rationes, v. g., in mortis periculo.

Quandocumque confirmatio plurimis administratur, statuimus schedulas quasdam, quibus nomina eorum qui confirmandi sunt inscribantur, a pastore unicuique dandas, quas episcopo sacramentum administraturo exhibeant.

253. Quanquam de necessitate hujus Sacramenti non sit, ut in eo recipiendo Patrinus vel Matrina adhibeatur, cum tamen id laudabilis Ecclesiae consuetudo suadeat; sacrique canones praescribant, Episcopi nullum non movebunt lapidem, ut disciplina hujusmodi, jam in nonnullis harum Provinciarum Dioecesibus invecta, ubique introducatur. Confirmati vero habebunt Patrinos singuli singulos, nec tamen foeminis mares nec maribus foeminae Patrini officium praestabunt. Quod si hoc fieri omnino nequeat, saltem duo pro pueris Patrini, et duae pro puellis Matrinae adhibeantur.

CODE

CANON 788

Licet sacramenti confirmationis administratio convenienter in Ecclesia Latina differatur ad septimum circiter aetatis annum, nihilominus etiam antea conferri potest, si infans in mortis periculo sit constitutus, vel ministro id expedire ob iustas et graves causas videatur.

CANON 794

§ 1. Patrinus unum tantum confirmandum aut duos praesentet, nisi aliud iusta de causa ministro videatur.

§ 2. Unus quoque pro singulis confirmandis sit patrinus.

Concerning the Sacrament of Confirmation we have only two local laws. The first of these is in number 252 of the Second Plenary Council which repeats the twenty-first decree of the First Provincial Council. This statute in the first place, forbids the administration of Confirmation before the seventh year except for special reasons, such as the danger of death. Secondly, it requires in the case of a large number to be confirmed that each have a card with his or her name on it. These cards are to be given to the candidates by the Pastor and are to be shown to the confirming Bishop.

The other local statute is in number 253 of the same Council. This, while proposing the ideal of a separate sponsor of the same sex for each one to be confirmed, allows, when this is impossible, two men to act for the boys and two women for the girls. It is to be noted in connection with this decree that many of the Fathers voted for its omission, but that it was incorporated by the Sacred Congregation.[3]

Regarding the age for Confirmation the two laws agree. The Code is silent about the name card so in this respect the Council is *praeter codicem* and still binds.

Apropos of the sponsor the Code in canon 794 declares that each should stand for only one or two candidates unless the minister permit otherwise for a just cause.

Since the Council allows departure from the ancient discipline about individual sponsors only when this ideal is impossible of attainment, and the Code permits it only for a just cause, the two laws practically agree and Bishops can find ample justification for continuing to follow local custom in this regard.

TITLE III

The Holy Eucharist

Article 1

Easter Communion

Second Plenary Council

257. Praesules in primo Concilio Provinciali Baltimorensi suppliciter rogaverunt Sanctam sedem, ut, pro summa illius in leges ecclesiasticas potestate, facultas illis fieret, "prorogandi tempus communionis Paschalis a prima Dominica Quadragesimae ad Dominicam SS. Trinitatis inclusive;" et illorum precibus benigne annuit Rom. Pont. Pius VIII. Si cui vero Episcopo visum fuerit in ejus dioecesi eam dari sacerdotum copiam,

Code

Canon 859

§ 2. Paschalis communio fiat a dominica Palmarum ad dominicam in albis; sed locorum Ordinariis fas est, si ita personarum ac locorum adiuncta exigant, hoc tempus etiam pro omnibus suis fidelibus anticipare, non tamen ante quartam diem dominicam Quadragesimae, vel prorogare, non tamen ultra festum sanctissimae Trinitatis.

[3] *Conc. Plen. Balti. II Acta et Decreta*, p. 136, footnote 3.

ut facile coarctato tempore omnes praecepto satisfacere possint, laudandus erit, si paulatim ac prudenter ad universalem Ecclesiae disciplinam propius accedat.

The Second Plenary Council in number 257 records that the Fathers of the First Provincial Council petitioned the Holy See for the faculty to increase the period of time within which the Paschal Communion could be received from the first Sunday of Lent to Trinity Sunday both inclusively,[4] which request was granted by Pope Pius VIII on September 26, 1830, because of the scarcity of priests, the extent of the territory to be covered by them and the custom already existing here of prolonging the Paschal time.[5]

The Code in canon 859, § 2 places the time for the Easter Communion from Palm Sunday to the Sunday after Easter, but gives to Ordinaries, if conditions of person and place so require it, the right to extend this period with the fourth Sunday of Lent and Trinity Sunday inclusively as the extreme dates.

As is evident from a comparison of the two laws, the concession of the local indult gives our Bishops the advantage of increasing the Paschal time three weeks beyond the limit allowed by the common law.

Augustine in his Commentary [6] is of the opinion that this privilege ceased with the coming of the Code. Woywod [7] on the other hand, considers that it persevered and appeals to canon 4. This opinion seems correct,[8] though the supporting argument is not the strongest. The first two reasons that prompted the granting of the indult were the scarcity of priests and the extent of the territory to be covered by them. Regarding these the Fathers of the Second Council say in the decree under consideration that when and where the Bishop judges he has sufficient priests to enable him easily to curtail the period of satisfying the Easter precept, it will be praiseworthy for

---

[4] *Conc. Prov. Balti. Habita*, p. 46.

[5] *Conc. Prov. Balti. Habita*, p. 92.

[6] IV, 238.

[7] *A Practical Commentary*, I, 414.

[8] Cf. Ayrinhac, *Legislation on the Sacraments*, p. 177; Smith, *Notes on the Second Council*, p. 198.

him gradually and prudently to conform to the universal discipline of the Church. This seems nowhere to have been done and to the third reason for the granting of the indult, namely custom, now being of more than a hundred years' duration and immemorial, has become in virtue of canon 5 the most weighty argument for the perseverance of our privilege.

Article 2

The Holy Sacrifice of the Mass

Section I—The Place of Celebration

Second Plenary Council

362. Statuimus sacerdoti nulli, vi facultatum generalium sibi concessarum celebrandi in quocumque loco decenti, licere Missam celebrare in aedibus privatis, nisi in stationibus, et in iis aedibus quas Ordinarius designaverit; aut dum actu missionis exercitiis, procul ab aliqua ecclesia, dat operam. Quod si Ordinarii alias concedant licentiam celebrandi in privatis aedibus ob speciales circumstantias, iis commendamus eam pro una tantum vel altera vice concedere.

Code

Canon 822

§ 4. Loci Ordinarius aut, si agatur de domo religionis exemptae, Superior maior, licentiam celebrandi extra ecclesiam et oratorium super petram sacram et decenti loco, nunquam autem in cubiculo, concedere potest iusta tantum ac rationabili de causa, in aliquo extraordinario casu et per modum actus.

The Second Plenary Council in number 362 repeats the twenty-third decree of the First Provincial which declares that it is unlawful for any priest by reason of his general faculties of celebrating in any fitting place to say Mass in private homes except in stations and in those houses which the Ordinary designates; or while he is actually engaged in giving a mission far from any church. It seems evident from this statute that priests by reason of their general faculties to celebrate in any fitting place, could say Mass habitually in private houses of their stations and in those which the Ordinary would designate. However, Putzer maintains that it was not within the power of the Ordinary to permit the habitual celebration of Mass in private homes.[9] Judging from the local practice it must have been understood in this country that the permission could be given once and for all.

[9] *Op. cit.*, p. 280 and 281.

The Code in canon 822, § 4 decrees that the Ordinary of the place, or in the case of exempt religious and major Superior, can for a just and reasonable cause give permission to celebrate Mass outside a church or oratory on a consecrated altar-stone in a decent place, but never in a bedroom. This permission is to be given only in extraordinary cases and *per modum actus.*

The Commission for the Interpretation of the Code has said that this faculty must be strictly interpreted.[10] By such interpretation it is understood that the Bishop cannot grant the permission of the portable altar permanently, but only for a period of about eight to ten days at a time.[11] A priest must ask for it every time he has to celebrate outside of sacred places and there is no limit to the number of times it may be repeated as long as the just and reasonable cause is present.[12]

The faculty referred to by the Council, of saying Mass "in any fitting place" was given in number 23 of *Form* 1 of the ordinary quinquennial faculties formerly enjoyed by our Bishops.[13]

These faculties were withdrawn by the decree of the Sacred Consistorial Congregation of April 25, 1918.[14]

The new faculties given to our Bishops contain no special concessions in this regard so the Code is now our only rule. Wherever, therefore, it is necessary for a priest to say Mass in private houses, even in stations, and this is rather frequent in some of our dioceses, they must obtain frequent renewals of the necessary permission from the Bishop, or through him obtain an indult from the Holy See. The only possible justification that one can have for acting otherwise is to assure himself that there has been established an immemorial custom and apply canon 5.

[10] *A. A. S.*, XI (1919), 478; cf. *A. A. S.*, XVI (1924), 370.

[11] Cappello, *De Sacramentis*, I, No. 750; Bliley, *op. cit.*, p. 118.

[12] Cappello, *ibid.*, Bliley, *ibid.*

[13] Cf. Sabetti-Barrett, *Compendium Theologiae Moralis*, 23. ed., pp. 1081, 1085 and 1086, footnote 1.

[14] *A. A. S.*, X (1918), 190; cf. Ayrinhac, *General Legislation*, p. 175; Motry, *op. cit.*, p. 4.

Section II—Permission for a Visiting Priest to Say Mass

Third Plenary Council

295. Huic ergo malo nullum aliud remedium nacti, volumus et edicimus ut in posterum nullis qui ad colligendum venisse sciuntur, venia detur a rectoribus vel unica vice celebrandi missam (quod tamen de regularibus in monasteriis proprii ordinis privatim celebrantibus intelligi nolumus) donec ab Ordinario ipso hanc veniam acceperint.

Code

Canon 804

§ 1. Sacerdos extraneus ecclesiae in qua celebrare postulat, exhibens authenticas et adhuc validas litteras commendatitias sui Ordinarii, si sit saecularis, vel sui Superioris, si religiosus, vel Sacrae Congregationis pro Ecclesia Orientali, si sit ritus orientalis, ad Missae celebrationem admittatur, nisi interim aliquid eum commisisse constet, cur a Missae celebratione repelli debeat.

§ 2. Si iis litteris careat, sed rectori ecclesiae de eius probitate apprime constet, poterit admitti; si vero rectori sit ignotus, admitti adhuc potest semel vel bis, dummodo, ecclesiastica veste indutus, nihil ex celebratione ab ecclesia in qua litat, quovis titulo, percipiat, et nomen, officium suamque dioecesim in peculiari libro signet.

§ 3. Peculiares hac de re normae, salvis huius canonis praescriptis, ab Ordinario loci datae, servandae sunt ab omnibus, etiam religiosis exemptis, nisi agatur de admittendis ad celebrandum religiosis in ecclesia suae religionis.

The Third Plenary Council in number 295 decrees that in future no one who is known to have come to collect money be given permission by the Rector to say Mass even once (which, however, does not apply to Regulars celebrating privately in monasteries of their own Order) until they have received this permission from the Ordinary himself.

The Code in canon 804 lays down the general rule that Rectors of churches are not to allow strange priests to say Mass unless they have a *celebret.* However, a visiting priest without a *celebret* but whose good standing is well known to the Rector may be permitted to say Mass.

In the case of one entirely unknown to the Rector and not having a *celebret* permission to say Mass once or twice may be granted provided the visiting priest wears the clerical dress, accepts nothing under any pretext from the church in which he says Mass and enters his name, office and diocese in the book specially kept for that purpose.

Finally, the Code makes provision for the completion of these regulations by diocesan statutes which, however, must not be opposed to the common law. Such local prescriptions are binding upon all priests even religious except when they celebrate in a church of their own Order.

This provision for diocesan statutes and the exemption of religious in their own churches would seem by analogy to apply to local provincial laws, in which case the concession made to religious by both the particular and the common law would be the same.

The conciliar prohibition of granting permission to a visiting priest to say Mass even once simply because he has come to collect money seems to be a restriction of the right which the Code gives to Rectors to allow a priest under the condition stated to say Mass daily or at least once or twice. Such curtailing of the Rector's right is opposed to the Code and, therefore, according to canon 6, § 1 is abrogated.

Article 3

Taking the Blessed Sacrament Out of the Tabernacle

Second Plenary Council

264. Cum in ecclesia Sanctissimum e tabernaculo extrahunt, semper superpelliceo et stola sint induti.

Code

Canon 2

Codex, plerumque, nihil decernit de ritibus et caeremoniis quas liturgici libri, ab Ecclesia Latina probati, servandas praecipiunt in celebratione sacrosancti Missae sacrificii, in administratione Sacramentorum et Sacramentalium aliisque sacris peragendis. Quare omnes liturgicae leges vim suam retinent, nisi earum aliqua in Codice expresse corrigatur.

Canon 847

Ad infirmos publice sacra communio deferatur, nisi iusta et rationabilis causa aliud suadeat.

CANON 849

§ 1. Communionem privatim ad infirmos quilibet sacerdos deferre potest, de venia saltem praesumpta sacerdotis, cui custodia sanctissimi Sacramenti commissa est.

§ 2. Quando privatim sacra communio infirmis ministratur, reverentiae ac decentiae tanto sacramento debitae sedulo consulatur, servatis a Sede Apostolica praescriptis normis.

The Second Plenary Council in number 264 says that, when in church priests remove the Blessed Sacrament from the tabernacle, they are always to be vested in surplice and stole.

The Code says nothing specifically about this matter but in canon 2 declares that all liturgical laws retain their force except in so far as they are explicitly corrected by it. Now according to the Roman Ritual [15] when removing the Blessed Sacrament from the tabernacle to go on a sick-call, the priest is to be vested in surplice and stole. That this rubric applies also when preparing to carry the Blessed Sacrament to the sick privately is the opinion of Wapelhorst who in treating of the permission which the Code in canons 847 and 849 grants for this private carrying of the Blessed Sacrament says that when a priest uses this faculty, the following rules are to be observed. Having lit two candles and washed his hands, vested in surplice and white stole, he places the Blessed Sacrament according to the customary manner in the pyx. Then having closed the tabernacle he leaves the Blessed Sacrament on the altar or on a table in the sacristy, makes the proper genuflections, removes the stole, surplice and cassock and finally hangs the burse around his neck and places it on his breast.[16]

This law of the Council, then, is still in force and applies even in the case of sick-calls. It goes without saying, of course, that in an emergency, such as the probable danger of death one is excused from the full carrying out of the rubrics.

[15] Tit. IV, cap. 4, No. 12.

[16] *Rituale Romanum*, pp. 279, 280 and 281, footnote 2.

Article 4

Carrying the Blessed Sacrament

Second Plenary Council

264. Dolendum sane est rerum adjuncta, quae apud nos obtinent, impedire quominus eâ cum pompâ, quam vult Ecclesia, ad infirmos deferatur Sanctissimum Sacramentum. Studeant itaque sacerdotes, ut interna animi devotione hujus pompae defectum suppleant, simulque haud negligant, quantum in ipsis est, reverentiae externae, quae Christo revera praesenti debetur, prospicere. Dum Sanctissimum deferunt, vana et inutilia evitent colloquia; piae potius contemplationi vel precibus dent operam. "Delatio Sanctissimi Sacramenti ad urgentes tantum causas, atque ad actuale ministerii Sacerdotalis exercitium coarctetur." Quaenam vero sit urgens causa, ex loci, temporis, aliisque adjunctis erit dijudicandum. Injungimus "presbyteris strictam obligationem semper in hisce casibus Sanctam Hostiam super pectus deferendi." Nunquam, nisi in extrema necessitate vel ipsam Hostiam, vel vas sacrum in quo servatur, stola saltem non induti attrectent.

Code

Canon 847

Ad infirmos publice sacra communio deferatur, nisi iusta et rationabilis causa aliud suadeat.

Canon 849

§ 1. Communionem privatim ad infirmos quilibet sacerdos deferre potest, de venia saltem praesumpta sacerdotis, cui custodia sanctissimi Sacramenti commissa est.

§ 2. Quando privatim sacra communio infirmis ministratur, reverentiae ac decentiae tanto sacramento debitae sedulo consulatur, servatis a Sede Apostolica praescriptis normis.

The Second Plenary Council in number 264 expresses regret that owing to circumstances existing in this country the Blessed Sacrament cannot be carried to the sick with all the pomp that the Church wishes. It enjoins, however, on priests the strict obligation of keeping the Sacred Host upon the breast while carrying It to the sick, as prescribed by Pope Pius IX in his Encyclical Letter, "*De Sanctissima Eucharistia Deferenda.*" [17] Vain and useless talking is to be avoided on the way and the priest is rather to give himself to pious contemplation or prayer.

[17] Feb. 25, 1859.—*Conc. Plen. Balti. II Acta et Decreta*, Appendix, p. 297.

Among the ordinary faculties that used to be granted to our Bishops in *Formula* I the twenty-fourth provided for the private carrying of the Blessed Sacrament to the sick.[18]

The Holy See having been asked in 1912 whether the Blessed Sacrament could be carried to the sick privately without the observance of the prescribed rubrics, the Sacred Congregation for the Discipline of the Sacraments answered that this could be done for a just and reasonable cause, but with the observance of the rubric proposed by Benedict XIV in his decree "*Inter omnigenas*" of February 2, 1744,[19] that the priest wear the stole over his proper dress, put the pyx in a burse which is to hang by a cord around his neck and repose on his breast, and that he never go unaccompanied by at least a layman in defect of a cleric.[20]

The Code now grants this faculty in canon 847 wherein it decrees that Holy Communion is to be carried to the sick publicly, unless a just and reasonable cause excuses. It further prescribes in canon 849 that in the private administration of Holy Communion to the sick, the reverence and respect due to so great a Sacrament be zealously safeguarded and the regulations laid down by the Holy See be observed which are those summed up in the foregoing decree of Benedict XIV.[21]

Our practice, then of carrying the Blessed Sacrament privately and in the street dress finds justification not only in custom, but also in this concession of the Code for there is always present in this country a just and reasonable cause for so doing. We are still, however, bound by all the rubrics compatible with this among which is the above prescription of the Council that the priest keep the Host upon his breast. As for the avoidance of useless talking and the practice of contemplation or prayer while going on sick-calls, the common law makes no specific mention, but these precautions are obviously implied in its counsel on the reverence and respect due the Blessed Sacrament and our local statute suggests to priests the most fitting way of preserving due decorum.

[18] Sabetti-Barrett, *op. cit.* 23. ed., p. 1085.

[19] *Fontes*, No. 339.

[20] Dec. 23, 1912, *A. A. S.*, IV (1913), 725.

[21] *Rituale Romanum*, Tit. IV, cap. 4, Nos. 6, 12 and 13; cf. Wapelhorst. *op. cit.*, p. 280.

Article 5

Administering Holy Communion to the Sick

Second Plenary Council

264. Infirmis Sacram Eucharistiam ministrantes, praescripta Ritualis Romani, in quantum rerum circumstantiae sinunt, diligentissime servent.

Code

Canon 849

§ 2. Quando privatim sacra communio infirmis ministratur, reverentiae ac decentiae tanto sacramento debitae sedulo consulatur, servatis a Sede Apostolica praescriptis normis.

The Second Plenary Council in number 264 deals finally with the administration of Holy Communion to the sick. In this connection it states simply that in so far as circumstances allow it, the prescription of the Roman Ritual should be most diligently observed.

The corresponding legislation of the Code is that already quoted from canon 849, § 2, which decrees that when Holy Communion is administered privately to the sick the reverence and respect due to so great a Sacrament is to be safeguarded and the rules prescribed by the Holy See are to be observed.

The rubric of the Roman Ritual governing the act of giving private Holy Communion is that the priest wearing the stole already because he is carrying the Blessed Sacrament, puts on the surplice also, if he has not yet done so, upon entering the sick room.[22]

That this is a strict rubric is evident from the words of St. Alphonsus who says that to administer Holy Communion without stole and surplice is according to the common opinion of the Doctors a mortal sin *ex genere suo.*[23] The Sacred Congregation of Rites having been asked whether or not the practice, in vogue in some rural parishes where long journeys had to be made, of priests wearing only the stole and not the surplice over their common dress in carrying and administering the Blessed Sacrament to the sick, could be continued, replied in the negative and ordered the custom stopped and the prescription of the Roman Ritual observed.[24]

[22] Tit. IV, cap. 4, No. 29.

[23] *Op. cit.*, Lib. VI, Tract. III de Euch. No. 241.

[24] Decree of Dec. 16, 1826.—*Decreta Authentica* S. R. C., No. 4474.

Kenrick [25] in speaking of the manner of giving Holy Communion to the sick says that the stole at least should be worn under pain of mortal sin, and if possible also the surplice according to the monition of the First Provincial Council of Baltimore.[26]

Smith believing that our American theologian could not have been ignorant of the foregoing decree of the Sacred Congregation of Rites concludes from this statement of his that he did not interpret it as strictly applying to our country.[27] Passing over the possibility of Archbishop Kenrick's knowledge of this decree, it actually does not seem to apply directly to us since it primarily treats of the public carrying and administering of the Blessed Sacrament. It shows, however, that the mind of the Church is to have the rubrics carried out as fully as possible even at the cost of some inconvenience; and in particular it enables us to interpret the local and common law requirement of observing the rubrics in the private administration of Holy Communion.

O'Kane in this connection says, "With us the priest goes to the house of the sick person in his ordinary dress; but he should bring with him, or contrive to send before him, the vestments which the rubric requires him to wear." [28]

Wapelhorst quoting this statement and the above decrees of the Sacred Congregation of Rites and of the Council of Baltimore says that the Holy See has granted the faculty of carrying the Blessed Sacrament privately, but not that of removing It from the tabernacle or administering It in houses without the surplice, etc.[29]

In virtue, then, of both the general and particular laws our priests have the obligation of wearing the surplice and stole in giving Holy Communion to the sick in their homes. The cassock, likewise, should be worn since the surplice presupposes it and would look unsightly without it.

[25] *Op. cit.*, III, 77.

[26] *Conc. Prov. Balti. Habita*, p. 82.

[27] *Notes on the Second Plenary Council*, pp. 204, ff.

[28] *Op. cit.*, p. 331, No. 797.

[29] *Op. cit.*, p. 281, footnote 2.

ARTICLE 6

Mass Stipends

SECOND PLENARY COUNCIL

369. Unde relinquentes singulis Ordinariis, ut rerum adjunctis bene consideratis quantitatem stipendii, quae ipsis justa esse videtur, pro clero suo determinent, hoc solum statuimus, nequis plus neve regulariter minus exigat, quam episcopo suo opportunum ac justum visum fuerit.

CODE

CANON 831

§ 1. Ordinarii loci est manualem Missarum stipem in sua dioecesi definire per decretum, quantum fieri potest, in dioecesana Synodo latum; nec sacerdoti licet ea maiorem exigere.

§ 2. Ubi desit Ordinarii decretum, servetur consuetudo dioecesis.

§ 3. Etiam religiosi, licet exempti, circa stipem manualem stare debent decreto Ordinarii loci aut dioecesis consuetudini.

The Second Plenary Council in number 369 leaves to the Ordinary the regulation of the Mass stipend and decrees that where this regulation exists the celebrant should never demand more nor as a rule less than the regular stipend.

The Code in canon 831 makes it the right of the local Ordinary to fix the amount of the stipend and forbids the priest to demand one larger than that fixed by the law of the Bishop.

The two laws agree in empowering the Bishop to determine the amount of the stipend and in forbidding priests to demand more than the fixed offering. The Code, however, is silent about the acceptance of less than the standard. Keller in his work, *Mass Stipends,* holds that if the priest wishes he may ordinarily accept less.[30] This is contrary to the Baltimore law which seems *praeter codicem* and still in force.

ARTICLE 7

Mass Foundations

SECOND PLENARY COUNCIL

370. Neque hic possumus quin declaremus, esse abusum non tolerandum et rei sacrae profanationem, quod, quemadmodum pluries factum est, invitationes, publicae et frequentes ad eleemosynas in hujusmodi fundationes erogandas, per plures menses continuos ephemeridibus popularibus inter alia

[30] P. 91.

negotia profana inserantur. Quem abusum sine mora per Episcopos et praelatos tolli et in posterum praecaveri volumus.

Finally, the Fathers of the Second Council in number 370 condemn, wish stopped, and for the future prevented by Bishops and Prelates the abuse of advertising in the newspapers for Mass foundations.

This decree, likewise, is *praeter codicem* and, therefore, remains in force.

TITLE IV

Matrimony

Article 1

Marriage Attempted After Civil Divorce

Third Plenary Council

124. Ad haec crimina compescenda poenam excommunicationis statuimus, Ordinario reservatam, *ipso facto* incurrendam ab eis, qui postquam divortium civile obtinuerint, matrimonium ausi fuerint attentare.

The Third Plenary Council in number 124 after remarking how grave a sin it is to appeal to the civil tribunal for the dissolution of the marriage bond and, what is worse, for those validly married to attempt a new marriage after civil divorce, decrees an *ipso facto* excommunication reserved to the Ordinary to be incurred by those who having obtained a civil divorce would dare to attempt marriage.

This censure is incurred by those and only those who, already validly married, attempt after a civil divorce a new marriage, and applies whether they go before a priest, a non-Catholic minister or a representative of the State.[31]

There being in the Code no corresponding penalty nor anything to abrogate it, this local censure continues among those reserved to the Ordinary.

Article 2

Marriage Attempted Before a Non-Catholic Minister

Third Plenary Council	Code
127. Item decernimus Catholicos, qui coram ministro cujuscumque sec-	**Canon 1063** **§ 1. Etsi ab Ecclesia obtenta sit**

[31] Slater-Martin, *op. cit.*, II, 193, footnote.

tae acatholicae matrimonium contraxerint vel attentaverint, extra propriam dioecesim, in quolibet statu vel territorio sub ditione praesulum qui huic concilio adsunt vel adesse debent, excommunicationem incurrere Episcopo reservatam, a qua tamen quilibet dictorum Ordinariorum sive per se, sive per sacerdotem ad hoc delegatum absolvere poterit. Quod si in propria dioecesi ita deliquerint, statuimus eos ipso facto innodates esse excommunicatione, quae, nisi absque fraude legis alium Episcopum adeant, eorum Ordinario reservatur.

dispensatio super impedimento mixtae religionis, coniuges nequeunt, vel ante vel post matrimonium coram Ecclesia initum, adire quoque, sive per se sive per procuratorem, ministrum acatholicum uti sacris addictum, ad matrimonialem consensum praestandum vel renovandum.

CANON 2245

§ 4. Censura latae sententiae non est reservata, nisi in lege vel praecepto id expresse dicatur, et in dubio sive iuris sive facti reservatio non urget.

CANON 2319

§ 1. Subsunt excommunicationi latae sententiae Ordinario reservatae catholici:

1.° Qui matrimonium ineunt coram ministro acatholico contra praescriptum can. 1063, § 1.

The same Council in number 127 decrees that Catholics who would contract or attempt marriage before a minister of any non-Catholic sect whatsoever, outside their own dioceses in any state or territory under the authority of the Bishops who are present at this Council, incur excommunication reserved to the Bishop from which, however, any of the aforesaid Ordinaries either *per se* or through the delegation of a priest can absolve. But, if the couple should be guilty of this delinquency within their own diocese, they incur *ipso facto* an excommunication which is reserved to their own Ordinary unless without acting *in fraudem legis* they approach another Bishop.

The Code has a similar censure in canon 2319, § 1, 1°, wherein it declares under excommunication *latae sententiae* and reserved to the Ordinary, Catholics who enter matrimony before a non-Catholic minister against the prescription of canon 1063, § 1, which canon in turn forbids a couple even with a dispensation from the impediment of mixed religion to go before a non-Catholic minister as such for the purpose of giving or renewing matrimonial consent either before or after a marriage *coram ecclesia*.

The validity of the Baltimore censure has been called into

question [32] on the grounds that at the time of its promulgation there was a like common law censure and it was forbidden then [33] as now [34] to reserve to the Ordinary cases already reserved to the Holy See. This objection, however, seems without weight, in view of the fact that the local censure received Papal approbation after diligent examination and mature consideration along with the other decrees of the Third Plenary Council, and hence was evidently recognized in spite of the apparent contradiction.[35]

Granted the validity of the Baltimore censure, the next consideration is its present binding force. This is to be ascertained by comparison with the kindred penalty of the Code. In this connection one is confronted by other disputes as to the real force of the common law sanction. The first of these concerns the ceremony and whether one must have appeared before both a non-Catholic and Catholic minister to incur excommunication, or whether the non-Catholic ceremony alone suffices. The second concerns the parties and whether the penalty is incurred when both parties are Catholic or only in the case of mixed or disparate marriage.

Arguing from the Constitution, "*Aposticae Sedis,*" which specifically censured the non-Catholic ceremony alone [36] and the faculty for *senatio* given our Bishops which implies only the non-Catholic ceremony, it would seem that this alone and not the double ceremony is censured. From the wording of the Code, however, it would seem that only the double ceremony is punished by the sanction of excommunication.[37]

Again some authors think that in the case of two Catholics the censure is not incurred because canon 1063, § 1 seems to be concerned only with mixed or disparate marriage.[38] Some on the other hand

[32] Schenk, *op. cit.*, p. 266, ff.; Slater-Martin, *op. cit.*, II, 197.

[33] *Fontes,* 1302 and 1615.

[34] Can. 2247, § 1.

[35] *Conc. Plen. Balti. III Acta et Decreta,* pp. xv and xvi.

[36] Schenk, *op. cit.*, pp. 261, ff.

[37] Neuberger, *op. cit.*, p. 52; Linneborn, *op. cit.*, p. 171; Woywod, *Homiletic Review,* XXIV (1923-24), 510 and 511; Schenk, *op. cit.*, pp. 260 and 261.

[38] Chelodi, *Jus Paenale,* p. 66, footnote 3; Cappello, *De Censuris,* p. 320, No. 369, § 4; Leech, *op. cit.*, p. 93.

maintain that the penalty of canon 2319, § 1, 1° applies whether one or both of the parties be Catholic.[39]

In the first controversy the opinion favoring the sanction of the double ceremony seems the stronger. The wording of the law might first be considered and this is its obvious meaning. It appears unnecessary to appeal to the Constitution, "*Aposticae Sedis,*" for an interpretation. Besides this appeal is weak in view of the change the Code has made in penal legislation. Nor is the argument from the faculty for *sanatio* strong since faculties are not intended to be interpretative of a law, but would logically be expected to cover the broadest interpretation of the law.

The sanction for the single ceremony is at least doubtful and according to canon 2245, § 4 in doubt of law or fact a censure is not reserved.

In the second controversy there seems no solid reason to question the application of the censure to cases involving two Catholics. The fact that the law stresses its application in cases of mixed religion (which term according to canon 1071 includes also that of disparity of cult) even when a dispensation has been obtained does not imply that it does not include other cases.

Comparing the local law with the various interpretations of the Code, one comes to the following conclusions:

If the common law includes all marriages whether involving one or two Catholics and one or two ceremonies, then the particular and general censures are identical. In this case, however, those guilty of a breach of the law would incur only one excommunication.[40]

If, however, the common law applies only to the double ceremony and this in mixed or disparate marriages only, then the two laws differ. In this case Catholics attempting marriage before a non-Catholic minister alone would be excommunicated only by the local censure.

If, finally, the common law applies to the double ceremony only,

[39] Petrovits, *op. cit.*, N. 270; Leitner, *op. cit.*, p. 241; Cocchi, *Commentarium*, VIII, 234, No. 147; Cipollini, *De Censuris*, Lib. II, No. 70; Augustine, *Commentary*, VIII, 297; Neuberger, *op. cit.*, pp. 52 and 53; Blat, *op. cit.*, Lib. V, par. III, Tit. XI, No. 157.

[40] Chelodi, *Jus Poenale*, p. 33, footnote 4; Schenk, *op. cit.*, p. 268.

but to all marriages thus attempted whether between two Catholics or a Catholic and a non-Catholic, and this seems to be the best interpretation, then the two laws again would differ. In this case offending Catholics would be excommunicated by the Council only, if they attempt marriage before a non-Catholic minister alone, and by both the Council and the Code if they go also before a priest. Since this latter contingency would evidently involve two crimes, namely, marriage before a non-Catholic minister and the double ceremony, two distinct censures would be incurred in accordance with canon 2244, § 2, 1° which decrees: *Censura latae sententiae multiplicatur, si diversa delicta, quorum singula censuram secumferunt, eadem vel distincta actione committantur.*

The practical conclusion from all these distinctions is that, granted the validity of the Baltimore penalty, and this can hardly be questioned, any Catholic attempting marriage before a non-Catholic minister is under at least one censure of excommunication reserved to the Ordinary whether the source of that punishment be the Council or the Code or both.

After examining these local censures it might well be remarked here that those who already validly married and having obtained a civil divorce attempt a new marriage before a non-Catholic minister incur both censures in accordance with canon 2244, § 2, 1° quoted above. For here again two distinct crimes would be involved, namely, that of attempting marriage before a non-Catholic minister and that of making this attempt after a civil divorce in the case of a valid marriage.

CHAPTER V

SACRED PLACES AND SEASONS

TITLE I

Christian Burial

Article 1

The Burial of Catholics in Non-Catholic Cemeteries

Second Plenary Council

391. In Superiori Concilio Plenario de ritibus funereis haec decreta sunt: Ritus ecclesiasticos nolumus adhiberi in sepultura fidelium, quandocumque eorum corpora sepeliuntur in coemeteriis sectarum; vel etiam in coemeteriis profanis, quando adsunt coemeteria Catholica.

392. Cum tamen conditionem, in qua nostrates versantur, consideremus, legis hujus rigor mitigari aliquantulum posse videtur. Si cujus itaque Catholici defuncti, si fuerit ad fidem conversus, consanguinei superstites sint Acatholici, et fundum in alieno coemeterio jam possideant, permittimus ut exequiae in domo vel etiam publice in Ecclesia celebrentur, si pastori id eorundem bono spirituali profuturum vel alias expedire visum fuerit. Si superstites Catholici sint, fundum vero in alieno coemeterio sine ulla fraude legis vel ab anno 1853 habuerint, in quo cadavera jam sint humata, pastoris arbitrio et conscientiae relinquimus, ut preces pro exequiis in Rituali praecriptas privatim in domo recitet, antequam cadaver efferatur; at in Ecclesia, ut nonnisi praehabita Ordinarii venia exequiae fiant, praecipimus.

Praeterea, si in Coemeterio profano separata terrae pars obtineri nequeat, in qua Corpora Catholicorum exclusive inhumentur, saltem loculus ubi cadaver deponitur benedicatur, ea oratione adhibita quae in Romano Rituali expresse praescribitur (Tit. de Exequiis), "Deus cujus miseratione animae, &c.

Third Plenary Council

318. Ad haec igitur mala praecavenda, et ad omnem ambiguitatem a Patrum verbis amovendam; quum agitur de sepultura eorum qui fuerunt ad fidem conversi, et quorum superstites acatholici fundum domesticum in alieno coemeterio habent; vel etiam de istis Catholicis, qui pariter ante legem latam proprium fundum habuerunt, vel certe sine ulla fraude post legem acquisierunt, declaramus, in istis casibus licere ritus ecclesiasticos adhiberi, sive domi sive in ecclesia, quotiescumque id ab Episcopo, ob graves rationes, interdictum non fuerit; et declaramus insuper, correctionem S. Congr. de Prop. Fide de loculo benedicendo, et supradicto decreto adjunctam, in istis etiam casibus esse observandam. His casibus exceptis, nunquam rectori animarum licebit dictos ritus adhibere in sepultura fidelium in alieno coemeterio, nisi de expressa Ordinarii licentia.

Code

Canon 1205

§ 1. Cadavera fidelium sepeliendo sunt in coemeterio quod, secundum ritus in probatis liturgicis libris traditos, sit benedictum, sive solemni sive simplici benedictione ab iis data de quibus in can. 1155, 1156.

Canon 1206

§ 1. Ius est catholicae Ecclesiae possidendi propria coemeteria.

§ 2. Sicubi hoc Ecclesiae ius violetur nec spes sit ut violatio reparetur, curent locorum Ordinarii ut coemeteria, societatis civilis propria, benedicantur, si, qui in eis condi solent, sint maiore ex parte catholici, aut saltem ut in eis catholici spatium habeant, idque benedictum, sibi reservatum.

§ 3. Si ne hoc quidem obtineri possit, toties quoties benedicantur, secundum ritus in probatis liturgicis libris traditos, singuli tumuli.

In number 391 the Second Plenary Council repeats a part of the third decree of the First Plenary Council,[1] in which the Fathers express their wish that Christian burial should not be granted to those who are to be buried in sectarian cemeteries or in such as are non-sectarian where there are Catholic ones. In number 392 they state, however, that owing to conditions here it would seem that the rigor of this law could be mitigated a little. They go on, then, to state that a deceased convert whose surviving relatives are non-Catholics and have a lot in a non-Catholic cemetery, can be buried from the house or even publicly from the church if the Pastor judge it spiritually helpful to the relatives or otherwise expedient. If the surviving relatives are Catholics and without being *in fraudem legis* or after 1853 (the year in which the First Plenary Council went into effect) have purchased a lot in a non-Catholic cemetery in which some bodies have already been buried, then it is left to the judgment and conscience of the Pastor to determine whether or not the prescribed prayers are to be said privately, at the home before the burial; not, however, without the permission of the Ordinary is the funeral to be held in the church.

The Third Plenary Council in number 318 in turn mitigated this law of the Second. It permits converts, whose surviving non-Catholic relatives have a lot in a non-Catholic cemetery, to have Catholic burial either at home or in the church as often as this has not for grave reasons been forbidden by the Bishop. The same concession is made to other Catholics who have such a lot without being *in fraudem legis.*

[1] *Conc. Plen. Balti. Habita,* p. 44.

The Fathers, moreover, order observed the Instruction of the Sacred Congregation of the Propagation of the Faith which is incorporated in number 392 of the Second Council and which requires that, where in non-sectarian cemeteries there is no part set aside for the exclusive burial of Catholics, each grave be blessed according to the form given in the Roman Ritual.[2]

The Council decrees, finally, that outside of the foregoing cases it shall not be lawful for Pastors to use the Catholic ritual for burials in non-sectarian cemeteries without the express permission of the Ordinary.

The Code in canons 1205, § 1 and 1206, § 2 and § 3 requires that the faithful be buried in cemeteries blessed with either the solemn or simple blessing according to the rite prescribed in liturgical books.

Where it is impossible to have Catholic cemeteries the Bishops are to see to it that the general ones be blessed if the majority of those to be buried there are Catholic; if they are not, then a certain portion is to be reserved for Catholics and this to be blessed. If neither of these arrangements is possible, then each grave is to be blessed according to the prescribed rite.

The greater liberty granted by the Council in this matter is evidently opposed to the Code and consequently abrogated. Nor can we appeal through custom to canon 5 for the continuance of the practice of burying Catholics in non-Catholic cemeteries where Catholic ones are available, since the required one hundred years had not elapsed between 1852, the furthest possible date, and 1918. Frequently a happy solution of the difficulties concerning the place of burial of members of a family of which some are Catholics and some non-Catholics is obtained by having such families purchase a lot in the unconsecrated section of the Catholic cemetery and have the graves of the Catholic members blessed. Where lots have already been purchased much will depend on the circumstances of each individual case and the matter should be referred to the Ordinary.

In answer to a query as to the effect of the Code upon this point of the local legislation the *Ecclesiastical Review* replied that the former did not change the law of the Third Plenary Council of Baltimore

[2] Instr. of Jan. 24, 1868, Article 17; *Conc. Plen. Balti. II Acta et Decreta*, p. cxl.

regarding the burial of Catholics in non-Catholic cemeteries, since the concessions it grants are dispensations from the ancient and universal discipline of the Church which is referred to in canon 1206, § 1.[8] This answer would be correct were the Baltimore decree in the nature of a privilege or indult as provided for in canon 4. It does not, however, appear to be such, but like most of the other local statutes is a particular law subject to the provision of canon 6, § 1. It had its incipiency in what the Fathers of the Council judged the exigencies of the time and place required, and the Holy See did nothing more than approve it with the added requirement that each grave be blessed according to the rubrics of the Roman Ritual. A particular law and an indult are two vastly different things canonically and must be interpreted accordingly. To consider this statute an indult would necessitate the same procedure for all of our local legislation and, indeed, for all particular law as a whole. In which hypothesis the reference to such laws in canon 6, §1 would have no purpose.

Article 2

The Burial of Non-Catholics in Catholic Cemeteries

Second Plenary Council

389. Ex mente Sedis Apostolicae toleratur, ut in sepulchris gentilitiis, quae videlicet privata et peculiaria pro Catholicis laicorum familiis aedificantur, cognatorum et affinium etiam Acatholicorum corpora tumulentur.

Code

Canon 1239

§ 1. Ad sepulturam ecclesiasticam non sunt admittendi qui sine baptismo decesserint.

§ 2. Catechumeni qui nulla sua culpa sine baptismo moriantur, baptizatis accensendi sunt.

§ 3. Omnes baptizati sepultura ecclesiastica donandi sunt, nisi eadem a iure expresse priventur.

Canon 1240

§ 1. Ecclesiastica sepultura privantur, nisi ante mortem aliqua dederint poenitentiae signa:

1.° Notorii apostatae a christiana fide, aut sectae haereticae vel schismaticae aut sectae massonicae aliisve eiusdem generis societatibus notorie addicti.

---

[8] LX (1919), 82.

The Second Plenary Council in number 389 incorporates from a decree of the Provincial Council of Prague of 1860 the following: "*Ex mente Sedis Apostolicae toleratur, ut in sepulchris gentilitiis, quae videlicit privata et peculiara pro Catholicis laicorum familiis aedificantur, cognatorum et affinium, etiam Acatholicorum corpora tumulentur.*" [4]

This statute of the Council of Prague in turn was based on a decree of the Sacred Congregation of the Holy Office of March 30, 1859.

Having been asked whether non-Catholics related by blood or affinity could be buried in the Catholic family lot, the Sacred Congregation replied: "*Curent episcopi totis viribus ut cuncta fiant ad norman Sacrorum Canonum; quatenus vero absque scandalo et periculo id obtineri non possit, tolerari posse.*" [5]

The same Congregation on January 4, 1888 declared that the foregoing decree of Baltimore was to be understood according to its response of March 30, 1859, and added: "*Adeo ut tolerantia de qua agitur sit tolerantia mere passiva ad praecavenda maiora mala.*" [6]

The Code in canon 1239 denies ecclesiastical burial to those not baptized and in canon 1240, §1, 1° to those notoriously affiliated with heretical or schismatic sects, as are non-Catholics, and, finally, in canon 1212 it excludes from interment in consecrated ground all those denied Christian burial.

The Baltimore law, then, is evidently opposed to the Code. However, interpreted according to the above decrees of the Holy Office it would seem to be an indult and continue in force in virtue of canon 4. Therefore, while the burial of non-Catholics in the lots of Catholic relatives is to be positively discouraged and reasonably avoided, it may still be tolerated when it is judged to be the lesser of two evils.

Article 3

Money Accruing from the Sale of Lots

Second Plenary Council

393. Si quis vero locum aliquem in coemeterio sibi et haeredibus suis in perpetuum reservatum velit, ita ut nullus alius ipsis nolentibus ibi sepeliri

---

[4] *Collectio Lacensis*, V, 486.

[5] *Fontes*, 949; *Coll. de Prop. Fide*, 1173.

[6] *Fontes*, *ibid.*, footnote 1; *Coll. de Prop. Fide*, *ibid.*, footnote 1.

unquam possit, pro jure istiusmodi *exclusivo*, ut ajunt, pretium solvi potest. Ex pecuniis ita comparatis dubium haud est, quin ea habeatur summa, quae coemeteriis servandis, restaurandis, et ornandis sufficiat. Si quid supersit, ad charitatis vel religionis opera promovenda Ordinarii judicio adhibeatur. Districte autem vetamus, ne unquam, quocunque sub praetextu, sine Ordinarii venia, pecunias quae ex coemeteriis derivantur, suas facere audeant viri ecclesiastici; id vero si attentaverint, poenis severissimis plectantur.

The Second Plenary Council in number 393 decrees that the money derived from the sale of lots is to be used for the upkeep of the cemetery. If there be any surplus, it is to be devoted to religious and charitable purposes according to the judgment of the Ordinary. Never under any pretext and without the permission of the Ordinary are ecclesiastics to dare to make their own money accruing from the cemetery. Those attempting to do so are to be punished.

As there is no corresponding law in the Code, this statute of Baltimore continues to be our rule regarding the use of the proceeds from cemetery lots.

Article 4

The Care of Cemeteries

Third Plenary Council

319. Demum omnes ecclesiarum rectores graviter monemus, ipsis veram incumbere obligationem de coemeteriis Catholicis rite et decenter custodiendis, ne ex eorum conditione sordida aut neglecta fideles justam conquerendi causam habeant, et suorum corpora in eis tumulare aversentur.

Code

Canon 1210

Quodlibet coemeterium sit undique apte clausum et caute custoditum.

Canon 1211

Caveant Ordinarii locorum, parochi ac Superiores, ad quos spectat, ne in coemeteriis epitaphia, laudationes funebres ornatusque monumentorum quidquam prae se ferant a catholica religione ac pietate absonum.

The Second Plenary Council in number 319 states that Pastors have a real obligation to see that the cemetery is in good condition, so that the faithful may not have just reason for complaint regarding its untidy and unkempt appearance, and for refusal to be buried there.

There is no such specific law on the care of cemeteries in the Code. Canon 1210 provides merely for its being fittingly enclosed and aptly guarded and canon 1211 orders the exclusion of epitaphs, inscriptions and ornaments discordant with Catholic faith and piety.

The Baltimore law is a fitting supplement to the general law and continues in force as a reminder to the parish clergy of this important obligation.

TITLE II

Holydays of Obligation

SECOND PLENARY COUNCIL

382. Principio autem ut de iis, quae ad Ecclesiae praecepta pertinent, loquamur, maximopere dolendum est tantum inter nos in Festis ac Jejuniis observandis discrepantiam inveniri. Aliquibus enim in locis Festa septem vel octo; in aliis vero quatuor tantum celebrantur. Jejunii quoque, praesertim Quadragesimalis, diversa est pro locorum diversitate observantia. Haud difficile quidem esset, Festorum numerum ad minimum reducendo, et indulgentiorem, quae se offerat, jejunandi rationem sectando, uniformitatem quandam inducere. Sed summopere cavendum est, ne falsa uniformitatis specie magis difformes ab universali Ecclesia reddamur.

383. Patribus visum est festos dies, quales nunc in unaquaque Provincia servantur, esse retinendos. Festum tamen Patronale Beatae Mariae Virginis sine labe Conceptae, tanquam festum de praecepto, ipso die Decembris octavo, per has Provincias ubique celebretur. Quod ad Provincias S. Francisci atque Oregonensem et Dioecesim Sanctae Fidei attinet, Sanctam Sedem orandam esse censemus, ut pro quinque illis festis diebus, quibus a Baltimorensi Provincia discrepant, concedatur dispensatio quoad praeceptum Missam audiendi et ab operibus servilibus abstinendi, non tamen quoad devotionem et solemnitatem externam. Supplicandum quoque duximus, ut S. Sedis auctoritate iisdem liceat se Baltimorensi Provinciae in servandis jejunii diebus conformare.

THIRD PLENARY COUNCIL

111. Hinc ad salutem animarum per majorem uniformitatem in festis promovendam, Patribus visum est Apostolicae Sedi supplices offerre preces ut ex omnibus festis apud nos jam vigentibus, illa tantum retineantur quorum observatio, attentis devotione fidelium et publicis moribus, felicius sperari potest. Talia autem videntur esse sex quae sequuntur:

Immaculata Conceptio B. M. V.;
Nativitas D. N. J. C.;
Circumcisio D. N. J. C.;
Ascensio D. N. J. C.;
Assumptio B. M. V.;
Festum Omnium Sanctorum.

Quoad reliqua vero ubi nunc sunt de praecepto, oranda est Sancta Sedes, ut quoad praeceptum missam audiendi et a laboribus servilibus abstinendi, non tamen quoad devotionem et solemnitatem externam, supprimantur et supradicti sex dies festi, omnes et soli, per omnes has provincias de praecepto servandi esse declarentur.

CODE

CANON 1247

§ 1. Dies festi sub praecepto in universa Ecclesia sunt tantum: Omnes et singuli dies dominici, festa Nativitatis, Circumcisionis, Epiphaniae, Ascensionis et sanctissimi Corporis Christi, Immaculatae Conceptionis et Assumptionis Almae Genitricis Dei Mariae, sancti Ioseph eius sponsi, Beatorum Petri et Pauli Apostolorum, Omnium denique Sanctorum.

§ 2. Ecclesiastico praecepto dies festi Patronorum non subiacent; locorum autem Ordinarii possunt sollemnitatem exteriorem transferre ad dominicam proxime sequentem.

§ 3. Sicubi aliquod festum ex enumeratis legitime sit abolitum vel translatum, nihil inconsulta Sede Apostolica innovetur.

The Fathers of the Second Plenary Council in number 382 expressed their regret at the lack of uniformity in the American Church regarding holydays, and in number 383 they determined that each diocese shall continue to observe its own special feasts, but they decided to ask the Holy See to dispense the provinces of San Francisco, Oregon and Santa Fe from the precepts of assisting at Mass and abstaining from servile work, not, however, from the liturgical solemnity on those feasts which they did not have in common with the province of Baltimore.

To this request the Sacred Congregation of the Propagation of the Faith replied on January 24, 1868 that the conformity of those three provinces with that of Baltimore in the observance of feasts was desirable, but that the Bishops concerned should send their own petitions for dispensation together with their reasons for asking it.[7]

The Fathers of the Third Council in number 111 determined to petition the Apostolic See for the sake of uniformity to limit the feasts or precept for this country to the following and only the following: Christmas, the Feast of the Circumcision, the Ascension, the Assumption, the Immaculate Conception and the Feast of All Saints.

This request was granted by an indult of December 31, 1885.[8]

The Code in canon 1247, § 1 gives the list of holydays for the universal Church. We continue to observe only the above-named feasts in virtue of our indult and canon 1247, § 3 which states that, if any-

[7] *Conc. Plen. Balti. II Acta et Decreta*, p. cxlv, No. XI.

[8] *Conc. Plen. Balti. III Acta et Decreta*, p. cv.

where any of the feasts mentioned in the canon have been legitimately abolished or transferred, no change is to be made without consulting the Holy See.

TITLE III

Fast and Abstinence

SECOND PLENARY COUNCIL

382. Principio autem ut de iis, quae ad Ecclesiae praecepta pertinent, loquamur, maximopere dolendum est tantum inter nos in Festis ac Jejuniis observandis discrepantiam inveniri. Aliquibus enim in locis Festa septem vel octo; in aliis vero quatuor tantum celebrantur. Jejunii quoque, praesertim Quadragesimalis, diversa est pro locorum diversitate observantia. Haud difficile quidem esset, Festorum numerum ad minimum reducendo, et indulgentiorem, quae se offerat, jejunandi rationem sectando, uniformitatem quandam inducere. Sed summopere cavendum est, ne falsa uniformitatis specie magis difformes ab universali Ecclesia reddamur.

383. Patribus visum est festos dies, quales nunc in unaquaque Provincia servantur, esse retinendos. Festum tamen Patronale Beatae Mariae Virginis sine labe Conceptae, tanquam festum de praecepto, ipso die Decembris octavo, per has Provincias ubique celebretur. Quod ad Provincias S. Francisci atque Oregonensem et Dioecesim Sanctae Fidei attinet, Sanctam Sedem orandam esse censemus, ut pro quinque illis festis diebus, quibus a Baltimorensi Provincia discrepant, concedatur dispensatio quoad praeceptum Missam audiendi et ab operibus servilibus abstinendi, non tamen quoad devotionem et solemnitatem externam. Supplicandum quoque duximus, ut S. Sedis

CODE

CANON 1250

Abstinentiae lex vetat carne iureque ex carne vesci, non autem ovis, lacticiniis et quibuslibet condimentis etiam ex adipe animalium.

CANON 1251

§ 1. Lex ieiunii praescribit ut nonnisi unica per diem comestio fiat; sed non vetat aliquid cibi mane et vespere sumere, servata tamen circa ciborum quantitatem et qualitatem probata locorum consuetudine.

§ 2. Nec vetitum est carnes ac pisces in eadem refectione permiscere; nec serotinam refectionem cum prandio permutare.

CANON 1252

§ 1. Lex solius abstinentiae servanda est singulis sextis feriis.

§ 2. Lex abstinentiae simul et ieiunii servanda est feria quarta Cinerum, feriis sextis et sabbatis Quadragesimae et feriis Quatuor Temporum, pervigiliis Pentecostes, Deiparae in caelum assumptae, Omnium Sactorum et Nativitatis Domini.

§ 3. Lex solius ieiunii servanda est reliquis omnibus Quadragesimae diebus.

§ 4. Diebus dominicis vel festis de praecepto lex abstinentiae, vel abstinentiae et ieiunii, vel ieiunii tantum cessat, excepto festo tempore Quadragesimae nec pervigilia anticipantur; item cessat Sabbato Sancto post meridiem.

auctoritate iisdem liceat se Baltimorensi Provinciae in servandis jejunii diebus conformare.

THIRD PLENARY COUNCIL

112. Quod vero ad jejunia attinet, difficilius adhuc esset in eis uniformitatem obtinere. Aliis enim in locis obstat climatis asperitas, in aliis escae esurialis caritas, in aliis demum diversi incolarum mores et consuetudines. Satius ideo videtur ut relinquatur judiciis Episcoporum ea statuere in synodis provincialibus quae suis provinciis magis in Domino judicaverint expedire.

CANON 1253

His canonibus nihil immutatur de indultis particularibus, de votis cuiuslibet personae physicae vel moralis, de constitutionibus ac regulis cuiusvis religionis vel instituti approbati sive virorum sive mulierum in communi viventium etiam sine votis.

CANON 1254

§ 1. Abstinentiae lege tenentur omnes qui septimum aetatis annum expleverint.

§ 2. Lege ieiunii adstringuntur omnes ab expleto vicesimo primo aetatis anno ad inceptum sexagesimum.

The Third Provincial was the first of our local Councils to ask special concessions in the matter of fast and abstinence. In their tenth decree the Fathers determined to request the Holy See that, in view of the diversity of discipline in this country, we be granted a general dispensation from fasting on the Fridays of Advent and from both fast and abstinence on the Wednesdays of this ecclesiastical season.

The answer of the Sacred Congregation of the Propagation of the Faith, dated September 2, 1837 made no mention of the Friday fast, but granted the requested dispensation from the fast and abstinence on the Wednesdays of Advent.[9]

As in the case of holydays the Fathers of the Second Plenary Council in number 382 expressed their regret at the lack of uniformity here regarding fasting. The Fathers in number 383 decided to petition the Holy See to grant to the provinces of San Francisco, Oregon and Santa Fe such dispensations as would bring them into conformity with the province of Baltimore in the matter of fast days as of holydays. The answer of the Sacred Congregation to this was the same as to the other request, namely, that uniformity was desirable,

[9] *Conc. Prov. Balti. Habita*, p. 150.

but that the Bishops of the three provinces concerned should send their own petitions with the reasons prompting them.[10]

The Fathers further asked for a general dispensation from the law of abstinence from flesh meat on the Saturdays of the year.[11] To this, likewise, the Sacred Congregation answered that each individual Bishop who thought he needed such an indult should personally apply to the Holy See, setting forth the reasons for his request.[12]

So our Ordinaries were obliged to continue to send separate petitions for exemption from this law which were usually granted as indults for a twenty-year period, and the disparity of observance continued.[13]

On January 20, 1880 Pope Leo XIII granted our Bishops for ten years the faculty of dispensing each year from the Saturday abstinence.[14]

The Fathers of the Third Council confronted by this lack of conformity decided in number 112 to leave the matter to the judgment of the Bishops of the individual provinces to decide in Council what, before God, they considered expedient.

The first important indult regarding fast and abstinence granted to this country was that of December 11, 1878 in favor of soldiers and sailors, by which they have permission to eat flesh meat on any day of the year except Ash Wednesday, the vigils of Christmas and the Assumption, and the last three days of Holy Week. This privilege was extended also to their families provided they were living together [15] and was without time limit.

In answer to a petition of the late Cardinal Gibbons on behalf of the American Hierarchy we were granted on August 3, 1887 our second important general indult in this matter.[16] This is called the *Quadragesimal* Indult because it refers to the Lenten abstinence.[17]

[10] Instr. of Jan. 24, 1868—*Conc. Plen. Balti. II Acta et Decreta*, p. cxlv, No. XI.

[11] *Conc. Plen. Balti. II Acta et Decreta*, p. 199.

[12] *Conc. Plen. Balti. II Acta et Decreta*, p. cxlv, No. X.

[13] Sabetti-Barrett, *op. cit.*, 22. ed., p. 296.

[14] Konings-Putzer, *op. cit.*, p. 297.

[15] *Conc. Plen. Balti II Acta et Decreta*, p. 343; *Eccl. Rev.*, LXII (1922), 311 and 312.

[16] Konings-Putzer, *op. cit.*, p. 295.

[17] Slater-Martin, *op. cit.*, I, 567.

According to this we were allowed in the first place the use of flesh meat, eggs and white meats during Lent at all meals on Sundays and at the principal meal, dinner, on Mondays, Tuesdays, Thursdays and Saturdays, except the Saturdays of Ember Week and those of Holy Week. The eating of fish and flesh meat at the same meal, however, was not permitted during Lent, even on Sundays. Secondly, eggs and white meats were permitted at dinner and the evening collation,[18] on all days of Lent on which flesh meat was forbidden.

Thirdly, in the morning was permitted a small piece of bread and a drink of coffee, tea, chocolate or the like. Fourthly, where dinner could not be taken at mid-day, the collation was allowed in the morning and the dinner in the evening. Fifthly, lard or the fat of any animal was permitted in the preparation of food. Sixthly, those exempt from fasting were allowed the free use of flesh meat, eggs, and white meats on those days of Lent on which these were permitted to all.

The first two of these concessions were apparently granted without any time limit while the last four were for ten years.[19]

The third indult granted us in this matter was that of March 15, 1895 whereby our Bishops were given for ten years the faculty to dispense workingmen and their families from the law of abstinence on all days of the year except Fridays, Ash Wednesday, the last three days of Holy Week and the vigil of Christmas.[20]

The Code treats of fast and abstinence in canons 1250 to 1254. The absence of any mention herein of abstinence on the ordinary Saturdays of the year and of any special fast or abstinence during Advent *ipso facto* abrogated the former common laws that made all Saturdays days of abstinence and the Wednesdays of Advent days of fast and abstinence and the Fridays of this season days of fast in addition to the abstinence regularly observed on all Fridays of the year. We no longer, therefore, have need of indults in this matter, and those we formerly enjoyed have ceased.

Again, since the Code in canon 1250 allows eggs, white meats and

[18] The use of eggs and white meats at the evening collation was not expressly permitted but has been allowed by interpretation. (Cf. Slater-Martin, *op. cit.*, I, 568.)

[19] Konings-Putzer, *op. cit.*, p. 295.

[20] *Eccl. Rev.*, XII (1895), 425.

fats for seasoning on all days of abstinence, and canon 1252 in accordance with previous indults [21] no longer requires abstinence on Sundays, Mondays, Tuesdays and Thursdays of Lent, our indults in this respect, likewise are obsolete.

Finally, since canon 1251 *per se* does not forbid a small quantity of food in the morning and evening of fast days nor the interchange of dinner and the evening collation and by interpretation [22] the taking of the collation in the morning and the morning repast in the evening, these concessions of our *Quadragesimal* Indult have fallen into disuse.

In conclusion, our fast and abstinence regulations can be summed up by saying that we now follow the Code, except for the abovementioned concessions made to soldiers and sailors and in favor of workingmen and the fact that we observe abstinence on the Wednesdays instead of the Saturdays of Lent. The indult to the service men and that regarding the Wednesday abstinence during Lent granted, as they were, without any time limit persevere in virtue of canon 1253.[23] The one regarding workingmen we enjoyed by reason of recent renewals up to and including the year 1931.[24] Though there is no public document to substantiate it, it is understood on good authority that this indult was renewed for the year 1932 only and that henceforth it must be requested by each Ordinary individually.

Our most recent concession regarding fast and abstinence is the faculty granted on August 5, 1931 by Pope Pius XI for five years to all the Ordinaries of the United States. This faculty empowers our Bishops to dispense their subjects from the obligation of fasting and abstaining whenever a civil holiday occurs on a day on which either one or both of these obligations would normally bind.[25]

[21] Ayrinhac, *Administrative Legislation*, p. 111.
[22] Vermeersch-Creuzen, *op. cit.*, II, 331; Noldin, *op. cit.*, II, 704.
[23] Woywod, *Practical Commentary*, II, 56.
[24] *Eccl. Rev.*, LX (1919), 574; LXXX (1929), 187.
[25] *Eccl. Rev.*, LXXXVI (1932), 65.

CHAPTER VI

DIVINE WORSHIP

TITLE I

Exposition and Benediction of The Most Blessed Sacrament

SECOND PLENARY COUNCIL

375. Quapropter, quoniam Ecclesia lege communi non definivit, sed potius episcopis determinandum reliquit, quam frequenter, spectatis locorum circumstantiis populique fidelis indigentiis, Sanctissimum Sacramentum utiliter exponatur, Nos certo sperantes fore, ut cultus erga tantum tamque venerabile Sacramentum ad pietatem populi fidelis augendam, ejusque amorem in amantissimum Redemptorem nostrum magis magisque inflammandum permultum conferat, statuere decrevimus, ut solemnis Sanctissimi Sacramenti Expositio et Benedictio, consueto ritu stricte observato, in omnibus nostrae ditionis ecclesiis et in sacellis monasteriorum et communitatum religiosarum, saltem quandocunque debita cum solemnitate fieri poterit, singulis totius anni Dominicis diebus, festisque de praecepto, vel festis etiam primae et secundae classis non de praecepto, semel tantum in die, dari possit. Per octavam vero Corporis Domini licebit eam solemniter fieri tum in Missa solemni, tum in Vesperis, Benedictione iterato data. Licebit insuper solemnem Benedictionem dare bis in hebdomade tempore Quadragesimali, singulis pariter diebus sacrarum Missionum tempore, in festo Sanctissimi Cordis Jesu, et ubicumque fit devotio Quadraginta Horarum; et in aliis diebus ab Ordinario designatis. Quod si Ordini alicui religioso vel Societati Sancta Sedes aliquid amplius indulserit, illud omnino incolume esse volumus. Extra autem hujusmodi privilegium, de quo certum Ordinario exhibeatur documentum, nolumus Benedictionem dari vel Expositionem fieri, nisi prout supra, venia Ordinarii expressa, salvis etiam in omnibus S. Congreg. Rituum hac in re decretis.

CODE

CANON 1274

§ 1. In ecclesiis aut oratoriis quibus datum est asservare sanctissimam Eucharistiam, fieri potest expositio privata seu cum pyxide ex qualibet iusta causa sine Ordinarii licentia; expositio vero publica seu cum ostensorio die festo Corporis Christi et intra octavam fieri potest in omnibus ecclesiis inter Missarum sollemnia et ad Vesperas; aliis vero temporibus nonnisi ex iusta et gravi causa praesertim publica et de Ordinarii loci licentia, licet ecclesia ad religionem exemptam pertineat.

The Fathers of the Second Plenary Council in number 375 declare that Solemn Exposition and Benediction of the Most Blessed Sacrament will be lawful, provided the proper solemnity of the rite can be strictly observed, once on all Sundays and feasts of precept and even on feasts of the first and second class that are not of precept. During the octave of Corpus Christi it will be lawful to have solemn Exposition during both the solemn Mass and Vespers, followed in each case by Benediction. Moreover, it will be lawful to give solemn Benediction twice a week during Lent, every day during a Mission, on the feast of the Most Sacred Heart of Jesus, during Forty Hours' Devotion and on other days appointed by the Ordinary. Any further privilege granted by the Holy See to religious Orders or Societies is to remain unaffected. Outside of such a privilege, however, documentary proof of which is to be given to the Ordinary, there is to be no Benediction or Exposition without the express permission of the Bishop, as stated above. However, in all things, the decrees of the Sacred Congregation of Rites in this matter are to be observed.

The Code in canon 1274, §1 which no doubt refers to Benediction also decrees that public Exposition of the Most Blessed Sacrament (that is with the ostensorium) may be held in all churches on the feast of Corpus Christi and during the octave, both during Holy Mass and at Vespers. At other times a just and grave, particularly public, cause and the permission of the Ordinary are required even in churches belonging to exempt religious.

The two laws are in agreement as to the feast and octave of Corpus Christi. They differ, however, in that the Council gives a general permission for the days mentioned, while the Code leaves the matter to the judgment of the Ordinary. The Baltimore law, therefore, is abrogated and the clergy can no longer avail themselves of the liberty it grants as regards Exposition and Benediction unless they have the consent of their Ordinaries.

TITLE II

Forty Hours' Devotion

Second Plenary Council

376. Quoniam vero in nostris regionibus plura obstant, quominus omnia, quae Instructione Clementina praescribuntur ad amussim observari queant,

Sedem Apostolicam humillime supplicandam esse censemus, ut solemnem hunc ritum eadem forma peragendum, quâ Dioecesis Baltimorensis ex Summi Pontificis concessione jam utitur, reliqui omnes Ordinarii in suas possint dioeceses introducere, videlicet:

1.° Ut, durantibus temporum locorumque peculiaribus circumstantiis, in omnibus ecclesiis et publicis Oratoriis per universas hasce Provincias alternis vicibus, semel vel bis quotannis, prout Ordinariis satius in Domino visum fuerit, Sanctissimum publicae adorationi per triduum, in forma Quadraginta Horarum, exponi possit horis diurnis tantum, a mane usque ad vesperam, de nocte autem recondatur;

2.° Ut processionem omittere liceat, si commode fieri nequit, ita ut neque intra ambitum ecclesiae haberi valeat;

3.° Ut universi utriusque sexus Christifideles, qui illam ecclesiam, in qua Venerabile per tres dies expositum manebit, devote visitaverint, et inibi pias ad Deum preces per aliquod temporis spatium effuderint, indulgentiam septem annorum totidemque quadragenarum semel singulis hujusmodi diebus lucrari possint et valeant;

4.° Ut iis vero, qui confessi et sacra communione refecti ecclesiam visitaverint, in qua Sacra Eucharistia publico cultui exposita est, ibique pie oraverint, indulgentiam plenariam, semel per Expositionis triduum lucrandam, quae applicari possit animabus fidelium defunctorum, Sanctitas Sua benignissime concedere dignetur, ea tamen lege, ut Christi fideles ecclesiam praedictam unoquoque tridui die visitent;

5.° Ut omnia altaria illius ecclesiae, in qua alternatim fiet Expositio, privilegiata, durante Expositione, declarentur.

The Fathers of the Second Plenary Council in number 376 decided to petition the Holy See to allow all Ordinaries to introduce the devotion of Forty Hours as then being carried out in the diocese of Baltimore, namely, with Exposition during the day only; without procession, if this could not conveniently be held even within the church; with an indulgence of seven years and seven quarantines to be gained once a day by all who would visit the church in which the devotion is being held and there pray piously to God for some time; that the Pope grant a plenary indulgence to be gained once during the devotion by all who having gone to confession and received Holy Communion visit the church of Exposition and there pray piously; finally, that all the altars of the church of Exposition be declared privileged during the time of the devotion.

This request was granted on January 24, 1868[1] and continues in force by virtue of canon 4.

[1] *Conc. Plen. Balti. II Acta et Decreta*, p. cxlix, Decree IV.

TITLE III

Vespers

SECOND PLENARY COUNCIL

379. Vesperae integrae ut decantentur, diebus Dominicis Festisque in omnibus ecclesiis, more Ecclesiae Romanae, quatenus fieri potest, volumus et mandamus. Atque hae quidem nunquam omittendae sunt ob alia exercitia pietatis. Cultus enim solemnis Ecclesiae Pontificibus probatus, et per tot saecula vigens Deo gratior censendus est.

THIRD PLENARY COUNCIL

118. Demum, ut ubi vesperarum officium peragitur, vesperae integrae id est psalmis non decurtatis, decantentur.

The Second Plenary Council in number 379 commands that, as far as possible, the entire Vespers be sung in all churches on Sundays and feasts after the manner of Rome and that these be not omitted on account of some other exercises of piety.

The Third Plenary Council orders that, when Vespers are sung, they be sung entirely, that is, without any curtailing of the psalms.

There is nothing specific in the Code regarding Vespers, but the above two Baltimore decrees are in harmony with the approved liturgy of the Church [2] and still bind.

TITLE IV

Zeal and Doctrine

ARTICLE 1

Prayers

SECOND PLENARY COUNCIL

399. Si vero aliquando, ob publicas calamitates vel necessitates, preces vernaculo sermone recitari in fidelium coetibus visum fuerit, id nonnisi statuente Ordinario fiat, eaeque tantum adhibeantur orandi formulae quas ipse praefinierit. Idem et de diebus pro gratiarum actione a Civili Magistratu designatis statuimus.

The Second Plenary Council in number 399 orders that, if on account of some public calamity or necessity it seems proper to say

[2] *Caerimoniale Episcoporum,* Lib. II, cap. I-III.

some vernacular prayers at gatherings of the faithful, this be done only at the Ordinary's command and by the use of such prayers as he designates. The same applies to days of thanksgiving appointed by the civil authority.

The Code contains no law that touches on this matter so the decree of the Council remains in force as something *praeter codicem.*

Article 2

The Indian and Negro Missions

Third Plenary Council

243. In universis harum regionum dioecesibus quotannis, prima Quadragesimae Dominica, collecta fiat, et summa inde proveniens mittatur ad commissionem pro missionibus domesticis instituendam. Hoc vero modo distributio fiet. Pecunia ex hac collecta primae Dominicae Quadragesimae derivata in dioecesibus, ubi Societas pii Operis de Propagatione Fidei jam existit, tota impendatur a commissione in juvandis Indorum et Nigrorum missionibus. Quod vero in illa collecta confertur a dioecesibus, ubi nondum existit illa societas, dispertiatur in duas partes, quarum una Lugdunum transmittatur, altera pro Indorum et Nigrorum missionibus retineatur.

Commissio autem sic constituatur. Revdmus. Archiepiscopus Baltimorensis adsciscat sibi duos ex Episcopis, quorum dioeceses hujusmodi ope non indigent. Eligant deinde secretarium sacerdotem, clericum puta ex pio clericorum S. Sulpitii instituto, qui quotannis ad Episcopos universos plane referet de collectis acceptis deque modo quo pecuniae omnes expensae fuerint. Etiam Episcopi qui de his collectis participant, singulis annis ad commissionem referent de numero Indorum et Nigrorum in suis dioecesibus, deque eorum statut spirituali, et de ceteris quae ipsorum judicio utiliter commissioni significari possunt aut debent.

The Third Plenary Council in number 243 decrees that on the first Sunday of Lent there be taken up in every diocese a collection the proceeds from which are to be sent to the Commission in charge of home missions.

The Commission is to be established according to the following method: The Archbishop of Baltimore is to associate with himself two Bishops whose dioceses are not in need of the collection in question. These in turn are to appoint from among the priests of St. Sulpice a secretary whose duty it will be to send each year to all the Bishops of the United States a detailed report of the results of the collection and the amounts expended.

To this Commission the Bishops who share in these expenditures are required to report the number and the spiritual condition of the Indians and Negroes in their dioceses and whatever else concerning them they may consider useful.

Regarding the proceeds of this collection in the individual dioceses, the Council decrees that where the Society of the Propagation of the Faith has been established, the full amount is to be sent to the Commission to aid the Indian and Negro Missions; while in those dioceses in which the former Society has not yet been introduced the collection is to be divided into two parts, one of which is to be sent to the Society of the Propagation of the Faith and the other to the Indian and Negro Missions.

This obligation towards the Indian and Negro Missions is obviously *praeter codicem* and hence continues to bind.

According to the present arrangement, which has the approval of the Holy See, sixty percent of the proceeds accruing from ordinary memberships in the Society of the Propagation of the Faith is given to the Foreign Missions while the remaining forty percent is devoted to the Home Missions. Of the mission collection taken up annually in our churches fifteen per cent goes to the Near East Relief, and of the balance sixty percent goes to the Foreign Missions and forty percent to the Home Missions.

TITLE V

Church Music

Second Plenary Council

361. Ut omnia juxta ordinem fiant, et solemnes Ecclesiae ritus integri serventur, monemus rectores ecclesiarum ut sedulo invigilent ad abusus eliminandos qui in cantu ecclesiastico in his regionibus invaluerunt. Curent igitur ut sacrosancto Missae Sacrificio et aliis divinis officiis musica, non vero musicae divina officia inserviant. Noverint, juxta Ecclesiae ritum, carmina vernaculo idiomate, inter Missarum solemnia, vel vesperas solemnes, decantare non licere.

Third Plenary Council

117. Praecepta itaque ac monita Patrum atque Summorum Pontificum attendentes, et decretum Plenarii Concilii Baltimorensis II. (No. 361.) renovantes, monemus pastores omnes ut sedulo invigilent ad eliminandos abusus qui in musica aut cantu in ecclesiis suis irrepere potuerunt. Insuper iisdem pastoribus, dum revocamus in mentem munus ipsis impositum dirigendi selectionem musicae in suis ecclesiis, districte mandamus ut nunquam tolerent templum Dei profanis melodibus resonare; et nonnisi eum cantum in illo admittant qui sit gravis, pius et vere ecclesiasticus. In eumdem finem praecipimus ut in missa cantus ille prorsus excludatur qui verba liturgiae mutilet, aut nimia repetione iteret, aut ita transponat ut significatio eorum totaliter vel quadantenus immutetur.

118. Praeterea volumus et mandamus ut cantus ea ratione moderetur, qua nonnisi ubi rubricae sinunt, missae cursus interrumpatur. Item, ut musica, quantum fieri potest, cum temporum varietate et cum qualitate festorum plane concordet.

Code

Canon 1264

§ 1. Musicae in quibus sive organo aliisve instrumentis sive cantu lascivum aut impurum aliquid misceatur, ab ecclesiis omnino arceantur; et leges liturgicae circa musicam sacram serventur.

The subject of Church music is treated brieby by the Second Plenary Council in number 361 and more at length by the Third in numbers 114 to 119.

The Second Council confirms and again promulgates number 8 of the Third Provincial Council which decrees that Rectors of churches are warned sedulously to see to the elimination of the abuses which have crept into ecclesiastical chant in this country. They are, therefore, to have the music subservient to the Divine Offices and not vice versa. Their attention is called to the fact that according to the rite of the Church it is not lawful during solemn Mass and solemn Vespers to sing hymns in the vernacular.

Renewing this decree the Fathers of the Third Plenary Council in number 117 remind Pastors of their duty of selecting the music for their churches and strictly command them never to tolerate profane melodies in the temple of God and to allow only that which is profound, pious and truly ecclesiastical. To attain this end they order further the exclusion from Mass of such singing as mutilates the words of the liturgy, repeats too much or so transposes the words that the meaning is totally or to a great extent destroyed.

The same Council in number 118 further commands that the singing be so controlled that the Mass will be interrupted only where the rubrics permit it; and, moreover, that the music be as much as possible in keeping with the ecclesiastical season and the dignity of the feast.

These laws are in keeping with an Instruction on Church music issued to the Archbishop of Baltimore by the Sacred Congregation of the Propagation of the Faith on June 22, 1884.[3]

The Code touches on this subject in canon 1264, § 1 where it orders absolutely excluded from the church all music in which there is any admixture of the lascivious and the voluptuous either in playing or singing; and requires the observance of the liturgical laws concerning sacred music.

The Councils are in complete accord with the liturgical laws referred to in the Code and which are to be found chiefly in the *Motu Proprio* of Pope Pius X issued on November 22, 1903.[4]

In further explanation of the mind of the Holy See on this matter the Sacred Congregation of Rites issued a decree to the Archbishop of Los Angeles in Mexico on January 17, 1908[5] and another to the Archbishop of New York on December 18 of the same year.[6]

In order further to impress upon the whole Church the importance of the liturgy and liturgical music in divine worship Pope Pius XI on December 20, 1928 published the Apostolic Constitution, "*Divini cultus sanctitatem.*" The strength and permanency of the binding force of this document on both the clergy and laity is evident from its very form. The main points considered by the Constitution are the instruction in sacred music from youth particularly in the case of future priests, the course of chant and sacred music in the seminary, the duties of those in charge of choirs and congregational singing.[7]

Finally, in the Apostolic Constitution, "*Deus scientiarum Dominus,*" of May 24, 1931 Pope Pius XI outlines the work to be done in universities by the Pontifical Institute of Sacred Music.[8]

[3] *Coll. de Prop. Fide,* 1621.
[4] *Coll. de Prop. Fide,* 2182.
[5] *Decr. Auth.,* 4210.
[6] *A. A. S.,* I (1909), 175.
[7] *A. A. S.,* XXI (1929), 33.
[8] *A. A. S.,* XXIII (1931), 241.

CHAPTER VII

THE TEACHING AUTHORITY OF THE CHURCH

TITLE I

Preaching

SECOND PLENARY COUNCIL

128. Ii qui curam animarum habent, caeterique, qui ad praedicandi munus assumuntur, debent non solum dominicis et festis diebus, verum etiam "tempore jejuniorum Quadragesimae et Adventus Domini quotidie, vel saltem tribus in hebdomada diebus, si ita oportere duxerit Episcopus, Sacras Scripturas, divinamque legem annuntiare; et alias quotiescumque id opportune fieri posse Episcopus judicaverit."

THIRD PLENARY COUNCIL

216. Postremo *assidua* sit verbi Dei praedicatio. Hinc Tridentini Patres jusserunt ut rectores animarum non solum dominicis et festis diebus solemnibus, verum etiam tempore jejuniorum Quadragesimae et Adventus Domini, quotidie, vel saltem tribus in hebdomada diebus, si ita oportere duxerit Episcopus, Sacras Scripturas, divinamque legem annuntient.

Efficacibus remediis tanto malo occurrere cupientes, praecipimus, ut diebus dominicis et festis solemnibus, etiam aestivo tempore, omnes qui curam habent animarum, per se aut, si legitime impediti fuerint, per alios idoneos inter celebrationem omnium omnino missarum quibus adstant fideles, sive illae missae sint cantatae, sive privatae, vel etiam valde mane celebrentur, Evangelium diei occur-

CODE

CANON 1332

Diebus dominicis aliisque festis de praecepto, ea hora quae suo iudicio magis apta sit ad populi frequentiam, debet insuper parochus catechismum fidelibus adultis, sermone ad eorum captum accommodato, explicare.

CANON 1344

§ 1. Diebus dominicis ceterisque per annum festis de praecepto proprium cuiusque parochi officium est, consueta homilia, praesertim intra Missam in qua maior soleat esse populi frequentia, verbum Dei populo nuntiare.

§ 2. Parochus huic obligationi nequit per alium habitualiter satisfacere, nisi ob iustam causam ab Ordinario probatam.

§ 3. Potest Ordinarius permittere ut sollemnioribus quibusdam festis aut etiam, ex iusta causa, aliquibus diebus dominicis concio omittatur.

CANON 1345

Optandum ut in Missis quae, fidelibus adstantibus, diebus festis de praecepto in omnibus ecclesiis vel oratoriis publicis celebrantur, brevis Evangelii aut alicuius partis doctrinae christianae explanatio fiat; quod si loci Ordinarius id praeceperit, opportunis datis instructionibus, hac lege tenentur non solum sacerdotes e clero saeculari, sed etiam religiosi,

rentis lingua vernacula distincte legant, atque si tempus patiatur, per duodecimam horae partem, populum in lege Domini erudiant, omni consuetudine aut praetextu in contrarium non obstante. Quod si quis obstinate neglexerit, ab Ordinario severe puniatur. Sermo vero proprie dictus habeatur in missa ultima quae apud nos missa communitatis sive parochialis reputatur.

exempti quoque, in suis ipsorum ecclesiis.

Canon 1346

§ 1. Curent locorum Ordinarii ut tempore Quadragesimae, itemque, si id expedire visum fuerit, tempore Adventus, in ecclesiis cathedralibus et paroecialibus sacrae conciones frequentius ad fideles habeantur.

§ 2. Canonici aliique de Capitulo huic concioni, si in propria ecclesia continuo post chorum habeatur, interesse tenentur, nisi iusto impedimento detineantur; et illos Ordinarius, poenis quoque adhibitis, ad id adigere potest.

Both the Second and Third Plenary Councils deal at length with the subjects of preaching, the former devoting to it numbers 127 to 146 and the latter numbers 214 to 216. For the most part this is mere pastoral advice on the importance of this duty and the manner of discharging it. Of positive legislation there is comparatively little.

The Second Council in numbers 128 decrees that priests in care of souls have the obligation to preach the Holy Scripture and the Divine law not only on Sundays and holydays throughout the year, but every day or at least three times a week during Lent and Advent according to the judgment of the Bishop.

The part of this decree dealing with Lenten and Advent sermons is given as a direct quotation from the Council of Trent,[1] while the first part, though not in quotation marks, expresses the spirit of this same Council.

The Third Plenary Council in number 216 repeats practically verbatim the above decree of the Second, but only as being the command of the Fathers of Trent and not as a local statute. It would seem from a study of these decrees of the two local Councils that the former intended to enact a local statute in the words of the then existing common law, while the latter intended only to call attention to the common law obligation without making it of particular binding force. The Code in canon 1344 orders the Pastors to preach

[1] Sess. XXIV, de Ref., cap. 4.

the customary homily during the Mass that is usually best attended on Sundays and holydays of obligation throughout the year, and specifies that this pastoral duty cannot be habitually fulfilled through another without a just cause approved by the Ordinary. It states, however, that the Ordinary may allow the omission of a sermon on certain of the more solemn feasts and for good reasons also on some Sundays.

According to canon 1332 the Pastor must give catechetical instructions to the adults in discourses suited to their capacity on Sundays and other feasts of obligation at an hour which he judges most convenient for their attendance.

Canon 1345 states that it is to be desired that, in all churches and public oratories where people assist at Mass on Sundays and holydays of obligation, a short explanation of the Gospel or of some point of Christian doctrine be given to the people.

Finally, canon 1346 decrees that local Ordinaries shall take care that during Lent and also during Advent, if they judge it useful, more frequent sermons are given in the Cathedral and parochial churches.

In view of the fact that the Third Council superseded the Second and that its law-makers evidently did not intend to enact a separate local statute, but merely to have the common law enforced, it seems legitimate to conclude that the spirit of the Baltimore law is fulfilled now by following the Code.

This latter would replace the above decrees even though they were certainly particular laws since it agrees with the Baltimore statute as regards Sundays and holydays while giving to Ordinaries in the matter of Lenten and Advent sermons a greater liberty then they formerly enjoyed under the old law.

The Fathers of the Third Plenary Council in number 216, after expressing regret that a number of the faithful almost never hear the word of God because they do not attend the parochial Mass on Sundays, decrees that in spite of any custom or pretext to the contrary all having the care of souls must themselves, or if legitimately prevented, through others, read the Gospel in the vernacular and if time permit, instruct the people for five minutes in the law of God at every Mass at which the faithful assist on Sundays and holydays even during the Summer and this whether the Masses are sung, private, or even very early in the morning.

The Code in canon 1345, referred to above, states that it is to be desired that in all churches and public oratories where people assist at Holy Mass on Sundays or holydays of obligation, a short explanation of the Holy Gospel or of some point of Christian doctrine be given. If the local Ordinary has issued orders concerning this matter, they must be obeyed not only by the secular clergy but also by the religious, even exempt, in their own churches.

The above decree of the Council is not only in no wise opposed to the Code but is amply provided for by it and, therefore, remains in force.

TITLE II

The Teaching of Catechism

Second Plenary Council

442. Omnibus animarum curam gerentibus in Domino injungimus, ut saltem quater unoquoque anno, et praesertim, si fieri possit, Quatuor Temporum feriis, pueros omnes spirituali ipsorum regimini commissos, qui nondum S. Eucharistiae participes facti sunt, in unum colligant, et per aliquot dies Doctrinam Christianam diligenter edoceant. Eos, qui ad septennium pervenerint, ad Confessionem accedere curent; qui vero id aetatis attigerint, ut Panem coelestem discernere valeant, ad primam Communionem, omni adhibita diligentia, disponantur.

Third Plenary Council

217. Ad rectores animarum spectat per seipsos pascere gregis sui agnos. Patris nomine prorsus indignus foret ille, qui filio fame pereunti panem frangere inique recusaret. Volumus ergo, ut rectores ecclesiarum vel eorum vicarii saepius adeant dominicis diebus scholas catechismi, ferialibus autem parochiales, ac etiam collegia seu gymnasia et academias puerorum et puellarum quae a sacerdotibus non reguntur. Praeceptores sacerdotali charactere non insigniti, sive religiosi sive laici, magno equidem sunt adjumento in juvenum institutione, at munus verbi Dei docendi sibi proprium non habent. "Labia enim sacerdotis custodient scientiam, et legem requirent ex ore ejus." (Mal. II. 7.)

218. Jubemus ergo ut parvulorum curam assiduam habeant animarum rectores, praesertim quo tempore parantur ad sacram synaxim prima vice recipiendam, et quidem ut ipsimet rectores vel eorum vicarii praedictos parvulos saltem per sex hebdomadas et ter in unaquaque hebdomada (saltem in loco ubi resident vel ad quem facilius accedere possunt), catechismum doceant. Nemo ad confirmationis susceptionem admittatur, quin diligenter

instruatur de iis, quae ad naturam effectumque hujus sacramenti spectant. Episcopum itaque, confirmationem adolescentibus collaturum hortamur ut confirmandos sive per se sive presbyterum in doctrina Christiana examinet. Satagant insuper rectores, ut pueri puellaeque post primam suam communionem per duos subsequentes annos Catholicam doctrinam suaque munera Christiana melius edoceantur.

219. Re igitur mature perpensa statuimus ut comitatus instituatur Rmorum. Episcoporum quorum erit: 1° Catechismum seligere et si opus fuerit emendare, aut de novo exarare, prout magis necessarium et opportunum aestimaverint. 2° Opus suum ita perfectum ad coetum Rmorum. Archiepiscoporum remittere qui denuo catechismum recognoscent, et typis accurate mandari curabunt. Hoc catechismo in lucem edito quamprimum uti teneantur omnes animarum curam habentes, et praeceptores tam religiosi quam laici.

CODE

CANON 1329

Proprium ac gravissimum officium, pastorum praesertim animarum, est catecheticam populi christiani institutionem curare.

CANON 1330

Debet parochus:

1.° Statis temporibus, continenti per plures dies institutione, pueros ad sacramenta poenitentiae et confirmationis rite suscipienda singulis annis praeparare;

2.° Peculiari omnino studio, praesertim, si nihil obsit, Quadragesimae tempore, pueros sic instituere ut sancte Sancta primum de altari libent.

The Second Plenary Council deals with the teaching of the Catechism in connection with its treatise on Parochial Schools.[2] Herein the Fathers insist on the importance of this work and on the fact that it is the personal duty of priests in care of souls.[3]

In number 442 they enjoin on those having the care of souls that at least four times a year for several days (particularly, if possible, during the Ember days) they assemble all those children who have not yet made their first Holy Communion for the purpose of instructing them diligently in Christian doctrine. Those who have attained the use of reason are to be prepared for confession and those old enough to make their first Communion are to be prepared for it.

The Third Plenary Council has a short chapter on this subject

[2] Tit. IX, Cap. I.

[3] No. 438.

including numbers 217 to 219. In number 217 this Council insists even more than did the preceding one that the teaching of Catechism is a personal duty of priests having the care of souls and states that this obligation cannot be entrusted entirely to religious or the laity.

In numbers 218 the Fathers order Pastors to care assiduously for the souls of children especially when they are preparing for their first Holy Communion. The Pastors themselves or their assistants are to give instructions in Catechism three times a week for at least six weeks before the children make their first Communion.

The Code in canon 1329 states that it is a proper and most serious duty especially of the Pastors of souls to provide for the Catechetical instruction of the Christian people. Canon 1330 states that the Pastors in the first place must at stated times each year prepare the children for the reception of the Sacraments of Penance and Confirmation by instructions over a number of days; and secondly they must with great diligence (preferably during lent if nothing stands in the way) so instruct the children that they may receive their first Holy Communion worthily.

The Code and the Councils are evidently in harmony and the latter, therefore, continues in force. The requirement of the Second Council that those having the care of souls gather the children at least four times a year, and that of the Third that Pastors or their assistants are to give the children instructions in Catechism three times a week for six weeks before their first Holy Communion, were legislated, no doubt, in view of the lack of parochial schools in many places. Where this condition continues, the letter of the law still binds. Where, however, there are parochial schools, the law would seem amply fulfilled provided the instruction is not left entirely to the sisters or brothers.

The Fathers of the Third Plenary Council in number 219 appointed a *Committee* to prepare a catechism which, after its approval by the Board of Archbishops, should become the official text-book that all those in care of souls and all teachers, both religious and lay, would be bound to use. Such a text-book, known as the Baltimore Catechism, was prepared but has never obtained the universal recognition expected. Because of its use of theological rather than popular language, it is considered too technical.

Since the promulgation of the Code several documents on the teaching of Christian doctrine have been issued by the Holy See.

On May 31, 1920 the Congregation of the Council with the approval of Pope Benedict XV sent a circular letter to the Bishops of Italy inquiring about the enforcement of the legislation on the teaching of Christian doctrine. Herein the Ordinaries in question were asked to answer according to their knowledge and conscience and with the least possible delay the following questions:

(a) What, if any, measures have been taken to secure the execution of the decrees regarding the explanation of the Gospel to the people and the teaching of Catechism?

(b) Have any penalties been enacted by the Bishops against offenders?

(c) Do all Pastors and others having the care of souls in the diocese explain the Gospel to the people on all Sundays and holydays of obligation and teach Christian doctrine to adults on these days throughout the year without any interruption?

(d) Do all Pastors hold for children the confession, first Communion and Confirmation classes as prescribed and do they have the Confraternity of Christian Doctrine?

Finally, the Bishops were requested to give the names of offenders in this matter; state what means had been used to coerce them; what coöperation the secular and regular clergy had showed themselves willing to give and what reasons they had for refusing it if they did. The Congregation wished to know the names also of those thus refusing and the suggestions which Ordinaries might have to make for the future.[4]

By the *Motu Proprio, "Orbem Catholicum,"* of June 29, 1923 Pope Pius XI wishing to extend to the whole world the discipline inaugurated by Pope Benedict XV for Italy and, by calling the attention of all to this most important work, to excite and sustain the diligence and zeal of Prelates created in connection with the Congregation of the Council a special Office or Department with mission to look after everything that pertains to religious instruction. On this occasion the Pontiff invited the coöperation of the Bishops, clerics and laity. The members of pious sodalities particularly were

[4] *A. A. S.*, XII (1920), 299.

urged to be faithful in their attendance at and active in their interest in catechetical instruction. Finally, religious communities were asked to have in their principal schools special classes for the religious instruction of the young and the training of catechists.[5]

This special Office created by Pope Pius XI commenced in 1924 an investigation of existing conditions in regard to the teaching of religion in the different parts of the world. For this purpose it sent on June 24 to all Bishops a series of questions. These dealt in general with religious instruction in parishes, Catholic colleges and public schools and in particular with the time devoted to this instruction, the method followed, the results obtained, possible defects and their remedies and, finally, the number who should and actually do attend.[6]

Previously, on April 16, of the same year this Office issued a decree requiring that for the future it will not be lawful to organize national or provincial catechetical societies or other bodies for the teaching of religion in schools without having first sent to the Sacred Congregation of the Council an announcement of each organization together with an outline of the work to be done by it.

The same procedure is declared proper and much to be desired in the case also of diocesan catechetical organizations.[7]

On September 8, 1926 the Sacred Congregation of Seminaries and Universities addressed a letter to the Ordinaries of the world on the importance of training seminarians in the art of catechizing children and others.[8] The Sacred Congregation of Religious on November 25, 1929 issued an Instruction to the Superiors of lay religious engaged in teaching. The purport of this Instruction was the stressing of the obligation of these Superiors to see to the thorough training of their young aspirants in the knowledge of and the art of explaining Christian doctrine.[9]

At the request of the Catechetical Commission of the Holy Office Pope Pius XI in an Apostolic Letter of March 12, 1930 granted new

[5] *A. A. S.*, XV (1923), 327.

[6] *A. A. S.*, XVI (1924), 332.

[7] *A. A. S.*, XVI (1924), 431; can. 711, § 2.

[8] *A. A. S.*, XVIII (1926), 453; cf. also *A. A. S.*, XXIII (1931), 128, Mod. II, 4.

[9] *A. A. S.*, XXII (1930), 28.

Indulgences for those teaching or attending classes of Christian doctrine. These Indulgences replace those granted by Popes Paul V and Clement XII. The first of these is a plenary Indulgence to be gained twice a month on the days of their choice and under the usual conditions by those who spend at least twenty minutes a week in teaching or attending classes of Christian doctrine. The second is a partial Indulgence of one hundred days to be gained each time one with at least a contrite heart devotes as much as twenty minutes to the above-mentioned Catechetical work.[10]

TITLE III

Seminaries

Article 1

The Establishment of Seminaries

Third Plenary Council

139. Concilii Tridentini decreto Summorumque Pontificum monitis inhaerens, Concilium Plenarium Baltimorense II. hoc tulit decretum: "Valde etiam optamus, ut praeter majus * * * seminarium, aliud quod parvum aut praeparatorium vocant, in unaquaque dioecesi existat. Quod si nondum fieri possit, unum omnino pro unaquaque provincia constituatur. Non parva sane ex parvis hisce seminariis capitur utilitas. In iis enim adolescentuli certiora in dies indicia prodent, quinam clericali militiae adscribendi sint, quinam ab ea repellendi. Praeterea tenerrima puerorum aetatula a pravis exemplis et mundana conversatione tuta defenditur, dum doctrina et moribus se parant, idoneosque reddunt, qui in seminaria majora admittantur. Habent etiam hoc commodi, ut cum in iis ea omnia quae ad literas ac scientiam profanam pertinent doceantur, in majori-

Code

Canon 1354

§ 1. Unaquaeque dioecesis in loco convenienti ab Episcopo electo Seminarium seu collegium habeat in quo, pro modo facultatum et dioecesis amplitudine, certus adolescentium numerus ad statum clericalem instituatur.

§ 2. Curandum ut in maioribus praesertim dioecesibus bina constituantur Seminaria: minus, scilicet, pro pueris litterarum scientia imbuendis maius pro alumnis philosophiae ac theologiae vacantibus.

§ 3. Si constitui Seminarium dioecesanum nequeat, aut in constituto Seminario conveniens institutio, praesertim in philosophicis ac theologicis disciplinis, desideretur, Episcopus alumnos in alienum Seminarium mittat, nisi Seminarium interdioecesanum vel regionale, auctoritate apostolica, constitutum fuerit.

---

[10] *A. A. S.*, XXII (1930), 343.

bus Theologia tantum et disciplinae sacrae discendae supersint." (No. 175.) Cujus decreti executionem, quatenus opus sit, maxime urgemus.

From the beginning one of the paramount cares of our Bishops was the training of a native clergy. The Fathers of the Second Provincial Council [11] recommended the institution of diocesan seminaries and those of the First Plenary Council [12] advised that where this was not practical there be at least one seminary in each province.

The Second Plenary Council has a whole chapter including numbers 170 to 181 on Seminaries, and the Third devotes three full chapters embracing numbers 135 to 185 to the subject.

For the most part these decrees are repetitions of the common law of the Church and contain a great deal of positive law.

In numbers 174 and 175 the Fathers of the Second Plenary Council express strongly the desire that every diocese have its own theological and preparatory seminaries and command that where this is an impossibility there must be at least one of each in every province. In this they were in harmony with the Council of Trent which allowed several dioceses to unite in the erection of a common seminary.[13]

The Fathers of the Third Plenary Council in number 139 repeat these decrees and urge their execution.

Practically the same legislation is found in canon 1354 of the Code which requires, where possible, the erection of a major and minor seminary in every diocese. Where this cannot be done, the Bishop is to send his students to an outside seminary unless an inter-diocesan or regional one has been established with the authority of the Holy See. Under the present discipline interdiocesan or provincial seminaries need the approval of the Congregation of Seminaries and Universities which will define also the obligations of the various Bishops towards them.[14]

[11] No. 8.

[12] No. 14.

[13] Sess. XXIII, de Ref., Cap. XVIII.

[14] Ayrinhac, *Administrative Legislation*, p. 243.

Article 2

The Length of the Seminary Course

Third Plenary Council

145. Ad studiorum rationem ut jam gradum faciamus, in omnibus puerorum seminariis quae etiam Parva vel Praeparatoria vocantur, studiorum cursus non pauciores quam sex annos complectetur.

153. In quibusdam hujusce regionis locis ea adhuc obtinet agendi ratio, qua clerici tyrones, donec seminarium majus ingrediantur, in collegiis educantur in quibus crescunt ac instituuntur juvenes qui laicali statui destinantur. Equidem ejusmodi educationis ratio non omni ex parte Concilii Tridentini praescriptis respondet, juxta quae clerici instituendi sunt in seminariis in quibus omnia ad unicum clericalis educationis scopum diriguntur. Verum quum pro temporali necessitate, iisdem in locis seminaria pure ecclesiastica, in praesenti erigi aut sustentari non queant: indulgendum erit ut, quoad per subsidiorum tenuitatem meliori modo provideri non possit, in memoratis locis mixtae educationis rationem retinere liceat.

162. In delectu alumnorum, qui in majus seminarium admittendi sint, magna adhibenda erit sollertia in expendenda eorum vocatione, indole ac moribus; nemini pateat aditus, quin studiorum curriculum pro seminariis minoribus praescriptum, integre ac cum sufficienti successu absolverit.

166. In omnibus igitur seminariis majoribus, tam provincialibus quam dioecesanis aut privatis, sive a sacerdotibus saecularibus sive a religiosorum institutis regantur, studiorum curriculum non pauciores quam sex annos complectetur, quorum duo philosophicis disciplinis attribuendi, theologicis vere quatuor.

Code

Canon 1365

§ 1. In philosophiam rationalem cum affinibus disciplinis alumni per integrum saltem biennium incumbant.

§ 2. Cursus theologicus saltem integro quadriennio contineatur, et, praeter theologiam dogmaticam et moralem, complecti praesertim debet studium sacrae Scripturae, historiae ecclesiasticae, iuris canonici, liturgiae, sacrae eloquentiae et cantus ecclesiastici.

§ 3. Habeantur etiam lectiones de theologia pastorali, additis practicis exercitationibus praesertim de ratione tradendi pueris aliisve catechismum, audiendi confessiones, visitandi infirmos, assistendi moribundis.

The Third Plenary Council in number 145 prescribes that the course in the preparatory seminary should cover a period of no less than six years and in number 162 it decrees that this preparatory course is normally to be one of the conditions for admission into the major seminary. In number 153, however, it provides that, when attendance at preparatory seminaries is not possible, aspirants to the priesthood may be permitted to go to mixed colleges.

According to number 166 of the same Council the course in the major seminary is likewise to be six years.

The Code does not specify over how many years the preparatory course should extend, but in canon 1365 it requires for the major seminary at least six years, two of which are to be devoted to Philosophy and four to Theology.

The Code and the Council are in agreement, therefore, as regards the length of the course in the major seminary. The silence of the common law as to the number of years to be devoted to the preparatory course makes our local requirement of six years something *praeter codicem* and, hence still binding.

The Code does not make attendance at the minor seminary a necessary condition for admission into the major one, but it is the wish of the Holy See that youthful aspirants to the priesthood receive their early training in a preparatory seminary as is evident from canon 1354.

Article 3

The Programme of Studies for Seminaries

Third Plenary Council

147. Praeterea ex aliis linguis recentioribus unusquisque unam saltem colat, sive Germanicam, sive Gallicam, aut Polonicam aliamve e Slavicis linguis, vel Italicam, Hispanicamve, prout Episcopus pro dioecesis necessitate ordinaverit.

150. Denique in singulis minoribus seminariis scholam instituendam esse jubemus, qua ars tabulas accepti et expensi conficiendi (*Book-keeping*) eatenus tradatur ut futuri sacerdotes in administrandis bonis temporalibus codices accepti et expensi accurrate et juxta ordinem redigere sciant.

Code

Canon 1364

In inferioribus Seminarii scholis:

1.° Praecipuum locum obtineat religionis disciplina, quae, modo singulorum ingenio et aetati accommodato, diligentissime explicetur;

2.° Linguas praesertim latinam et patriam alumni accurate addiscant;

3.° Ea in ceteris disciplinis institutio tradatur quae conveniat communi omnium culturae et statui clericorum in regione ubi alumni sacrum ministerium exercere debent.

Canon 1365

§ 1. In philosophiam rationalem

171. Quandoquidem linguae Hebraicae quaedam cognitio et peritia non parum confert ad sacram exegesim pleniori et accuratiori ratione pertractandam, huic linguae addiscendae unum saltem annum, Philosophiae postremum aut Theologiae primum impendere omnes cogantur. (Conc. Plen. Balt. II., No. 178.)

cum affinibus disciplinis alumni per integrum saltem biennium incumbant.

§ 2. Cursus theologicus saltem integro quadriennio contineatur, et, praeter theologiam dogmaticam et moralem, complecti praesertim debet studium sacrae Scripturae, historiae ecclesiasticae, iuris canonici, liturgiae, sacrae eloquentiae et cantus ecclesiastici.

§ 3. Habeantur etiam lectiones de theologia pastorali, additis practicis exercitationibus praesertim de ratione tradendi pueris aliisve catechismum, audiendi confessiones, visitandi infirmos, assistendi moribundis.

Both the Second and Third Plenary Councils go considerably into detail regarding the matter that is to make up the course of studies in both the major and the minor seminary. The Second Council devotes to this numbers 166 to 178 and the Third numbers 146 to 152 and numbers 166 to 175. These decrees are for the most part directional. What there is of positive law is so fundamental and essential that it cannot but be fulfilled in every seminary. As compared to the common law as set forth in canons 1364 and 1365 the local statutes are in perfect harmony though more detailed. In three respects only are they *praeter codicem.* The first of these is in number 147 of the Third Council which requires in the minor seminary a course in one of the living languages other than English according to the needs of the respective dioceses. The second is found in number 150 of the same Council which orders emphatically for the preparatory seminary a course in book-keeping. The last of these is in number 171 of the Third Council which following number 178 of the Second requires at least one year of Hebrew during the second year of Philosophy or the first of Theology. These three special requirements being something apart from the Code and in no sense opposed to it continue in force for our seminaries.

Article 4

Admission to the Seminary

Third Plenary Council

152. Insuper mandamus, ut nullo loco horum Statuum in seminarium majus admittantur alumni, nisi ab examinatoribus facto scientiae periculo probentur. Hi examinatores poterunt esse examinatores synodales vel pro-synodales illius dioecesis in qua seminarium illud majus situm est.

176. "Experientia docet," ajunt Patres superioris Concilii Plenarii, "saepius evenire, ut alumni unius seminarii in aliud migrent, sive quia ad ministerium haud idonei judicantur, sive disciplinae severioris fuga, sive tandem ex animi inconstantia et levitate. Praecipimus igitur, ut nemo hujusmodi in posterum in seminarium quodvis admittatur, nisi secum afferat literas testimoniales ab Episcopo et superioribus seminarii ex quo recens egressus est. Quod si eum hactenus Episcopus ille aut superiores seminarii suis sumptibus aluerint, ex justitia recuperare debent ab Episcopo aut superioribus seminarii, ad quod transiit, tantum quantum in ipso educando impensum fuit" (No. 180), si nempe in alteram dioecesim adscribatur. Quae ut accurate serventur, et Nos mandamus.

Code

Canon 1363

§ 3. Dimissi ex aliis Seminariis vel ex aliqua religione ne admittantur, nisi prius Episcopus etiam secreta a Superioribus aliisve notitias requisierit de causa dimissionis, ac de moribus, indole et ingeno dimissorum, et certo compererit nihil in eis esse quod sacerdotali statui minus conveniat; quas notitias, veritati conformes, eorum conscientia graviter onerata, suppeditare Superiores debent.

The Third Plenary Council in number 152 orders that no one be admitted to a major seminary without an examination before the Synodal or pro-Synodal Examiners of the diocese in which the seminary is located.

There is no corresponding law in the Code so this local requirement continues to bind us as something *praeter codicem.*

The same Council in number 176 quoting and confirming number 180 of the Second orders that students from one seminary be not admitted to another unless they can show testimonial letters from the Bishop and the superiors of the seminary they have just left.

Should one join another diocese and his former Bishop or seminary superiors have supported him, they have a right in justice to recover from the adopting Bishop or the superiors of his seminary only the cost of the aspirant's education.

The Code in canon 1363, § 3 makes a like demand for students dismissed from other seminaries, but does not specifically require testimonials in the case of those changing seminaries of their own accord. In this respect the Council which makes no distinction is *praeter codicem* and therefore still in force. So the general practice of requiring some kind of a recommendation from those who freely change seminaries, is in this country not merely a matter of prudence, but of legal obligation.

Regarding the recovery of expenditures involved in a change of dioceses the Code is silent and so the right granted by our local law is *praeter codicem* and can continue to be appealed to.

Article 5

Prayer for Those to be Ordained

Third Plenary Council

181. Mandamus ut Dominicis diebus, qui Quatuor Temporum jejunia proxime antecedunt, parochi nedum solemne illud jejunium ordinationum causa institutum fideles moneant, sed et eosdem ad frequentandum iis diebus missae sacrificium, precesque devote persolvendas, atque jejunia Deo offerenda suaviter excitent, quo fiat ut Dei sanctorumque ope implorata, tum Episcopus in eorum delectu, quibus ordines conferat, Spiritus Sancti lumine illustretur, tum illi quibus conferendi erunt, tales evadant, quales Dei honor cultusque et Ecclesiae utilitas, immo necessitas postulant.

The Third Plenary Council in number 181 orders that on the Sundays immediately preceding the Ember days Pastors should not only solemnly warn the faithful that this fast was instituted because of ordinations, but also excite them to assist at Holy Mass during these days, pray devoutly, and generously offer up their fast to God that by His help and that of the Saints the Bishop in choosing those to be ordained may be enlightened by the Holy Ghost, and those receiving Orders may become such as the honor and worship of God and the utility and necessity of the Church demand.

This decree of Baltimore is *praeter codicem* and still in force.

Article 6

The Seminarian's Vacation

Third Plenary Council

177. Ne alumni clerici, ubi villae nondum institutae sunt, vacationum tempore, illum rectae institutionis fructum amittant, quem non sine magno suo et suorum moderatorum praeceptorumque labore acquisierunt, superiores accedente feriarum tempore sedulo eos instruant, qua ratione in omni modestia et sanctitate debeant inter consanguineos et concives versari; quae pericula fugere, ut immaculatos se custodiant ab hoc saeculo; quali occupatione animi recreationes temperare, ne otio torpeant, ex quo tot enascuntur vitia; quibus demum exercitiis pietatis quotidie incumbere, ut clementissimus Deus feriarum tempus benedicere dignetur, quo alumni post exantlatos labores quiete fruuntur. (Conc. Prov. Ultraject. a. 1863.) Parochis etiam praecipimus, ut alumnorum clericorum feriarum tempore intra paroeciam degentium vitae et moribus sedulo invigilent, quo possint de tota eorum agendi ratione testimonium reddere. Ipsi juvenes statim ab initio parocho se sistant ejusque directioni et curae se subjiciant. Ut jam incipiant apostolico muneri quodammodo proludere caritatis et zeli operibus sese exercendo, atque clericalis vitae officiis assuescant, parochus eosdem adhibeat in operibus ministerii quae ipsis competunt, in tradendis scilicet puerulis christianae fidei elementis, in chori officiis inserviendo, in ceterisque id generis ministeriis ad divini cultus honorem ecclesiarumque decentiam et ornatum pertinentibus. Finitis vacationibus, parochus, gravata ejus conscientia, tenetur clausis literis Episcopum aut seminarii superiorem, si Episcopus voluerit, informare de moribus alumnorum, de eorum vivendi ratione, de frequentatione sacramentorum et assiduitate in aliis functionibus sacris, ac de habitu qualis clericos alumnos decet ab iis retento. Hoc testimonium illius parochi esse debet cujus directioni et vigilantiae alumni subjecti erant; quod si is aliorum sacerdotum informationibus indigeat, ut certa ad Episcopum vel seminarii superiorem referre valeat, eas necessario requirat..

The Fathers of the Third Plenary Council in number 177 decree that, as long as it is impossible to have villas, the seminarians may spend their vacations at home. In order that there may be no spiritual deterioration during the time of vacation, as these days approach, the seminary superiors are to instruct the students diligently regarding their conduct toward their relatives and associates; the proper use of their time; and the providing for their spiritual exercises. In this same number the Fathers further order Pastors to watch carefully over the life and character of the clerics who spend their vacations in their parishes that they may give a full report of their conduct.

From the very beginning these youths are to place themselves under the direction and care of the Pastor. As a prelude to their Apostolic mission and to accustom them to clerical life the Pastor should employ them in such works of the ministry as they are capable of, such as instructing children in the rudiments of their faith, in serving at the altar and the like.

At the end of the vacation the Pastor must as a matter of conscience inform the Bishop or, if the latter desires, the superior of the seminary in a sealed letter, of the character and the conduct of the students; how they have frequented the Sacraments; how assiduous they have been in other sacred functions; and whether their dress was such as becomes a cleric.

This testimony is to be given by the Pastor under whose direction and vigilance the clerics have been and, if he needs information from other priests in order to report with certainty to the Bishop or seminary superior, he is obliged to seek it.

The Code says nothing about the vacation of seminarians. Therefore, that part of the local decree which refers to seminary superiors continues to bind as something *praeter codicem.* The report of the pastor required by the Council has, however, been replaced by the more concise one ordered by the Instruction of the Sacred Congregation of the Sacraments of December 27, 1930.[15]

This Instruction deals with the examination of a seminarian's vocation before his admission to Orders. For the purpose of eliminating the unworthy a most careful investigation is prescribed. This duty is imposed primarily upon the Bishop for whose diocese the candidate is to be ordained. It devolves also upon officials and professors and especially upon Rectors of seminaries. Furthermore, the Pastor of the candidate is directed to report whether or not there is reason to fear coercion, unworthy motives, mental defects, particularly of an hereditary nature, how the seminarian conducts himself during the vacations and what reputation he enjoys among the parishoners. Even the laity are in certain circumstances to be questioned. Finally, personal interviews with the seminarian are to be sought by the Bishop

[15] *A. A. S.*, XXIII (1931), 120.

and the Rector of the seminary in order to ascertain the candidate's fitness, worthiness and motives.

A complete investigation is to precede the reception of Tonsure and Minor Orders. Before Major Orders a further examination covering particularly the period since the last ordination is to be made.

The Instruction itself and the Appendix to it give complete details for its fulfillment.

The Sacred Congregation of Religious issued a correspondingly similar Instruction to the Superiors of clerical religious on December 1, 1931.[16]

Article 7

The University

Third Plenary Council

182. Quamobrem magnopere optandum est, ut hisce in Statibus praeclarum quoddam scientiae existeret centrum, in quo juvenes ingenio et virtute praevalentes, consueto studiorum absoluto cursu, disciplinis theologicis, vel juri canonico, aut philosophicis una cum naturalibus scientiis aliisque quae viros ecclesiasticos nostrates decent, tres quatuorve annos impendere possent, ita ut, seminario tali semel incepto, haberetur nucleus vel germen quoddam unde, favente Dei gratia, perfecta suo tempore effloresceret studiorum universitas.

183. Re mature perpensa, convenerunt Patres, jam advenisse tempus, quo grande hoc opus inchoandum sit. Quod ut strenue urgeatur, visum est Concilio Commissionem instituere cujus erit, collatis consiliis id conniti, ut quamprimum fieri possit, Seminarium quoddam Principale pro Statibus Unitis Americae Septentrionalis prope civitatem quandam insignem ac populosam erigatur, ad quod undique clerici praestantioris ingenii, ordinarium studiorum curriculum emensi, et etiam sacerdotes confluere possint, ad eminentissimam sibi comparandam scientiam. Hujusmodi seminarium omnimodae jurisdictioni, directioni atque administrationi Episcoporum eorumdem Statuum subjectum erit, ad quos spectabit studiorum rationem definire, leges disciplinae praescribere, professores ceterosque officiales instituere, aliaque omnia ordinare quae ad rectum seminarii regimen pertinent. Quoniam de facultate theologica et philosophica juxta normam Universitatis Catholicae agitur, leges regiminis et disciplinae ac rationis studiorum, postquam de iis inter Archiepiscopos et Episcopos deliberatum erit, examini et approbationi S. Sedis subjicientur, nec nisi hac approbatione obtenta vigorem habebunt.

184. Quo vero citius tutiusque coeptum ad felicem perducatur eventum atque exitum, ne pigeat Episcopos, ut verbis utamur Pii IX s. m., exhortari

---

[16] *A. A. S.*, XXIV (1932), 74.

ac rogare egregios suarum dioecesium ecclesiasticos laicosque viros divitiis pollentes et in rem Catholicam praeclare animatos, ut suum aliorumque praeclarum sectantes exemplum, aliquam pecuniae vim perlibenter tribuere velint in Ecclesiae bono populorumque saluti tam utile opus. (Litt. App. ad Archiepp. et Epp. Imp. Austriaci, 17 Martii 1856.)

CODE

CANON 1380

Optandum ut locorum Ordinarii, pro sua prudentia, clericos, pietate et ingenio praestantes, ad scholas mittant alicuius Universitatis aut Facultatis ab Ecclesia conditae vel approbatae, ut inibi studia praesertim philosophiae, theologiae ac iuris canonici perficiant et academicos gradus consequantur.

Finally, it is interesting to note that the Fathers of the Third Plenary Council devote a whole chapter including numbers 182 to 185 to the subject, *De Seminario Principali.* Herein is brought out the importance of higher education for a certain number of our priests. It was decided to appoint a committee to devise ways and means of establishing for the whole of the United States, near one of our large cities and under the jurisdiction of the Hierarchy, a principal seminary where some of the more promising young priests could do post-graduate work. This was the germ of our present flourishing Catholic University of America the benefit of which to individuals and to the Church in this country has been invaluable.

The Code in canon 1380 states that it is much to be desired that local Ordinaries send pious and gifted clerics to the lectures of some university or faculty founded or approved by the Church in order that they may there pursue the studies particularly of Philosophy, Theology and Canon Law and obtain academic degrees.

The steps taken in this direction by the Fathers of the Third Plenary Council happily anticipated the wish of the Holy See as expressed in the Code.

Apropos of the Catholic University attention should be called here to the Apostolic Constitution, "*Deus Scientiarum Dominus,*" of Pope Pius XI. This Constitution issued on May 24, 1931 was directed to Universities and Faculties of Ecclesiastical Studies. After some introductory remarks and general rules the document considers in detail the personnel and government of universities, the method and subject-matter of the courses, examinations, degrees, buildings, libraries, salaries and the like.[17]

That this Constitution might be the more easily and faithfully carried out the Sacred Congregation of Seminaries and Universities issued on June 12, 1931 a more minute list of its requirements.[18]

TITLE IV

Parochial Schools

Article 1

The Erection and Support of Parochial Schools

THIRD PLENARY COUNCIL

199. Quibus omnibus bene perpensis statuimus et decernimus:

I. Prope unamquamque ecclesiam ubi nondum existit, scholam parochialem intra duos annos a promulgatione hujus Concilii erigendam et in perpetuum sustentandam esse, nisi Episcopus ob graviores difficultates dilationem concedendam esse judicet.

II. Sacerdotem, qui intra hoc tempus erectionem vel sustentationem scholae gravi sua negligentia impediat, vel post repetitas Episcopi admonitiones non curet, mereri remotionem ab illa ecclesia.

III. Missionem vel paroeciam quae sacerdotem in erigenda vel sustentanda schola adjuvare ita negligat, ut ob hanc supinam negligentiam schola existere non possit, ab Episcopo esse reprehendendam ac quibus efficacioribus et prudentioribus modis potest, inducendam ad necessaria subsidia conferenda.

CODE

CANON 1379

§ 1. Si scholae catholicae ad normam can. 1373 sive elementariae sive mediae desint, curandum, praesertim a locorum Ordinariis, ut condantur.

§ 2. Itemque si publicae studiorum Universitates doctrina sensuque catholico imbutae non sint, optandum ut in natione vel regione Universitas catholica condatur.

§ 3. Fideles ne omittant adiutricem operam pro viribus conferre in catholicas scholas condendas et sustentandas.

Both the Second and Third Plenary Councils devote a chapter to the question of the Parochial School. The former in numbers 423 to 442 and the latter in numbers 194 to 207.

[17] *A. A. S.*, XXIII (1931), 241.

[18] *A. A. S.*, XXIII (1931), 263.

The Fathers of the Second Council, after declaring that experience has proved that attendance at public schools constitutes a great danger to the faith and morals of Catholic children, conclude that parochial schools are the necessary remedy.

The Fathers of the Third Council, likewise, insist on the necessity of parochial schools and in number 199 lay down the following commands on their erection and support: First, that, within two years from the date of the promulgation of the decrees of the Council, there be erected and perpetually supported a parochial school near each and every church unless the Bishop decides that on account of serious difficulties a delay should be granted. Secondly, that a priest, who within this time fails to erect or seriously neglects to support his school, or who after repeated admonitions of the Bishop fails to take care of his school, should be removed from that church. Thirdly, that a mission or parish which so neglects to aid the priest in the erection or the support of a school that the school cannot exist is to be rebuked by the Bishop and induced by as efficacious and prudent means as possible to give the necessary support.

The Code treats of schools in canons 1372 to 1383. Herein it insists on the religious training of youth, the teaching of religion in schools, the Church's right to establish schools of every grade and the erection of such schools. Canon 1379 decrees that it is the duty especially of local Ordinaries to see to the establishment of elementary and secondary schools where these do not already exist. The faithful are not to refuse to aid according to their means in the building and maintaining of Catholic schools.

The decrees of the Council are more detailed than the Code, but in no wise opposed to it and, therefore, continue to have their full force.

Article 2

The School Board

Third Plenary Council

203. Quoniam vero status et incrementum scholarum nostrarum maxime ab idoneitate magistrorum dependet, summa cura in eo ponenda est, ut non nisi boni et idonei praeceptores iis praeficiantur. Itaque statuimus ac mandamus, ut nemo ad munus docendi in schola parochiali in futuro admittatur, nisi qui praevio examine se habilem et idoneum probaverit.

Episcopi igitur intra annum a promulgatione Concilii unum vel plures

sacerdotes rerum ad scholas pertinentium peritissimos nominabunt, qui "Dioecesanam Commissionem Examinationis" constituent. Nominabuntur usque ad revocationem, et nominati Episcopo in manus solemniter promittent, se munere suo juxta normam ab Episcopo sibi tradendam et ad finem, ob quem examen instituitur, pro viribus assequendum esse functuros. Hujus commissionis erit omnes magistros ac magistras, sive religiosos pertinentes ad congregationem aliquam dioecesanam, sive saeculares, qui munere docendi in scholis parochialibus in futuro fungi cupiunt, examinare, eisque, si idoneos repererint, testimonium idoneitatis vel diploma praebere, sine quo nulli sacerdoti fas erit magistrum vel magistram ullam (nisi jam ante celebrationem Concilii docuerint) pro schola sua conducere. Quod diploma ad quinque annos ac pro omnibus dioecesibus valebit. Quo tempore elapso, alterum et ultimum examen a magistris requiretur. Iis autem, quos in uno vel altero examine idoneos non repererint, diploma nequaquam dabunt, sed ad examen anni sequentis eos relegabunt.

Hoc examen semel in anno instituetur; pro sodalibus ex congregationibus dioecesanis in domibus et temporibus de quibus examinatores cum superioribus convenerint; pro saecularibus tempore et loco ab examinatoribus designandis. Materiae et quaestiones pro examine in scriptis conficiendo a commissariis conjunctim praeparabuntur et die examinis vel ab uno ex ipsis vel ab alio sacerdote a praeside commissionis deputato, in epistola sigillo praesidis munita et coram examinandis aperienda proponentur, qui sub oculis commissarii vel deputati solutiones et responsa exarabunt. Scripta parte examinis ab examinatoribus cognita et recensita, examen orale quam primum habebitur coram tota commissione. Antequam e loco examinis discedant, examinatores triplicem elenchum conficient eorum qui in examine satisfecerunt, quorum unum pro sodali congregationis dioecesanae tradent ejusdem superiori, aut ipsi candidato si sit saecularis; alterum apud praesidem commissionis retinebunt; tertium autem ad cancellarium dioecesis transmittent.

204. Praeter hanc commissionem ad magistros examinandos pro tota dioecesi institutam, Episcopi pro locorum et linguarum diversitate plures "Commissiones Scholarum," ex uno vel pluribus sacerdotibus compositas ad scholas in civitatibus et districtibus ruralibus examinandas constituent. Munus autem harum commissionum erit, semel vel etiam bis in anno unamquamque scholam districtus sui visitare et examinare et accuratam de statu scholarum relationem ad praesidem commissionis dioecesanae pro notitia et actione Episcopi transmittere.

The Third Plenary Council in number 203 orders Bishops to appoint within a year after the promulgation of its decrees a *Diocesan Board of Examiners.* These are to remain in office until recalled. After their appointment they are solemnly to promise the Bishop that they will do their duty to the best of their ability in accordance wih the rules which he lays down and the purpose for which examinations have been instituted.

This Board is to examine all, whether secular or religious, who are to teach in parochial schools and to issue to them testimonials or diplomas of fitness if they pass a satisfactory examination. Henceforth it will not be right for a priest to employ as teacher one who has no such certificate. These diplomas are good for five years and are to be recognized in every diocese. At the end of the first five years a second and final examination is required. Those who fail after two attempts in one year are to be put off until the following year.

The examination is to be held once a year. For diocesan religious their Superiors will determine the time and place. For seculars the Examiners themselves will decide.

The matter and questions for the examination are to be prepared in writing by the Board and on the day of the examination in the presence of those to be examined they are to be taken from the letter bearing the seal of the Chairman by one of the members of the Board or by another priest appointed by them who will also preside over the examination.

As soon as possible after the written examination has been corrected an oral examination is to be given before the whole Board.

Before leaving the place of examination the Examiners are to make three copies of the list of successful candidates one of which is for the candidate himself or his Superior in the case of a religious, one for the Chairman of the Board and one for the Chancellor of the diocese.

Finally, no one is to be accepted as a teacher in a parochial school without having first proved himself fitted by an examination.

These laws are *praeter codicem.* However, they seem either never to have been enforced or to have fallen into desuetude in nearly all of our dioceses. The general practice now is to appoint a Superintendent of schools whose duties include that of ascertaining the competency of parochial school teachers. This method, while not according to the letter of the law, is quite in keeping with its spirit especially in view of the present-day educational system, with its credits, diplomas and degrees. By means of these the Superintendent can learn about the intellectual ability of those aspiring to be teachers what in the days of the Council could be found out only by such examinations as it legislated.

The Third Council in number 204 orders further according to diversity of place and language the appointment of several School

Boards composed of one or more priests to examine the children in city and rural schools.

These are to visit once or even twice a year every school of their district to examine the pupils after which they are to send an accurate account of the condition of the schools to the chairman of the diocesan Board for the knowledge and the action of the Bishop. As far as the Code is concerned, this law still stands as something *praeter codicem*. However, what has been said above about the Board of Examiners for teachers applies here also. According to the modern system of education the examinations of the pupils are provided for by the Superintendent of schools.

Article 3

The Obligation of Sending Children to Parochial Schools

Third Plenary Council

198. Cum igitur ob causam sufficientem et ab Ordinario probatam, parentes ad scholas publicas filios mittere velint, dummodo necessariis cautionibus proxima pericula removeantur, stricte praecipimus ne quis sive Episcopus sive presbyter, quod Pontifex per Sacram Congregationem diserte vetat, hujusmodi parentes a sacramentis quasi indignos sive intentis minis sive actu ipso repellere audeat. Quod multo magis de pueris ipsis intelligendum est. Quare pastores animarum dum fideles sibi commissos de scholarum harum periculis monent, summopere caveant ne immodico zelo ducti sapientissima Sanctae Sedis consilia et praecepta verbis aut factis violare videantur.

199. Omnes parentes Catholicos prolem suam ad scholas parochiales mittere teneri, nisi vel domi vel in aliis scholis Catholicis Christianae filiorum suorum educationi sufficienter et evidenter consulant, aut ob causam sufficientem, ab Episcopo approbatam, et cum opportunis cautionibus reme-

Code

Canon 1374

Pueri catholici scholas acatholicas, neutras, mixtas, quae nempe etiam acatholicis patent, ne frequentent. Solius autem Ordinarii loci est decernere, ad normam instructionum Sedis Apostolicae, in quibus rerum adiunctis et quibus adhibitis cautelis, ut periculum perversionis vitetur, tolerari possit ut eae scholae celebrentur.

diisque eos ad alias scholas mittere ipsis liceat. Quaenam autem sit schola Catholica Ordinarii judicio definiendum relinquitur.

The Second Plenary Council has no direct legislation on the obligation of sending children to parochial schools.

The Third, however, in number 199 decrees that all Catholic parents are obliged to send their children to the parochial school unless they provide otherwise for their Catholic education or have the Bishop's permission to send them to other schools.

The Code in canon 1374 forbids Catholic children to frequent non-Catholic or mixed schools, that is such as are open to non-Catholics. It is for the local Ordinary to decide, according to the Instructions of the Holy See, in what circumstances and with what precautions attendance at such schools may be tolerated without danger of perversion to the pupils.

These two laws agree in requiring the attendance of Catholic children at Catholic schools and in leaving it to the Ordinary to decide when exceptions can safely and justifiably be made.

The Instructions of the Holy See referred to by the Code are undoubtedly such as our Bishops received on November 24, 1875.[19]

Finally, in this connection the Third Plenary Council in number 198 forbids both Bishops and priests to dare either by threats or acts to keep from the Sacraments parents who, for a reason approved by the Ordinary, and having removed the proximate dangers by the necessary precautions, send their children to the public school.

There is no corresponding legislation in the Code and so this decree of the Council continues in force as something *practer codicem.*

[19] *Coll. de Prop. Fide,* 1449.

CHAPTER VIII

CHURCH PROPERTY

A relatively large proportion of the legislation of the Councils is devoted to the subject of Church property. The American Church had to face conditions very different from those of the settled countries of Europe. In most places here there was neither property nor endowments and Bishops and priests had to devise ways and means of obtaining from the faithful the funds necessary to build churches, schools and rectories and to support themselves. Many things were tried which were more or less successful and more or less in harmony with the general laws of the Church. A certain unity was desirable and above all questionable methods were to be eliminated. Another problem equally acute was the question of the tenure of or title to Church property in the eyes of the civil authorities. Most of the provisions made by the legislatures of the vast majority of the States were inspired by the organization of Protestant churches in which lay trustees elected by members of the congregation formed a legal corporation to hold and manage church property and to appoint and dismiss ministers. It soon became evident that this trustee system is not suited to our organization and the Bishops had to devise other means. In the third place and as a result of the preceding the management of Church property fell to the lot of the priest and this was something for which the general law had little help to give. Hence, on this matter is to be found some of the most original and practical legislation of our Councils.

The Second Plenary Council devotes a whole chapter including numbers 182 to 204 to this subject. These decrees are concerned chiefly with the tenure of Church property and the correction of the abuses resulting from trusteeism; but they contain also several prescriptions on the administration of Church property, which to all practical purposes have been embodied in the decrees of the Third Council.

The Third Plenary Council devotes to the consideration of Church property; five chapters, including numbers 264 to 296. Herein a detailed development of the subject is given under the following heads:

The rights of the Church regarding property, the duties of Bishops, Pastors and Trustees and finally, some unlawful means of raising money.

TITLE I

The Tenure of Church Property

Third Plenary Council

267. In Statibus in quibus civilis parochiarum vel coetuum ecclesiasticorum incorporatio legalis quae cum legibus ecclesiasticis concordet, non existit, Episcopus ipsemet, lege in comitiis ferenda, corpus publicum seu persona moralis (*Corporation sole*) constitui poterit ad bona totius dioecesis habenda et administranda; vel poterunt simili lege dioecesis bona committi Episcopi fidei (*In trust*) ut eadem nomine dioeceseos teneat in ejusque bonum juxta mentem Ecclesiae administret; vel denique Episcopus bona dioeceseos temporalia possideat et administret nomine suo proprio, illo nempe absoluto plenoque juris titulo, qui anglice vocatur *in fee simple;* quo in casu Episcopus omnino memor sit, se, quantumvis a potestate saeculari plenum ecclesiasticarum rerum sibi datum fuerit dominium, ex sacrorum canonum monitu dominum earum non esse, sed mere procuratorem. (C. *Fraternitatem* 2, de Donat., l. II. Decret.)

268. Ne unquam bona cultui divino piisque operibus dicata ad alios usus divertantur, statuimus ac omnibus istarum provinciarum Episcopis in Domino praecipimus, ut duplex rerum inventarium rite confectum habeant; unum in quo res omnes ecclesiasticae, quas sive nomine proprio (*in fee simple*), vel suae fidei commissas nomine aliorum (*in trust*), vel soli ut corpus morale (*corporation sole*) possident, accurate describantur; alterum in quo res suae propriae (*personal property*) aeque fideliter notentur. Hac enim ratione optime de bonis tam Ecclesiae quam Episcoporum sine ullo confusionis et quae inde sequi posset scandalose contentionis aut sacrilegae alienationis periculo provisum erit. "Et justum est hoc apud Deum et homines, ut nec Ecclesia detrimentum patiatur ignoratione rerum Episcopi, nec Episcopus vel ejus propinqui sub obtentu Ecclesiae proscribantur." (Can. Ap. 40.)

269. Summorum Pontificum ac Praedecessorum nostrorum cura de bonis externis Ecclesiae hac in regione secure firmiterque servandis quanta fuerit, ex actis et decretis conciliorum nostrorum tam provincialium quam plenariorum apertum est. Nec minori Nos sollicitudine bonorum illorum securitati providere intenti, Episcopos iterum iterumque monemus, oneratam esse suam conscientiam, ut testamento vel alio legali documento, prout spectatis locorum adjunctis vel legum in suo Statu vigentium indole melius videtur, securae bonorum ecclesiasticorum quae penes se sunt ad successores transmissioni consulant. Hujus porro instrumenti duo exemplaria conficiant, quorum uno apud se in archivo dioecesano retento, alterum apud Archiepiscopum deponant; Archiepiscopus autem apud seniorem suffraganeum. Haec testamentorum depositio intra tres menses a sua cujusque consecratione omnino fiat. (Conc. Plen. Balt. II., No. 191. Cfr. etiam Nm. 204.)

Neque omittant de bonis suis propriis testamento accurate et solerter confecto tempestive providere quo nulla, ipsis vita decedentibus, de privata proprietate difficultas oriatur.

CODE

CANON 1495

§ 1. Ecclesia catholica et Apostolica Sedes nativum ius habent libere et independenter a civili potestate acquirendi, retinendi et administrandi bona temporalia ad fines sibi proprios prosequendos.

§ 2. Etiam ecclesiis singularibus aliisque personis moralibus quae ab ecclesiastica auctoritate in iuridicam personam erectae sint, ius est, ad normam sacrorum canonum, bona temporalia acquirendi, retinendi et administrandi.

The tenure of Church property sems to have been the chief concern of our Bishops. This is especially true of the Fathers of the First and Second Plenary Councils who had so painfully experienced the mismanagement and abuse of power on the part of the trustees and the reaction to these evils on the part of the Bishops and priests who to secure full control of ecclesiastical affairs had begun to hold Church property in their own names with the resulting danger of confusion especially after death between what belonged to them personally and what belonged to the Church.

The Fathers of the Second Plenary Council, therefore, proclaim the right of the Church to obtain and own such temporal goods as are necessary to carry out her mission; they condemn the pretensions of lay trustees and express their regret that the civil law in some of the States does not recognize religious corporations organized according to Catholic principles. In numbers 188 to 204 they declare that the Bishop must take the necessary means to safeguard the Church property of his diocese and to provide for its transmission at death to his sucessor whenever circumstances necessitated the holding of it in his own name.

The Third Plenary Council is more explicit and goes more into detail on this point. In numbers 267 to 269 it decrees that where the State law does not recognize the incorporation of parishes as provided for by ecclesiastical law, the Bishop must obtain for himself from the legislature the right of holding all Church property of the diocese as a *corporation sole* or *in trust,* and if this cannot be done, he may hold the property *in fee simple* in which case he is obliged by taking inventory and making a will to avoid confusing ecclesiastical and personal property and to prevent all danger of having the former claimed by his heirs.

Any one of the three above mentioned ways of holding Church property continued legitimate for our Bishops generally until 1911. On July 29 of that year the Sacred Congregation of the Council issued a decree on ways of possessing and administering ecclesiastical property in the United States. Herein the method known as *in fee simple* was absolutely forbidden. It was further declared that of all the methods then in vogue in this country the one commonly called the *parish corporation* with the conditions and safeguards it then enjoyed in the State of New York is the most desirable. This was to be introduced immediately wherever compatible with the civil law and, where not, untiring efforts were to be made to have it legalized as soon as possible. In the meantime Bishops were to use the *corporation sole* with the obligation in conscience of obtaining in matter of lesser importance the advice of the Diocesan Consultors and interested parties, and in transactions of greater moment their consent.[1]

The Code in canons 1495 and the following lays down the general principle that every diocese, parish and religious organization has legal personality and that every legal person has the right to own property. It is to be concluded, then, that all parochial property is to be held in the name of the parish and all diocesan property in the name of the diocese. This has always been the common law of the Church and is what the decree of 1911 sought to enforce locally for the sake of conformity and to do away with the dangers of the *corporation sole* and the *fee simple*. Wherever, therefore, it has been possible to carry out this decree of the Sacred Congregation, the precepts of the Councils of Baltimore no longer apply. Where, however, because of the civil law the *corporation sole* must still be used, our local legislation remains in force.

TITLE II

The Administration of Church Property

Third Plenary Council

268. Ne unquam bona cultui divino piisque operibus dicata ad alios usus

---

[1] *Eccl. Rev.*, XLV (1911), 585 and 586.

divertantur, statuimus ac omnibus istarum provinciarum Episcopis in Domino praecipimus, ut duplex rerum inventarium rite confectum habeant; unum in quo res omnes ecclesiasticae, quas sive nomine proprio (*in fee simple*), vel suae fidei commissas nomine aliorum (*in trust*), vel soli ut corpus morale (*corporation sole*) possident, accurate describantur; alterum in quo res suae propriae (*personal property*) aeque fideliter notentur.

270. Quum securitas bonorum nostrarum dioecesium a dispositione legum civilium plane dependeat, Episcopis summae religionis esse debet curare, ut quaecumque documenta vel instrumenta in qualicumque demum bonorum illorum negotio vel ministerio adhibenda, ea ratione formaque legali describantur, conficiantur ac deponantur, ut negotia peracta non tantum in facie Ecclesiae vel foro conscientiae, sed etiam coram lege et judice saeculari valida, rata, fixaque sint. Neque in iis negotiis quae et omissis legum formis sat firma apparent, cautiones et formas a lege civili statutas negligi permittant, quo firmissima et ab omni periculo secura transactio sit. In omnibus istis rebus viros in jure peritos et in tractandis negotiis versatissimos consulere nec Episcopi nec sacerdotes detrectent.

271. Volumus itaque ut singuli Episcopi in loco tuto ac commodo archivum seu tabularium dioecesanum erigant, in quo instrumenta et scripturae quae negotia dioecesana tum temporalia cum spiritualia spectant, juxta mentem Benedicti XIII. et normam a S. C. Conc. statutam apte disposita et diligenter clausa custodiantur.

272. Summa rationum, in qua plene et distincte missionis proprietates, reditus, debita, census annui et foenora solvenda notata sint, a rectore ac duobus aedituis vel auditoribus, quos vocant, signata ad cancellarium mittatur, qui eam ab Episcopo recognitam in archivo dioecesano reponat.

275. Ut omnia recte ordinateque procedant, rectores missionum praeter regesta in Rituali Romano praescripta (ubi Libri status animarum expressa mentio fit) habeant librum computus, in quo receptae et expensae, jura et debita, perspicue et accurate suo quaeque ordine describantur.

276. Praeterea, ne rectores et piorum locorum curatores proprias suas res rebus Ecclesiae immisceant cum famae suae discrimine, fidelium offensione, vel injuria Ecclesiae, duplex conficiant rerum inventarium. In utroque hoc inventario diligenter bona tam mobilia quam immobilia, quae ad missionem vel locum spectant, notentur; in eo vasa sacra sacramque omnem supellectilem describant; omnia recenseantur quaecumque pertinent ad domum presbyteralem, scholas et coemeterium, neque omittant indicare reditus permanentes, si qui sint, et onera quibus ecclesia vel locus subjicitur. Inventarii unum exemplar a rectore vel curatore et aedituis vel consiliariis subscriptum ad cancellarium mittatur ut in archivo dioecesano servetur, alterum in archivo missionis vel loci asservabitur. Inventarium singulis annis a rectore et aedituis vel consiliariis recognoscatur, bona intra annum acquisita vel onera suscepta addantur, quorum item catalogus rite signatus cancellario transmittatur. (Conc. Plen. ap. Maynutiam, 1876, c. XXIX.) Ne contentioni inter successorem et decessorem locus relinquatur, decernimus ut quoties sacerdos missionis cui praesit possessionem assumit, inventarium hujus missionis ad illud usque tempus rite descriptum, eidem a praedecessore vel a vicario foraneo exhibeatur. Quia de quibusdam muneribus, ut quidam ex Nobis alia occasione prudenter notarunt, maxime rerum mobilium, ut supellectilis, ornamentorum sacerdotalium, vasorum aureorum argenteorumque, sive ab individuis fidelibus sive a sodalitatibus sponte ecclesiae rectori oblatis dubium sat frequenter oritur, utrum ad hunc pertineant an ad missionem vel ecclesiam: decernimus, nisi contrarium explicite fuerit a donatoribus declaratum, res istas esse ecclesiae proprietatem, atque ideo neque rectorem in discessu a missione, neque ejus haeredes post ipsius obitum, jus habere ad eas removendas vel vendendas. Servetur itaque regula statuta, ea scilicet quae ecclesiasticis usibus apta rectori missionario donantur, esse missioni donata, nisi contrarium clare et indubitanter pateat.

278. Quo melius prospiciatur securitati pecuniarum, si quas penes se habeant, potissimum vero libris et documentis parochialibus, i. e. regestis, libro computus, inventario, testamento, contractuum syngraphis, aliisque hujusmodi scripturis, monemus, ut unusquisque rector in domo sua, vel alio loco tuto ac convenienti, habeat arcam ferream (*Safe*) quae Archivi parochialis vices impleat. In hac igitur arca libri praedicti et omnia instrumenta officialia, sive dioecesana sive civilia, tam quae res spirituales quam temporales missionis spectant, sedulo ac tuto custodiantur.

279. Si nova aliqua ecclesia sit erigenda, vel schola et domus presbyteralis, vel si hujusmodi aedificium notabiliter immutandum sit vel augendum, aut ruinosum diruendum, rectores tale opus non aggrediantur, priusquam Ordinarii licentiam scriptam obtinuerint. Hac lege non solum cavere volumus, ne aedibus ecclesiasticis supervacanee aut imprudenter constructis querelarum et murmuris ansa praebeatur, sed multo potius impedire quominus ecclesiae aere alieno temere et incaute graventur. Igitur strictissime prohibemus, vetamus et interdicimus, ne quis rector, sacerdos, et pii loci curator, sive ecclesiae sive missionis sive Episcopi nomine ecclesiam suam vel locum aere alieno gravare quocumque titulo vel colore audeat, sine expressa et scriptis exarata licentia Ordinarii.

280. Ad omne praecavendum injustae alienationis periculum, decernimus nulli dehinc presbytero licere, seclusa venia Ordinarii in scriptis data, nomine ac jure proprio retinere sive ecclesiam, sive scholas, sive domum presbyteralem, sive coemeterium, aut bona alia ecclesiastica, pro quorum acquisitione fideles qualicumque modo subsidia contulerint; sed ea quamprimum transferet in Ordinarium aut in societatem seu corporationem ab eodem sancitam. Quod si quis sacerdos absque permissione Ordinarii titulum talium bonorum proprio nomine per tres menses retinuerit, volumus ut canonica poena plectatur, quam singuli Episcopi pro suis dioecesibus statuant. Edicimus etiam ne quis rector aut quilibet sacerdos ecclesiae pecuniam in mensa numularia privato suo nomine depositam teneat, aut mensae libellum (*Bank book*) suae privatae personae inscribi permittat. (Conc. Plen. Balt. II., No. 188.)

281. Praeterea, si quis sacerdos pecuniam propriam in ecclesiae seu missionis usum mutuo conferre velit, id omnino non fiat nisi probante in scriptis Ordinario. Conficiatur insuper accurata rei notitia ab aedituis signanda, quae in archivo parochiali servetur. Item in libro rationum res referatur. (Conc. Plen. Balt. II., No. 193.)

282. Rectores summam adhibere debent curam in obtinendis proprietatum ecclesiasticarum titulis (*Deeds*). Postquam a viris peritis diligentissime recogniti fuerint, eos Episcopo probandos exhibeant, ut demum formis et cautelis tum a lege civili tum dioecesana requisitis vestiti in archivo dioecesano deponantur.

283. Propter semper imminens incendiorum periculum mandamus, ut omnia aedificia ecclesiastica contra damnum ex incendio oriundum, ab una vel pluribus societatibus fiducia publica merito gaudentibus, nomine corporationis vel Ordinarii tempestive assecurentur.

284. Sacris Literis saepe monemur, viri sapientis esse quaerere consilia prudentium. "Salus autem, ubi consilia multa." (Prov. xi., 14.) Cui veritati innixa Ecclesia nullo non tempore Episcopis aliisque ministris quibus rerum temporalium cura commissa fuit, probos viros consociavit, quorum prudenti consilio in negotiis tractandis uterentur. Hinc et nostra concilia constanter probarunt, ut parochi seu missionum rectores in administrandis Ecclesiae bonis consilium adhibeant virorum prudentium, quos inter optimos sui gregis fideles, Episcopo confirmante, selegerint, quo alacrius atque felicius pastores, negotiis externis haud ita distenti ac distracti, ovium suarum salutem promovere possint.

285. Constanter autem Ecclesia docuit nullam esse laicis et ipsis suis membris, auctoritatem in rebus Ecclesiae gerendis; aedituos et curatores laicos privilegio fuisse in atrium templi admissos, non jure. "Ad eorum munus quod attinet," ita Gregorius XVI. (Brevi, 12 Aug. 1841), "neminem ignorare volumus, illud pendere omnino ex auctoritate Episcopi, nihilque ab aedituis ecclesiae geri unquam posse, nisi quod eis fuerit ab Antistite demandatum." Et Praedecessores nostri, cum de aedituis laicis sermo fieret, declararunt: "universalem Catholicae Ecclesiae legem esse, omnes illos qui ecclesiae bona quocumque modo administrant, nonnisi consentiente Sede Apostolica vel Episcopo id licite facere, eosque in illorum administratione auctoritati et jurisdictioni Episcoporum * * * esse subjectos." (No. 202.) Igitur quicunque viri laici, approbante Episcopo, sive a rectore missionis sive a coetu fidelium electi sint, ut in bonorum temporalium administratione Ecclesiae ministris verbo et opere auxilium ferant, maxime vero aeditui quibus a lege civili facultas data est administrandi bona ecclesiastica, graviter serioque recogitent, se omnino legibus Ecclesiae teneri; quaecunque contra canonum sanctiones vel Episcopi statuta ab eis peracta fuerint, quantumvis in foro saeculari rata firmaque habeantur, coram Deo et Ecclesia invalida haberi et nulla; seipsos vero, si bona et jura Ecclesiae usurparint, incurrisse poenas ab eadem statutas.

286. Cum in pluribus provinciis nostris rectores ecclesiarum ipsa lege constituantur ex officio ecclesiarum suarum aeditui, caute nobis providendum est ne, quando necesse fuerit rectorem aliquem munere suo privare, ipse per interjectam appellationem sententiae executionem impediat, et sic officium aeditui coram potestate civili conservet. Statuimus ergo, annuente Apostolica

Sede, nullum rectorem etiam inamovibilem juridice remotum, depositum, vel munere suo privatum, contra sententiam Ordinarii *in suspensivo*, ut aiunt, appellare posse, sed *in devolutivo* tantum, ita ut desinat esse aedituus ecclesiae cujus rector erat, vel perpetuo, vel usque ad tempus quo judex *ad quem*, definitive litem terminans, eum in munus suum redintegret. Quapropter usque ad litis terminationem non definitive alius rector, sed administrator cum juribus competentibus instituetur, et Episcopus interim utriusque, tum amoti rectoris tum administratoris, honestae sustentationi providebit.

287. Ad unitatem disciplinae per omnes fere nostras provincias vigentis promovendam, quantum lex saecularis permittit, et quo certius viri optimi et fidelissimi in aedituorum, curatorum et consiliariorum numerum assumantur, sequentes regulas observatu commendamus.

I. Episcopi est judicare tum de necessitate tales auxiliarios laicos adhibendi, tum de numero eorum, tum de modo eos designandi.

II. Sicubi Episcopus hos auxiliarios a coetu fidelium eligendos esse melius judicaverit, ex iis solummodo seligendi sunt, quorum nomina ab ipso rectore ecclesiae fuerint ad hoc proposita.

III. Auxiliarii quocunque modo selecti necessario, antequam munus suscipiant, ab Ordinario in scriptis sunt approbandi; manent vero ad nutum Episcopi amovibiles.

IV. In ipsis seligendis ii tantum viri congregationis vocem sive activam sive passivam habeant, qui annos nati unum et viginti: 1. Praecepto Paschali satisfecerint; 2. Unam saltem sedem in ecclesia propria per annum elapsum conduxerint ejusque pretium solverint, aut alio debito modo, juxta ordinem constitutum ad sustentationem ecclesiae propriae contribuerint; 3. Prolem suam instituendam scholis Catholicis committere minime neglexerint, juxta normam Tit. vi, c. i. § 1 statutam; 4. Nulli societati secretae vel alias prohibitae adscripti sint.

V. Coetus aedituorum (consiliariorum, auxiliariorum) sic constituti (*Board of Trustees, Councilmen, etc.*), missionis rector ex officio suo erit praeses, sine cujus consensu nihil in coetu agendum vel statuendum est.

VI. Si qua ullo tempore discrepantia rectorem inter et aedituos vel consiliarios de rebus gerendis exoriatur, nec dissensionem pacifice componere ipsi per se valeant, controversia ad Episcopum referatur, cujus judicio ac sententiae omnes parebunt. (Conc. Plen. Balt. II., No. 201, 6°.)

Code

Canon 1519

§ 1. Loci Ordinarii est sedulo advigilare administrationi omnium bonorum ecclesiasticorum quae in suo territorio sint nec ex eius iurisdictione fuerint subducta, salvis legitimis praescriptionibus, quae eidem potiora iura tribuant.

§ 2. Habita ratione iurium, legitimarum consuetudinum et circumstantiarum, Ordinarii, opportune editis peculiaribus instructionibus intra fines iuris communis, universum administrationis bonorum ecclesiasticorum negotium ordinandum curent.

CANON 1521

§ 1. Praeter hoc dioecesanum Consilium administrationis, Ordinarius loci in administrationem bonorum quae ad aliquam ecclesiam vel locum pium pertinet et ex iure vel tabulis fundationis suum non habent administratorum, assumat viros providos, idoneos et boni testimonii, quibus, elapso triennio, alios sufficiat, nisi locorum circumstantiae aliud suadeant.

§ 2. Quod si laicis partes quaedam in administratione bonorum ecclesiasticorum vel ex legitimo fundationis seu erectionis titulo vel ex Ordinarii loci voluntate competant, nihilominus universa administratio nomine Ecclesiae fiat, ac salvo iure Ordinarii visitandi, exigendi rationes et praescribendi modum administrationis.

CANON 1522

Antequam administratores bonorum ecclesiasticorum, de quibus in can. 1521, suum munus ineant:

1.° Debent se bene et fideliter administraturos coram Ordinario loci vel vicario foraneo iureiurando cavere;

2.° Fiat accuratum ac distinctum inventarium, ab omnibus subscribendum, rerum immobilium, rerum mobilium pretiosarum aliarumve cum descriptione atque aestimatione earundem; vel factum antea inventarium acceptetur, adnotatis rebus quae interim amissae vel acquisitae fuerint;

3.° Huius inventarii alterum exemplar conservetur in tabulario administrationis, alterum in archivo Curiae; et in utroque quaelibet immutatio adnotetur quam patrimonium subire contingat.

CANON 1523

Administratores bonorum ecclesiasticorum diligentia boni patrisfamilias suum munus implere tenentur; ac proinde debent:

1.° Vigilare ne bona ecclesiastica suae curae concredita quoquo modo pereant aut detrimentum capiant;

2.° Praescripta servare iuris tam canonici quam civilis, aut quae a fundatore vel donatore vel legitima auctoritate imposita sint;

3.° Reditus bonorum ac proventus accurate et iusto tempore exigere exactosque loco tuto servare et secundum fundatoris mentem aut statutas leges vel normas impendere;

4.° Pecuniam ecclesiae, quae de expensis supersit et utiliter collocari potest, de consensu Ordinarii, in emolumentum ipsius ecclesiae occupare;

5.° Accepti et expensi libros bene ordinatos habere;

6.° Documenta et instrumenta, quibus iura ecclesiae in bona nituntur, rite ordinare et in ecclesiae archivo vel armario convenienti et apto custodire; authentica vero eorum exemplaria, ubi commode fieri potest, in archivo vel armario Curiae deponere.

CANON 1525

§ 1. Reprobata contraria consuetudine, administratores tam ecclesiastici

quam laici cuiusvis ecclesiae etiam cathedralis aut loci pii canonice erecti aut confraternitatis singulis annis officio tenentur reddendi rationem administrationis Ordinario loci.

§ 2. Si ex peculiari iure aliis ad id designatis ratio reddenda sit, tunc etiam Ordinarius loci vel eius delegatus cum his admittatur, ea lege ut aliter factae liberationes ipsis administratoribus minime suffragentur.

Canon 1527

§ 1. Nisi prius ab Ordinario loci facultatem impetraverint, scriptis dandam, administratores invalide actus ponunt qui ordinariae administrationis fines et modum excedant.

§ 2. Ecclesia non tenetur respondere de contractibus ab administratoribus sine licentia competentis Superioris initis, nisi quando et quatenus in rem suam versum sit.

Canon 1536

§ 1. Nisi contrarium probetur, praesumendum ea quae donantur rectoribus ecclesiarum, etiam religiosorum, esse ecclesiae donata.

The Second Plenary Council in numbers 186 and 197 and the Third in numbers 265 and 285 lay down the principle that laymen as such have no rights in the administration of Church property which, as said above, is to be under the control of the Ordinary of the diocese. Since the Second Council was concerned chiefly with the subject of tenure, it did not treat so thoroughly the subject of administration. For this latter one must consult the decrees of the Third Council which lays down the rules to be followed in this matter by Bishops, Pastors and lay trustees.

As regards the Bishops over and above the general obligation of acting as good *patresfamilias* their specific duties are set forth in numbers 266 to 274 of this Third Council. Herein it is prescribed first, that they have two separate and accurate lists, one of which contains a complete account of all Church property, and the other giving an equally faithful record of all personal property; secondly, that they see to it that all the formalities of the civil law are observed in the management of Church property; thirdly, that deeds to all property be provided and kept in the diocesan archives; and fourthly, that Rectors render a yearly account of their administration signed by themselves and two of the lay trustees.

The section of the Council outlining the duties of Pastors in this matter including numbers 275 and 283 and number 286 is considerably more detailed than that concerning Ordinaries.

In number 275 of the Third Council Pastors are ordered to have a kind of day-book in which are to be recorded all receipts and expenditures, credits and debts.

In 276 the Council further orders Pastors to have two lists of all movable and immovable possessions belonging to the parish. In these he is to note all sacred vessels and all other sacred furnishings; everything pertaining to the rectory, schools and cemetery; nor is he to omit the permanent income nor the expenses to which the church or place is exposed. One copy of this list signed by the Pastor or the one in charge and the trustees is to be sent to the Chancellor to be preserved in the diocesan archives; the other is to be kept in the archives of the parish. This list each year is to be reviewed by the Pastor and the trustees and, with the acquisitions and expenditures of the current year added, duly signed and sent to the Chancellor.

The Council further requires that whenever a priest takes possession of a parish, he be shown by his predecessor or the Vicar Forane an inventory of it from the beginning to date.

In this same number the Council declares, moreover, that unless the contrary has been explicitly stated by the donors, gifts such as furniture, vestments and vases made to the Rector are to be considered Church property and, therefore, neither the Rector at his departure nor his heirs at his death may remove or sell them.

The following number, 278, requires the keeping of all important parochial, diocesan and civil documents in a safe that will be easy of access to the Pastor.

In number 279 Pastors are forbidden to undertake to build, tear down or notably change or enlarge a church, school or rectory without the written permission of the Ordinary. Moreover, a most strict prohibition is pronounced against the burdening of a church or other sacred place with debt without the permission of the Ordinary expressed in writing.

In number 280 the Third Council decrees that henceforth it will be unlawful for any priest without the written permission of his Ordinary to hold in his own name and right any Church property toward the acquisition of which the faithful have in any way contributed. Likewise, priests are forbiden to put Church funds in the bank in their own names or to allow them to be recorded in their own personal bank books.

Number 281 forbids priests to lend their own money at interest to the Church without the written approval of the Ordinary. Should the latter consent, a written account of the transaction signed by the trustees is to be put in the parish archives and parish account book.

According to number 282 Pastors are obliged to secure deeds to all Church property under their management. These drawn up according to the requirements of civil and diocesan law are to be put in the diocesan archives.

Again number 283 orders that all Church buildings are to be insured against fire in the name either of the Corporation or of the Ordinary.

Finally, since according to the Fathers of the Third Council in many of our provinces the Rectors of churches are by civil law *ex officio* trustees of their churches, number 286 provides that a Pastor who has been juridically removed, deposed or deprived of his office can appeal from the sentence of the Ordinary only *in devolutivo* and that he ceases to be a trustee of his church either perpetually or until, his appeal having been sustained, he is reinstated.

The lay trustees are treated of in numbers 284 to 287 of the Third Plenary Council.

In the first of these decrees is laid down the general principle that it has always been the policy of the Church for Bishops and other ministers having the care of temporal goods to associate with themselves laymen of probity whose prudent advice they would seek in business transactions; and that our Councils have always advocated the practice of Pastors consulting in the administration of Church property some prudent men chosen from among their most outstanding parishioners and approved by the Bishop.

With equal force and clarity number 285 reiterates a second principle to the effect that the Church has always taught that the laity enjoy no authority by right in the management of ecclesiastical goods, but act always as the subjects of the Holy Father or their Bishop.

For the sake of uniformity, in so far as this is possible in view of the divergencies of the civil law in the various States, and the better to insure the choice of the most competent laymen as trustees, the Fathers in number 287 recommend the following rules:

1. It is for the Bishop to judge concerning the necessity of lay trustees, their number, and the method of choosing them.

2. Wherever the Bishop considers it better to have the trustees elected by the body of the faithful, they are to be chosen only from the names proposed by the Pastor.

3. Before assuming their office trustees must be approved by the Bishop who, moreover, always retains the right to remove them at will.

4. In the election only the male members of the congregation who have attained their majority should have a voice. Those selected must be male parishoners in good standing. Which means they must have made their Easter duty; they must during the past year have had at least one seat in their parish church and paid their pew rent, or otherwise, according to the custom of the place contributed to the support of their parish; they must have their children in a Catholic school; and finally, they must not be members of secret or other forbidden societies.

5. The pastor is to be *ex officio* president of the Board and nothing is to be done without his consent.

6. In case of differences between the Pastor and the trustees which they cannot amicably settle among themselves the Bishop is to act as arbiter and all are to be subject to his judgment.

The Code treats of the administration of Church property in canons 1518 to 1528.

Canon 1519 declares that it is the duty of the Ordinary diligently to supervise the administration of all ecclesiastical goods under his jurisdiction and to issue instructions in this matter compatible with the common law and the rights of others.

Canon 1521 provides for the appointment by the Ordinary of a Board of lay administrators as trustees for each parish.

Canon 1522 prescribes an accurate and specific inventory of all immovable and precious movable goods and all other property.

Canon 1523 requires the guarding against any loss of or damage to the ecclesiastical goods confided to one's care, orderly records of receipts and expenditures, and the keeping of documents and papers on which the property rights of the church are based in the archives or in a suitable safe. Authentic copies of these latter should, whenever it can conveniently be done, be kept also in the archives or safe of the diocesan Curia.

By canon 1525 all administrators both clerical and lay are bound to make an annual report to the local Ordinary of their administration of all churches, including cathedrals, of all pious places canonically erected, and of all confraternities.

Again canon 1527 states that administrators act invalidly when, without first having obtained the written faculty of the local Bishop, they exceed the limits of ordinary administration.

Finally, canon 1536, § 1 says that unless the contrary be proved, the presumption is that donations made either to secular or religious Rectors of churches are given to the church.

These excerpts from the Code suffice for a comparison with the Council and serve to show that, while some of our local provisions for the administration of Church property are more specific and detailed than the common law, none are to be set aside because of opposition except that which leaves the Bishop free to decide regarding the need of lay trustees. These have been made of obligation by canon 1521.

TITLE III

Some Prohibited Means of Raising Money

Second Plenary Council

119. Cum ex sacerdotum vagorum et ignotorum discursu ad eleemosynas a fidelibus colligendas gravia oriantur incommoda, visum est districte prohibere ne sacerdos aliquis, absque episcopi sui venia, scripto concessa, extra congregationem sibi commissam eleemosynas petat, vel in alia dioecesi absque Ordinarii licentia. Quod si sacerdos aliquis hanc legem transgredi praesumpserit, hortamur episcopos ut suspensionis censura eum statim innodent. Religiosi autem meminerint sui Superioris licentiam secum afferre.

Third Plenary Council

288. Praxis, sicubi forte existat, pecuniam exigendi ad fores ecclesiae Dominicis ac Festis diebus, ut quis ingredi possit ac sacrosancto missae sacrificio interresse, jampridem eliminari debuisset. Eam enim damnavit Summus Pontifex Pius IX. et prorsus tollendam significavit. Decessores quoque nostri supremo ejus judicio obsequentes finem pravae huic consuetudini omnino imponendum esse statuerunt. (Conc. Plen. Balt. II, No. 397.)

289. In unaquaque ecclesia constituatur spatium liberum ubi fideles Sacro adesse et verbum Dei audire possint. In hoc autem spatio eligendo et in eorum usum aptando, nunquam obliviscatur ille, qui ecclesiae praeest, hos homines esse Christi pauperes, et Boni Pastoris exemplo misericorditer cum illis agat, seduloque vitet quidquid eos contemnendi aut pudefaciendi specimen prae se ferre possit. Secus enim (quod Apostolus expresse vetat), exhonorantur pauperes (Jac. II 2-6), et timeri aliquando potest ne per pastorem ecclesiae ii, pro quorum aeque ac pro divitum animabus rationem est redditurus, a divino cultu et a vita Christiana penitus arceantur.

290. Plerisque in locis pecunia in pios usus haud exigua comparari solet per conventus quosdam, qui animorum oblectandorum causa fiunt, quique apud nos vulgo *Picnics*, *Excursions* aut simili nomine vocantur. Quum vero hujusmodi conventus, praesertim prope urbes opulentas et populosas, peccatorum et scandalodum seminaria saepe evadant, dubitatur a piis ac prudentibus viris, utrum amplius tolerandi sint an penitus prohibendi. Provida mens eorundem Patrum (No. 396) omnibus serio perpensis, decrevit eos nonnisi omni adhibita cautela posse permitti. Quo melius igitur prudens eorum consilium finem optatum consequatur, quoque facilius via ad mala quae timenda sunt et scandala praecludatur, statuimus ut hujusmodi conventus nunquam habere liceat nocturno tempore, neque Dominicis, Festis aut esurialibus diebus, neque cum usu liguorum (ut aiunt) inebriantium, vino et cerevisia inclusis. Insuper, ut haberi possint, necessario requiratur in singulis casibus Episcopi licentia. Item de nundinis, vulgo *Fairs*, statuimus eas haberi non posse Dominicis diebus neque sine Episcopi licentia, nec cum usu liquorum inebriantium, vini et cerevisiae. Mandamus quoque ut sacerdotes illum abusum, quo convivia parantur cum choreis (*Balls*) ad opera pia promovenda, omnino tollendum curent.

293. Gravissima sunt verba Concilii superioris, quibus damnavit perversam agendi rationem illorum sacerdotum, qui ipsa intra missarum solemnia ab altari recedunt, aedemque sacram circumeunt, a singulis fidelibus eleemosynam petentes. Tanta vero apparet quorundam pertinacia ac in observandis etiam strictissimis legibus socordia, ut qui constituti sumus legum ecclesiasticarum custodes, alta voce decretum Antecessorum nostrorum de novo promulgare et inculcare constringamur. Notatum itaque "turpissimum abusum, Ecclesiae sacrisque ejus ritibus injurium, quique Catholicorum ruborem et indignationem, acatholicorum vero irrisionem et contemptum provocat, reprobamus et prorsus exstirpandum decernimus. Qua in re singulorum Episcoporum conscientia oneratur." (No. 364.)

295. [Volumus et edicimus] utque nullis hujusmodi quaestoribus colligendi concedatur licentia, nisi eorum Ordinarius vel Ordinis Praefectus ipsi per litteras praevias eam pro iisdem obtinuerint ab Episcopis in quorum dioecesibus eleemosynas rogare desiderant. Praeterea continuo exposcatur ab eorum Episcopo vel Superiori, ut eos revocent; qui si id facere noluerint vel neglexerint, ad S. Congregationem de Prop. Fide sine mora abusus corrigendus deferatur.

296. Magnopere sane dolendum est, decretum a Praedecessoribus nostris in ultimo Concilio Plenario sapientissime latum No. 370, multis in casibus observatum plane non fuisse. Hinc iterum iterumque declaramus, "esse abusum non tolerandum et rei sacrae profanationem," quod sive in ephemeridibus sive in foliis encyclicis (*Circulars*) publice offerantur missae pro iis omnibus dicendae, qui ad aedificandas ecclesias, conventus aliasque hujusmodi aedes, aut ad solvenda harum institutionum debita. aut ad quodcumque aliud pium

14

opus eleemosynas contulerint. Hunc abusum vehementer reprobamus, et prohibemus; Episcopos vero et Praelatos enixe obsecramus ut praedictum abusum, ubi viget, tolli et in posterum ubique praecaveri curent.

CODE

CANON 1181

Ingressus in ecclesiam ad sacros ritus sit omnino gratuitus, reprobata qualibet contraria consuetudine.

CANON 1499

§ 1. Ecclesia acquirere bona temporalia potest omnibus iustis modis iuris sive naturalis sive positivi, quibus id aliis licet.

§ 2. Dominium bonorum, sub suprema auctoritate Sedis Apostolicae, ad eam pertinet moralem personam, quae eadem bona legitime acquisiverit.

CANON 1503

Salvis praescriptis can. 621-624, vetantur privati tam clerici quam laici sine Sedis Apostolicae aut proprii Ordinarii et Ordinarii loci licentia, in scriptis data, stipem cogere pro quolibet pio aut ecclesiastico instituto vel fine.

The Third Plenary devotes its last chapter on Church property including numbers 288 to 296 to the condemnation of some of the ways used to raise money and to kindred abuses. Number 288 repeats the condemnation previously decreed by the Second Council in number 397 of the practice of charging money at the church door.

The Code in canon 1181 declares that entrance to the church for sacred rites must be absolutely gratuitous and explicitly reprobates all contrary customs.

The two laws are evidently in perfect accord in their efforts to suppress this evil which has proved a scandal to both Catholics and non-Catholics alike.[2]

According to number 289 of the Third Council every church is to set aside some rent-free pews for the accommodation of the poor.

Since there is no identical requirement in the Code, this local statute obviously in keeping with the spirit of the common law continues in force as something *praeter codicem*.

Though recognizing the danger of sin and scandal in such socials as picnics, excursions, fairs and the like, the Fathers of the Third Council in number 290 decided, as their Predecessors had done,[3] to

[2] Cf. Letter of the Apostolic Delegate—*Eccl. Rev.*, XLV (1911), 594.

[3] *Conc. Plen. Balti. II Acta et Decreta,* No. 396.

continue to tolerate them as means of raising money, but conditioned on every possible precaution.

As an aid to the preclusion of the dangers inherent in such socials the following rules are prescribed:

1. The permission of the Bishop must be obtained in every individual case.
2. It is forbidden to hold fairs on Sundays, and picnics and excursions on Sundays, holydays and fast days and at night.
3. All intoxicants are prohibited.
4. Priests are commanded to see to the absolute stamping out of the abuse of holding entertainments accompanied by dancing for the purpose of promoting good works.

The Code has nothing on this matter beyond the general remark in canon 1499 that the Church can acquire temporal goods by all just means which are sanctioned in the case of others by the natural and the positive law.

This not only in no wise interferes with the foregoing decrees of the Third Council, but rather leaves the way open to their greater detail.

The Holy See added its authority to that of our Bishops, moreover, regarding this part of our local legislation by the decree of the Sacred Consistorial Congregation of March 31, 1916. Herein the Fathers of the Congregation call attention to the Baltimore statute forbidding the holding of dances for the benefit of pious projects, which prohibition, they say, after a period of faithful observance began gradually to fall into oblivion. After mature consideration of the subject and the consulting of many of our Ordinaries the Sacred Congregation decided that this local statute must stand. Furthermore, it decreed that all priests both secular and religious and all other clerics are absolutely forbidden to promote and foster dances even for any pious purpose whatsoever; nor are they allowed to be present if such dances are sponsored by the laity.[4]

Some time later one of our Ordinaries asked the Sacred Congregation whether or not this decree comprehended in its reprobation dances held during the day or the early hours of the night, and also those conducted without dinners or held in connection with picnics.

[4] *A. A. S.*, VIII (1916), 147; *Eccl. Rev.*, LV (1916), 63, 84 and 193.

To this the Sacred Congregation replied on December 10, 1917 in the affirmative and reiterated its prohibition against clerics fostering dances and being present at those sponsored by the laity.[5]

In number 293 the Fathers of the Third Council quoting from number 364 of the Second condemn and order stopped the practice of some priests who leave the altar during the Holy Sacrifice to take up the collection. The burden of remedying this abuse they place on the conscience of each Bishop.

There is no such definite prohibition in the Code, but this local statute continues to bind since it comes under the general principle laid down in canon 2.[6]

The Second Plenary Council in number 119 strictly prohibits any priest to collect money outside his own congregation without the written permission of his Ordinary, or outside his own diocese without the written permission of the proper Ordinary.

With practically the same idea in mind the Fathers of the Third Council order in number 295 that no one known to have come to collect be given permission to do so unless his Ordinary or the Superior of his Order has previously obtained it for him by letters from the Bishops in whose dioceses he desires to seek alms. Otherwise his recall is to be asked at once of his Bishop or Superior; which, if he is unwilling or neglects to do so, the abuse is to be referred without delay to the Holy See for correction.

The Code in canon 1503 decrees that, the prescriptions of canons 621 to 624 (which refer to religious) remaining in force, private persons whether cleric or lay are forbidden to collect alms for any charitable or Church institution or purpose without the written permission of the Apostolic See or of their own and the local Ordinary.

The case of religious has been dealt with under that heading in chapter 3. As regards secular priests the law of the Second Council has been absorbed by that of the Third. Since this latter is in agreement with the common law, it has been replaced in form by the Code.

Finally, in number 296 the Fathers of the Third Council repeat and forcefully confirm a decree incorporated in number 370 of the Second Council. This statute condemns as a profanation and an intolerable abuse the practice of advertising in newspapers and cir-

[5] *A. A. S.*, X (1918), 17.

[6] Gasparri, *Tract. de Eucharistia*, II, No. 847, p. 156.

culars that Masses will be offered for those who contribute toward the erection of churches and any other such buildings, the payment of debts incurred thereby or any like pious cause. The Bishops are urged to stamp out this abuse where it already exists and to take means to prevent its arising in the future.

This, as the preceding, has no specific correspondent in the Code and, therefore, likewise continues in full force as something *praeter codicem.*

CONCLUSION

This study of the Councils of Baltimore in the light of the Code of Canon Law leads to the following general conclusions:

First, that a great deal of the matter of the Councils especially of the Second Plenary was never law in the proper sense of the word.

Secondly, that some of the decrees that have the form of law are simply a promulgation of the common law then, as now, binding and so have no present practical utility.

Thirdly, that a few of our particular laws are in the form of indults granted by the Holy See and continue in force in virtue of canon 4.

Fourthly, that some laws, as for example those concerning the Diocesan Consultors, which before the Code were particular for us are now incorporated into the common law.

Fifthly, that a fair proportion of the statutes of our Councils has been abrogated by reason of opposition to the Code.

Sixthly, and finally, that a number of the laws of the Councils of Baltimore continue to bind as before because they are *praeter codicem.*

For the sake of convenient reference the Baltimore laws remaining in force and those abrogated are indicated in the two appendices that follow.

APPENDIX I

CONCILIAR LAWS STILL IN FORCE

1. The need of the written permission of the Ordinary for one cleric to take another before the civil court. (Chap. III, Tit. III.)
2. The prohibition against a cleric suing a layman before the civil court for any Church debts. (Chap. III, Tit. III.)
3. The freedom of laymen in bringing a cleric before the civil court. (Chap. III, Tit. III.)
4. The method of supporting incapacitated priests. (Chap. III, Tit. IV.)
5. The frequency of retreats for diocesan clergy. (Chap. III, Tit. V., Art. 1.)
6. The requirement of holding the junior-clergy examinations once a year for at least five years. (Chap. III, Tit. V, Art. 3, Sec. I.)
7. The holding of theological conferences four times a year in cities. (Chap. III, Tit. V, Art. 3, Sec. II.)
8. The prohibition against managing the money of the laity. (Chap. III, Tit. V, Art. 6.)
9. The prohibition against clerics' attendance at horse races. (Chap. III, Tit. V, Art. 7.)
10. The obligation of the Peter's Pence collection. (Chap. III, Tit. VI.)
11. The obligation of inquiring into the temporalities during the visitation of the diocese. (Chap. III, Tit. IX, Art. 4.)
12. The obligation of completing the visitation of the diocese within three years. (Chap. III, Tit. IX, Art. 4.)
13. Regarding the meetings of the Diocesan Consultors. (Chap. III, Tit. XIII, Art. 4.)
14. The method of fixing the Pastor's salary. (Chap. III, Tit. XV, Art. 4.)
15. The forfeiture of the Pastor's salary for failure to claim it within the year. (Chap. III, Tit. XV, Art. 4.)
16. The requirement of a written agreement between the Bishop and Religious taking up diocesan work. (Chap. III, Tit. XVI, Art. 1.)
17. The requirement that Religious give the Bishop six months' warning before giving up any diocesan work. (Chap. III, Tit. XVI, Art. 1.)
18. The prohibition against the Brothers of certain Orders entering seminaries without the permission of the Holy See. (Chap. III, Tit. XVI, Art. 4.)
19. The requirement of documentary proof of the ownership of ecclesiastical goods on the part of Religious doing diocesan work. (Chap. III, Tit. XVI, Art. 2.)
20. The privilege of solemn vows for certain Visitation nuns in this country. (Chap. III, Tit. XVI, Art. 4.)
21. That all Catholic societies be under the auspices and patronage of the Bishops. (Chap. III, Tit. XVII, Art. 1.)

22. The obligation of Pastors to foster special societies for the young people. (Chap. III, Tit. XVII, Art. 1.)
23. Regarding the Commission established to ascertain the status of questionable societies. (Chap. III, Tit. XVII, Art. 2.)
24. The permission to repeat in the vernacular the prayers used in the administration of the Sacraments and the burial of the dead. (Chap. IV, Introduction.)
25. The requirement that each candidate for Confirmation have a card with his or her name on it. (Chap. IV, Tit. II.)
26. The permission granted to our Bishops to lengthen the Paschal season? Chap. IV, Tit. III, Art. 1.)
27. The laws governing the removal of the Blessed Sacrament from the tabernacle. (Chap. IV, Tit. III, Art. 3.)
28. The laws governing the carrying of the Blessed Sacrament to the sick. (Chap. IV, Tit. III, Art. 4.)
29. The prohibition against accepting less than the standard stipend for Mass. (Chap. IV, Tit. III, Art. 6.)
30. The prohibition against the practice of advertising in newspapers for Mass foundations. (Chap. IV, Tit. III, Art. 7.)
31. The censure for attempting marriage after a civil divorce. (Chap. IV, IV, Tit. IV, Art. 1.)
32. The censure for attempting marriage before a non-Catholic minister. (Chap. IV, Tit. IV, Art. 2.)
33. The toleration of the burial of non-Catholics in Catholic cemeteries. (Chap. V, Tit. I, Art. 2.)
34. Regarding the use of the proceeds from the sale of cemetery lots. (Chap. V, Tit. I, Art. 3.)
35. Regarding the care of cemeteries. (Chap. V, Tit. I, Art. 4.)
36. Regarding holydays of obligation. (Chap. V, Tit. II.)
37. The indults to service men and workingmen regarding the law of abstinence, and that permitting us to observe abstinence on the Wednesdays instead of the Saturdays of Lent. (Chap. V, Tit. III.)
38. The local privileges regarding the Forty Hours' Devotion. (Chap. VI, Tit. II.)
39. Regarding the singing of Vespers. (Chap. VI, Tit. III.)
40. Regarding special times of prayer. (Chap. VI, Tit. IV, Art. 1.)
41. Regarding the five-minute instruction at Mass on Sundays and solemn feasts. Chap. VII, Tit. I.)
42. Regarding the teaching of Catechism. (Chap. VII, Tit. II.)
43. The requirement of a six-year course in the preparatory seminary. (Chap. VII, Tit. III, Art. 2.)
44. Regarding the programme of studies for seminaries. (Chap. VII, Tit. III, Art. 3.)
45. Regarding the examination before admission to the major seminary. (Chap. VII, Tit. III, Art. 4.)

46. Regarding the testimonial letters required of those changing seminaries. (Chap. VII, Tit. III, Art. 4.)
47. Regarding reimbursement for the education of a seminarian who changes dioceses. (Chap. VII, Tit. III, Art. 4.)
48. The Pastor's obligation to ask the prayers of the congregation before ordinations. (Chap. VII, Tit. III, Art. 5.)
49. The obligation of seminary superiors to give a pre-vacation instruction to the students. (Chap. VII, Tit. III, Art. 6.)
50. Regarding the erection and support of parochial schools. (Chap. VII, Tit. IV, Art. 1.)
51. Regarding the Sacraments and parents who send their children to the public school. (Chap. VII, Tit. IV, Art. 3.)
52. All the laws governing the tenure of Church property except the toleration of the *fee simple.* (Chap. VIII, Tit. I.)
53. All the laws governing the administration of Church property except the freedom given to the Ordinary in the matter of appointing lay trustees. (Chap. VIII, Tit. II.)
54. Regarding prohibited means of raising money. (Chap. VIII, Tit. III.)

APPENDIX II

CONCILIAR LAWS ABROGATED

1. Regarding affiliation with a diocese. (Chap. III, Tit. I.)
2. Regarding the method of changing dioceses after ordination. (Chap. III, Tit. II.)
3. The permission to hold theological conferences only twice a year in rural districts. (Chap. III, Tit. V, Art. 3, Sec. II.)
4. Regarding the subject matter for theological conferences. (Chap. III, Tit. V, Art. 3, Sec. II.)
5. Regarding those obliged to attend theological conferences. (Chap. III, Tit. V, Art. 3, Sec. II.)
6. Regarding the length of the clerical coat. (Chap. III, Tit. V, Art. 4.)
7 The strict prohibition against clerics' attendance at certain amusements. (Chap. III, Tit. V, Art. 7.)
8. Regarding the frequency of Provincial Councils. (Chap. III, Tit. VIII.)
9. The method of choosing candidates for the Episcopacy. (Chap. III, Tit. IX, Art. 1.)
10. Regarding the law of residence for Bishops. (Chap. III, Tit. IX, Art. 2.)
11. Regarding the visit *ad limina.* (Chap. III, Tit. IX, Art. 3.)
12. The obligation of having co-visitors during the visitation of the diocese. (Chap. III, Tit. IX, Art. 4.)

13. Regarding the frequency of the Diocesan Synod. (Chap. III, Tit. X.)
14. Regarding the faculties of the Vicar General. (Chap. III, Tit. XI.)
15. Regarding the number of Synodal Examiners. (Chap. III, Tit. XII.)
16. Regarding the number of Diocesan Consultors. (Chap. III, Tit. XIII, Art. 1.)
17. Regarding the appointment of the Diocesan Consultors. (Chap. III, Tit. XIII, Art. 2.)
18. Regarding the advice of the Diocesan Consultors relative to the calling of a Synod and the alienation of Church property. (Chap. III, Tit. XIII, Art. 3.)
19. Regarding the method of appointing a Diocesan Administrator. (Chap. III, Tit. XIV, Art. 1.)
20. Regarding the power of the Diocesan Administrator. (Chap. III, Tit. XIV, Art. 2.)
21. The method of appointing and removing Pastors. (Chap. III, Tit. XV, Art. 1.)
22. The method of determining stole fees. (Chap. III, Tit. XV, Art. 2, Sec. I.)
23. Regarding the division of stole fees. (Chap. III, Tit. XV, Art. 2, Sec. II.)
24. The exemption of Pastors from the obligation of the *Missa pro populo.* (Chap. III, Tit. XV, Art. 3.)
25. Regarding the permission for Mendicants to collect. (Chap. III, Tit. XVI, Art. 3.)
26. Regarding the need of the Ordinary's permission to collect in the case of Mendicant women and others enjoying the privilege of exemption on this score. (Chap. III, Tit. XVI, Art. 4.)
27. The general permission to administer solemn Baptism in private houses. (Chap. IV, Tit. I.)
28. The general permission for priests to say Mass in any decent place. (Chap. IV, Tit. III, Art. 2, Sec. I.)
29. The obligation of Rectors of churches to refuse permission to say Mass to priests who have come to collect. (Chap. IV, Tit. III, Art. 2, Sec. II.)
30. Regarding the burial of Catholics in non-Catholic cemeteries. (Chap. V, Tit. I, Art. 1.)
31. The liberty granted in the matter of Exposition and Benediction of the Most Blessed Sacrament. (Chap. VI, Tit. I.)
32. The holding of Church property *in fee simple.* (Chap. VIII, Tit. I.)

BIBLIOGRAPHY

SOURCES

Acta Apostolicae Sedis, Romae, 1919—.

Acta Sanctae Sedis, 41 vols., Romae, 1865-1908.

Bullarium SSmi. Domini Nostri Benedicti Papae XIV, 4 vols., 4. ed., Venetiis, 1778.

Canones Et Decreta Concilii Tridentini, 19. ed., Taurini, 1913.

Codex Iuris Canonici Pii X Pontificis Maximi iussu digestus Benedicti Papae XV auctoritate promulgatus, Romae, 1917.

Codicis Iuris Canonici Fontes Cura Emi. Petri Card. Gasparri Editi, 5 vols., Romae, 1923—.

Collectanea Sacrae Congregationis de Propaganda Fide, 2 vols., Romae, 1907.

Collectio Lacensis, Acta et Decreta Sacrorum Conciliorum Recentiorum, 7 vols., Friburgi, 1870-1890.

Concilia Provincilia Baltimori Habita 1829-1849, 2. ed., Baltimore, 1851.

Concilii Plenarii Baltimorensis II, Acta et Decreta, Baltimorae, 1868.

Concilii Plenarii Baltimorensis III, Acta et Decreta, Baltimorae, 1886.

Concilium Plenarium Baltimori Habitum Anno 1852, Baltimori, 1853.

Rituale Romanum, Auctoritate SSmi. D. N. Pii Papae XI ad Normam C. I. C. Accomodatum, 2. ed., Ratisbonnae, 1926.

REFERENCE WORKS

Alphonsus, Maria de Liguori, *Theologia Moralis*, ed. nova, 4 vols., Romae, 1905-1912.

Ayrinhac, H. A., *Marriage Legislation in The New Code of Canon Law*, New York, 1918.

———, *Penal Legislation in The New Code of Canon Law*, New York, 1920.

———, *General Legislation in The New Code of Canon Law*, New York, 1923.

———, *Constitution of The Church in The New Code of Canon Law*, New York, 1925.

———, *Legislation on The Sacraments in The New Code of Canon Law*, New York, 1928.

———, *Administrative Legislation in The New Code of Canon Law*, New York, 1930.

(Bachofen), Charles Augustine, *A Commentary on Canon Law*, 8 vols., St. Louis, 1920-1922.

———, *Rights and Duties of Ordinaries according to The Code and Apostolic Faculties*, St. Louis, 1924.

———, *The Pastor according to The New Code of Canon Law*, St. Louis, 1926.

Bartlett, Chester Joseph, *The Tenure of Parochial Property in The United States of America*, Washington, 1926.

Benedict, XIV, *De Synodo Dioecesana*, 2 vols., Ferrariae, 1775.

Blat, Albertus, *Commentarium Textus Codicis Iuris Canonici*, 5 vols., Romae, 1921-1925.

Bliley, Nicholas M., *Altars according to The Code of Canon Law*, Washington, 1925.

Brent, J. C., *Life of Archbishop Carroll*, Baltimore, 1843.

Bouix, Marie Dominique, *Du Concile Provincial*, Paris, 1850.

———, *Tractatus de Parocho*, Parisiis, 1855.

———, *Tractatus de Episcopo*, 2. ed., 2 vols., Parisiis, 1873.

Cappello, Felix M., *Tractatus Canonico-Moralis de Sacramentis*, 3 vols., Taurinorum Augustae, 1921-1923.

———, *De Censuris*, Romae, 1923.

Cathedral Records, Baltimore, 1926.

Catholic Encyclopedia, The, 17 vols., New York, 1907.

Chelodi, Ioannes, *Ius Poenale*, Tridenti, 1920.

———, *Ius Matrimoniale*, 3. ed., Tridenti, 1921.

———, *Ius de Personis*, Tridenti, 1922.

Cimetier, F., *Pour Etudier Le Code de Droit Canonique*, 2. ed., Paris, 1927.

Cipollini, Albertus D., *De Censuris Latae Sententiae iuxta C. I. C.*, Taurini, 1925.

Clarke, R. H., *Lives of Deceased Bishops*, New York, 1886.

Coady, John Joseph, *The Appointment of Pastors*, Washington, 1929.

Cocchi, Guidus, *Commentarium in Codicem Iuris Canonici*, 2. and 3. ed., 8 vols., Taurini, 1925-1927.

Corpus Scriptorum Ecclesiasticorum Latinorum, Vindobonae, 1871.

Creagh, John T., *The Code of Canon Law and the Church in the United States*, Washington, 1919.

Dilhet–Browne, *Beginnings of the Catholic Church in the United States*, Washington, 1922.

Doheny, William J., *Church Property: Modes of Acquisition*, Washington, 1927.

Droste-Messmer, *Canonical Procedure in Disciplinary and Criminal Cases of Clerics*, New York, 1887.

Ferry, William A., *Stole Fees*, Washington, 1930.

Fortescue, Adrian, *The Ceremonies of the Roman Rite Described*, London, 1920.

Griffin, Martin, *History of the Right Reverend Michael Egan, D. D.*, Philadelphia, 1893.

Guilday, Peter, *A History of the Councils of Baltimore 1791-1884*, New York, 1932.

———, *The Life and Times of John Carroll*, New York, 1922.

———, *The Life and Times of John England*, 2 vols., New York, 1927.

———, *The National Pastorals of the American Hierarchy, 1792-1919*, Washington, 1922.

Hefele, C. J. von, *Conciliengeschichte*, 2. ed., 9 vols., Freiburg in Br., 1875-1890.

Hefele–Leclerc, *Histoire des Conciles*, 8 vols., Paris, 1908-1921.

Keller, Charles, *Mass Stipends*, Washington, 1925.

Kenrick, Francis Patrick, *Theologia Moralis*, 3 vols., Philadelphia, 1841-1843.

Kirlin, Joseph L. J., *Catholicity in Philadelphia*, Philadelphia, 1909.

Klekotka, Peter J., *Diocesan Consultors*, Philadelphia, 1920.

Konings, A., *Theologia Moralis*, 7. ed., 2 vols., Neo-Eboraci, 1889.

Konings–Putzer, *Commentarium in Facultates Apostolicas*, 4. ed., New York, 1897.

Labbé and Cossart, *Sacrorum Conciliorum Nova et Amplissima Collectio*, 30 vols., Florence, 1759-1792.

Leech, George Leo, *A Comparative Study of The Constitution "Apostolicae Sedis" and The "Codex Juris Canonici"*, Washington, 1922.

Leitner, Martin, *Lehrbuch des Katholischen Eherechts*, 3. ed., Paderborn, 1920.

Linneborn, Johannes, *Grundriss des Eherechts nach dem Codex Juris Canonici*, 2. and 3. ed., Paderborn, 1922.

Lucidi, Angelico, *De Visitatione Sacrorum Liminum*, 2. ed., 3 vols., Romae, 1878.

Mansi, J. D., *Sacrorum Conciliorum Nova et Amplissima Collectio*, Venice, 1727.

Memorial Volume, A History of the Third Plenary Council, Baltimore, 1885.

Migne, *Patrologia Latina*, 221 vols., Paris, 1847-1870.

Maroto, Philippo, *Institutiones Juris Canonici*, 2 vols., Romae, 1921.

Motry, Hubert L., *Diocesan Faculties*, Washington, 1922.

Niedermeyer, A., *The Council in Baltimore*, Baltimore, 1914.

Nilles, Nicolaus, *Commentaria in Concilium Plenarium Baltimorense Tertium*, Oeniponte, 1890.

Noldin, H., *Summa Theologiae Moralis*, 3 vols.: Vol. I, 18. ed., 1925; Vol. II, 17. ed., 1924; Vol. III, 15. et 16. ed., Oeniponte, 1923.

O'Gorman, Thomas, *The American Church History*, Vol. IX, New York, 1895.

O'Hara, Edwin V., *Pioneer Catholic History of Oregon*, Portland, 1911.

O'Kane, James, *Notes on The Rubrics of The Roman Ritual*, New York, 1883.

O'Reilly, John Anthony, *Ecclesiastical Sepulture in The New Code of Canon* Law, 1923.

Petrovits, Joseph, *The New Church Law on Matrimony*, 2. ed., Philadelphia, 1926.

Quigley, Joseph A. M., *Condemned Societies*, Washington, 1927.

Reiffenstuel, Anacletus, *Jus Canonicum Universum*, 4 vols., Romae, 1838.

Riordan, A., *Cathedral Records*, Baltimore, 1806.

Roelker, Edward G., *Principles of Privilege according to The Code of Canon Law*, Washington, 1926.

Rothensteiner, John, *History of the Archdiocese of St. Louis*, 2 vols., St. Louis, 1928.

Sabetti–Barrett, *Compendium Theologiae Moralis*, 22. ed., New York, 1915.

Schenck, Francis J., *The Matrimonial Impediments of Mixed Religion and Disparity of Cult*, Washington, 1929.

Shea, J. G., *Hierarchy of The Catholic Church in The United States*, New York, 1886.

———, *History of The Catholic Church in The United States*, 4 vols., New York, 1886-1892.

———, *The Life and Times of Archbishop Carroll*, New York, 1888.

Smith, S. B., *Elements of Ecclesiastical Law*, 3 vols., New York, 1887-1888.

———, *New Procedure in Canonical and Disciplinary Causes of Ecclesiastics in The United States*, 1887.

———, *Notes on The Second Plenary Council of Baltimore*, New York, 1874.

Suarez, Franciscus, *De Legibus*, Naples, 1872.

Thomassinus, Ludovicus, *Vetus et Nova Ecclesiae Disciplina Circa Beneficia et Beneficiarios*, Magontiaci, 1787.

Vermeersch–Creusen, *Epitome Juris Canonici*, 2. ed., 3 vols., Mechliniae et Romae, 1924.

Wapelhorst, Innocentius, *Compendium Sacrae Liturgiae*, 11. ed., New York, 1931.

Wernz–Vidal, *Jus Canonicum*, 3 vols., Romae, 1923-1927.

Woywod, Stanislaus, *Practical Commentary on The Code of Canon Law*, 2 vols., New York, 1925.

———, *The New Canon Law*, New York, 1918.

PERIODICALS

American Catholic Historical Researches.

American Catholic Quarterly Review, Philadelphia.

Catholic Historical Review, The, Washington.

Ecclesiastical Review, The, New York and Philadelphia.

Homiletic and Pastoral Review, The, New York.

Irish Ecclesiastical Record, The, Dublin.

Records of The American Catholic Historical Society of Philadelphia.

United States Catholic Magazine, The, Baltimore.

Universitas Catholica Americae

WASHINGTONII, D. C.

FACULTAS IURIS CANONICI

No. 83

1932

DEUS LUX MEA

TITULI

QUOS

AD DOCTORATUS GRADUM

IN

IURE CANONICO

APUD UNIVERSITATEM CATHOLICAM AMERICAE

CONSEQUENDUM

PUBLICE PROPUGNABIT

IOANNES DANIEL MARIA BARRETT

SACERDOS SOCIETATIS SANCTI SULPITII

IURIS CANONICI LICENTIATUS

HORA XI A.M., DIE XXI MAII A.D. MCMXXVII

TITULI

DE IURE CANONICO

I. De Fontibus Iuris Canonici.
II. De Relatione inter Ecclesiam et Statum.
III. De Dissertatione.

IV.	Canones 1-7.	De Canonibus Introductoriis.
V.	Canones 8-24.	De Legibus Ecclesiasticis.
VI.	Canones 25-30.	De Consuetudine.
VII.	Canones 31-35.	De Temporis Supputatione.
VIII.	Canones 36-62.	De Rescriptis.
IX.	Canones 63-79.	De Privilegiis.
X.	Canones 80-86.	De Dispensationibus.
XI.	Canones 87-107.	De Personis in Genere.
XII.	Canones 329-349.	De Episcopis.
XIII.	Canones 451-470.	De Parochis.
XIV.	Canones 487-491.	De Religiosis Canones Introductorii.
XV.	Canones 492-498.	De Erectione et Suppressione Religionis.
XVI.	Canones 499-517.	De Superioribus et de Capitulis.
XVII.	Canones 518-530.	De Confessariis et Cappellanis Religiosorum.
XVIII.	Canones 531-537.	De Bonis Temporalibus Religiosorum.
XIX.	Canones 539-541.	De Postulatu Religiosorum.
XX.	Canones 893-900.	De Reservatione Peccatorum.
XXI.	Canones 1058-1066.	De Impedimentis Impedientibus Matrimonii.
XXII.	Canones 1067-1080.	De Impedimentis Dirimentibus Matrimonii.
XXIII.	Canones 1081-1093.	De Consensu Matrimoniali.
XXIV.	Canones 1094-1103.	De Forma Celebrationis Matrimonii.
XXV.	Canones 1108-1109.	De Tempore et Loco Celebrationis Matrimonii.
XXVI.	Canones 1138-1141.	De Sanatione in Radice.
XXVII.	Canones 1142-1143.	De Secundis Nuptiis.
XXVIII.	Canones 1960-1992.	De Causis Matrimonialibus.
XXIX.	Canones 1993-1998.	De Causis Contra Sacram Ordinationem.
XXX.	Canones 2142-2146.	De Modo Procedendi in Nonnullis Expediendis Negotiis.
XXXI.	Canones 2147-2156.	De Modo Procedendi in Remotione Parochorum Inamovibilium.
XXXII.	Canones 2157-2161.	De Modo Procedendi in Remotione Parochorum Amovibilium.
XXXIII.	Canones 2162-2167.	De Modo Procedendi in Translatione Parochorum.
XXXIV.	Canones 2168-2175.	De Modo Procedendi Contra Clericos Non Residentes.

XXXV. Canones 2176-2181. De Modo Procedendi Contra Clericos Concubinarios.
XXXVI. Canones 2182-2185. De Modo Procedendi Contra Parochum Negligentem.
XXXVII. Canones 2186-2194. De Suspensione ex Informata Conscientia.
XXXVIII. Canones 2215-2219. De Poenarum Notione et Speciebus.
XXXIX. Canones 2226-2240. De Poenarum Remissione.
XL. Canones 2257-2267. De Excommunicatione.

ROMAN LAW

XLI. Sources of Roman Law.
XLII. Personality.
XLIII. Freedom.
XLIV. Slavery.
XLV. Citizenship.
XLVI. The Roman Family.
XLVII. *Cura et Tutela.*
XLVIII. The Distinction of Things.
XLIX. Acquisition *Titulo Singulari.*
L. Acquisition *Titulo Universali.*
LI. Ownership.
LII. Possession.

INTERNATIONAL LAW

LIII. Nature of International Law.
LIV. Sources of International Law.
LV. State Rights.
LVI. The Monroe Doctrine.
LVII. The Drago Doctrine.
LVIII. Consuls.
LIX. Immunity of Diplomatic Agents.
LX. Extradition.

Vidit Facultas:

Philippus Bernardini, S.T.D., I.U.D., *Decanuc.*
Ludovicus Motry, S.T.D., I.C.D., *a Secretis.*
Valentinus Schaaf, O.F.M., I.C.D.
Franciscus Lardone, S.T.D., I.U.D.
Manoel De Oliviera Lima, L.H.B.

Vidit Rector Universitatis:

✠ Thomas J. Shahan, S.T.D., I.U.L., LL.D.

BIOGRAPHICAL NOTE

John Daniel Mary Barrett was born in Frostburg, Maryland, on September 12, 1895 and moved to Cumberland, Maryland, in August, 1907. He received his primary education in St. Michael's Parochial School, Frostburg, and LaSalle Institute, Cumberland. In September, 1914 he entered St. Charles' College, Catonsville, Maryland, from which institution he was graduated in June, 1919. In the following September he entered St. Mary's Seminary, Baltimore, where for two years he pursued the courses in Philosophy. In September, 1921 he began his Theological studies at the Sulpician Seminary in Washington and was ordained on September 29, 1925 by His Excellency, the Most Reverend William J. Hafey. Two weeks later he entered the graduate School of Canon Law at the Catholic University of America and in June, 1927 he completed the prescribed course of studies for the degree of Doctor of Canon Law. During the Scholastic year 1927 to 1928 he was professor of Canon Law at St. Mary's Seminary, Baltimore. In September, 1928 he entered the novitiate of the Sulpicians at Catonsville, Maryland, and became a member of that Society in the following June. In September, 1929 he resumed his studies at St. Mary's Seminary.

CANON LAW STUDIES

1. Freriks, Rev. Celestine A., C.PP.S., J.C.D., Religious Congregations in Their External Relations, 121 pp., 1916.
2. Galliher, Rev. Daniel M., O.P., J.C.D., Canonical Elections, 117 pp., 1917.
3. Borkowski, Rev. Aurelius L., O.F.M., De Confraternitatibus Ecclesiasticis, 136 pp., 1918.
4. Castillo, Rev. Cayo, J.C.D., Disertacion Historico-canonica sobre la Potestad del Cabildo en Sede Vacante o Impedida del Vicario Capitular, 99 pp., 1919 (1918).
5. Kubelbeck, Rev. William J., S.T.B., J.C.D., The Sacred Penitentiaria and Its Relations to Faculties of Ordinaries and Priests, 129 pp., 1918.
6. Petrovits, Rev. Joseph J. C., S.T.D., J.C.D., The New Church Law on Matrimony, x, 461 pp., 1919.
7. Hickey, Rev. John J., S.T.B., J.C.D., Irregularities and Simple Impediments in the New Code of Canon Law, 100 pp., 1920.
8. Klekotka, Rev. Peter J., S.T.B., J.C.D., Diocesan Consultors, 179 pp., 1920.
9. Wannenmacher, Rev. Francis, J.C.D., The Evidence in Ecclesiastical Procedure Affecting the Marriage Bond, 1920. (Not Printed.)
10. Golden, Rev. Henry Francis, J.C.D., Parochial Benefices in the New Code, iv, 119 pp., 1921. (Printed 1925.)
11. Koudelka, Rev. Charles J., J.C.D., Pastors, Their Rights and Duties According to the New Code of Canon Law, 211 pp., 1921.
12. Melo, Rev. Antonius, O.F.M., J.C.D., De Exemptione Regularium, x, 188 pp., 1921.
13. Schaaf, Rev. Valentine Theodore, O.F.M., S.T.B., J.C.D., The Cloister, x, 180 pp., 1921.
14. Burke, Rev. Thomas Joseph, S.T.B., J.C.D., Competence in Ecclesiastical Tribunals, iv, 117 pp., 1922.
15. Leech, Rev. George Leo, J.C.D., A Comparative Study of the Constitution "Apostolicae Sedis" and the "Codex Juris Canonici," 179 pp., 1922.
16. Motry, Rev. Hubert Louis, S.T.D., J.C.D., Diocesan Faculties According to the Code of Canon Law, ii, 167 pp., 1922.
17. Murphy, Rev. George Lawrence, J.C.D., Delinquencies and Penalties in the Aministration and the Reception of the Sacraments, iv, 121 pp., 1923.
18. O'Reilly, Rev. John Anthony, S.T.B., J.C.D., Ecclesiastical Sepulture in the New Code of Canon Law, ii, 129 pp., 1923.
19. Michalicka, Rev. Wenceslas Cyrill, O.S.B., J.C.D., Judicial Procedure in Dismissal of Clerical Exempt Religious, 107 pp., 1923.
20. Dargin, Rev. Edward Vincent, S.T.B., J.C.D., Reserved Cases According to the Code of Canon Law, iv, 103 pp., 1924.
21. Godfrey, Rev. John A., S.T.B., J.C.D., The Right of Patronage According to the Code of Canon Law, 153 pp., 1924.
22. Hagedorn, Rev. Francis Edward, J.C.D., General Legislation on Indulgences, ii, 154 pp., 1924.
23. King, Rev. James Ignatius, J.C.D., The Administration of the Sacraments to Dying Non-Catholics, v, 141 pp., 1924.
24. Winslow, Rev. Francis Joseph, A.F.M., J.C.D., Vicars and Prefects Apostolic, iv, 149 pp., 1924.

25. Correa, Rev. Jose Servelion, S.T.L., J.C.D., La Potestad Legislativa de la Iglesia Católica, iv, 127 pp., 1925.
26. Dugan, Rev. Henry Francis, M.A., J.C.D., The Judiciary Department of the Diocesan Curia, 87 pp., 1925.
27. Keller, Rev. Charles Frederick, S.T.B., J.C.D., Mass Stipends, 167 pp., 1925.
28. Paschang, Rev. John Linus, J.C.D., The Sacramentals According to the Code of Canon Law, 129 pp., 1925.
29. Piontek, Rev. Cyrillus, O.F.M., S.T.B., J.C.D., De Indulto Exclaustrationis necnon Saecularizationis, xiii, 289 pp., 1925.
30. Kearney, Rev. Richard Joseph, S.T.B., J.C.D., Sponsors at Baptism According to the Code of Canon Law, iv, 127 pp., 1925.
31. Bartlett, Rev. Chester Joseph, A.M., LL.B., J.C.D., The Tenure of Parochial Property in the United States of America, v, 108 pp., 1926.
32. Kilker, Rev. Adrian Jerome, J.C.D., Extreme Unction, v, 425 pp., 1926.
33. McCormick, Rev. Robert Emmett, J.C.D., Confessors of Religious, viii, 266 pp., 1926.
34. Miller, Rev. Newton Thomas, J.C.D., Founded Masses According to the Code of Canon Law, vii, 93 pp., 1926.
35. Roelker, Rev. Edward G., S.T.D., J.C.D., Principles of Privilege According to the Code of Canon Law, xi, 166 pp., 1926.
36. Bakalarczyk, Rev. Richardus, M.I.C., J.U.D., De Novitiatu, viii, 208 pp., 1927.
37. Pizzuti, Rev. Lawrence, O.F.M., J.U.L., De Parochis Religiosis, 1927. (Not Printed.)
38. Bliley, Rev. Nicholas Martin, O.S.B., J.C.D., Altars According to the Code of Canon Law, xix, 132 pp., 1927.
39. Brown, Brendan Francis, A.B., LL.M., J.U.D., The Canonical Juristic Personality with Special Reference to its Status in the United States of America, v, 212 pp., 1927.
40. Cavanaugh, Rev. William Thomas, C.P., J.U.D., The Reservation of the Blessed Sacrament, viii, 101 pp., 1927.
41. Doheny, Rev. William J., C.S.C., A.B., J.U.D., Church Property: Modes of Acquisition, x, 118 pp., 1927.
42. Feldhaus, Rev. Aloysius H., C.PP.S., J.C.D., Oratories, ix, 141 pp., 1927.
43. Kelly, Rev. James Patrick, A.B., J.C.D., The Jurisdiction of the Simple Confessor, x, 208 pp., 1927.
44. Neuberger, Rev. Nicholas J., J.C.D., Canon 6 or the Relation of the Codex Juris Canonici to the Preceding Legislation, v, 95 pp., 1927.
45. O'Keefe, Rev. Gerald Michael, J.C.D., Matrimonial Dispensations, Powers of Bishops, Priests, and Confessors, viii, 232 pp., 1927.
46. Quigley, Rev. Joseph, A.M., A.B., J.C.D., Condemned Societies, 139 pp., 1927.
47. Zaplotnik, Rev. Ioannes Leo, J.C.D., De Vicariis Foraneis, x, 142 pp., 1927.
48. Duskie, Rev. John Aloysius, A.B., J.C.D., The Canonical Status of the Orientals in the United States, viii, 196 pp., 1928.
49. Hyland, Rev. Francis Edward, J.C.D., Excommunication, Its Nature, Historical Development and Effects, viii, 181 pp., 1928.
50. Reinmann, Rev. Gerald Joseph, O.M.C., J.C.D., The Third Order Secular of Saint Francis, 201 pp., 1928.
51. Schenk, Rev. Francis J., J.C.D., The Matrimonial Impediments of Mixed Religion and Disparity of Cult, xvi, 318 pp., 1929.
52. Coady, Rev. John Joseph, S.T.D., J.U.D., A.M., The Appointment of Pastors, viii, 150 pp., 1929.

53. Kay, Rev. Thomas Henry, J.C.D., Competence in Matrimonial Procedure, viii, 164 pp., 1929.
54. Turner, Rev. Sidney Joseph, C.P., J.U.D., The Vow of Poverty, xlix, 217 pp., 1929.
55. Kearney, Rev. Raymond A., A.B., S.T.D., J.C.D., The Principles of Delegation, vii, 149 pp., 1929.
56. Conran, Rev. Edward James, A.B., J.C.D., The Interdict, v, 163 pp., 1930.
57. O'Neil, Rev. William H., J.C.D., Papal Rescripts of Favor, vii, 218 pp.,
58. Bastnagel, Rev. Clement Vincent, J.U.D., The Appointment of Parochial Adjutants and Assistants, xv, 257 pp., 1930.
59. Ferry, Rev. William A., A.B., J.C.D., Stole Fees, x, 107 pp., 1930.
60. Costello, Rev. John Michael, A.B., J.C.D., Domicile and Quasi-Domicile, vii, 201 pp., 1930.
61. Kremer, Rev. Michael Nicholas, A.B., S.T.B., J.C.D., Church Support in the United States, vi, 136 pp., 1930.
62. Angulo, Rev. Luis, C.M., J.C.D., Legislación de la Iglesia sobre la intención en la aplicación de la Santa Misa, vii, 104 pp., 1931.
63. Frey, Rev. Wolfgang Norbert, O.S.B., A.B., J.C.D., The Act of Religious Profession, viii, 174 pp., 1931.
64. Roberts, Rev. James Brendan, A.B., J.C.D., The Banns of Marriage, xiv, 140 pp., 1931.
65. Ryder, Rev. Raymond Aloysius, A.B., J.C.D., Simony, ix, 151 pp., 1931.
66. Campagna, Rev. Angelo, Ph.D., J.U.D., Il Vicario Generale del Vescovo, vi, 205 pp., 1931.
67. Cox, Rev. Joseph Godfrey, A.B., J.C.D., The Administration of Seminaries, vi, 124 pp., 1931.
68. Gregory, Rev. Donald J., J.U.D., The Pauline Privilege, xv, 165 pp., 1931.
69. Donohue, Rev. John F., J.C.D., The Impediment of Crime, viii, 110 pp., 1931.
70. Dooley, Rev. Eugene A., O.M.I., J.C.D., Church Law on Sacred Relics, ix, 143 pp., 1931.
71. Orth, Rev. Clement Raymond, O.M.C., J.C.D., The Approbation of Religious Institutes, 171 pp., 1931.
72. Pernicone, Rev. Joseph M., A.B., J.C.D., The Ecclesiastical Prohibition of Books, xii, 267 pp., 1932.
73. Clinton, Rev. Connell, A.B., J.C.L., The Paschal Precept, 1932.
74. Donnelly, Rev. Francis B., A.M., S.T.L., J.C.L., The Diocesan Synod, 1932.
75. Torrente, Rev. Camilo, C.M.F., J.C.L., Las Processiones Sagradas, 1932.
76. Murphy, Rev. Edwin J., C.PP.S., J.C.L., Suspension Ex Informata Conscientia, 1932.
77. MacKenzie, Rev. Eric F., A.M., S.T.L., J.C.L., The Delict of Heresy in its Commission, Penalization, Absolution, 1932.
78. Lyons, Rev. Avitus E., S.T.B., J.C.L., The Collegiate Tribunal of First Instance, 1932.
79. Connolly, Rev. Thomas A., J.C.L., Appeals, 1932.
80. Sangmeister, Rev. Joseph V., A.B., J.C.L., Force and Fear as Precluding Matrimonial Consent, 1932.
81. Jaeger, Rev. Leo A., A.B., J.C.L., The Administration of Vacant and Quasi-Vacant Episcopal Sees in the United States, 1932.
82. Rimlinger, Rev. Herbert T., J.C.L., Error Invalidating Matrimonial Consent, 1932.
83. Barrett, Rev. John Daniel Mary, S.S., A.M., J.C.L., A Comparative Study of the Councils of Baltimore and The Code of Canon Law, 1932.

www.ingramcontent.com/pod-product-compliance
Lightning Source LLC
LaVergne TN
LVHW050246080826
844660LV00012B/600